Made to Count will give you a new set of lenses so that you see your workplace as your God-given opportunity to advance the kingdom of Christ right where you are. May this book encourage you to fulfill your most important mission in life—to share the love of Jesus Christ with others.

—DR. JACK GRAHAM
President, Southern Baptist Convention
Pastor, Prestonwood Baptist Church

This book has the potential to transform our society, if readers will take the authors' message to heart. I believe the authors are speaking what the Spirit of God is saying to the church today—that our work, calling, and ministry are all the same! I wish every believer would read this book. It's one of the best books to date in the faith and work movement. Great job, Bob and Randy!

—OS HILLMAN
Director, International Coalition of Workplace Ministries

Bob Reccord and Randy Singer, who know the heart of the laity, have captured a challenging subject for every true believer desiring to fulfill a life of Christian signif-icance. These denominational leaders challenge both laity and clergy to fulfill the role of the lay believer in ministry at work. In a powerful manner, they undergird the significant role of the laity in their everyday activity as ministers. To serve Christ in the workplace does not mean every believer must attend seminary; as they point out, they must be with Jesus and then fulfill the Great Commission given to all of us.

—GIL STRICKLIN
President & CEO, Marketplace Ministries
Dallas, Texas

Randy Singer, a New York lawyer and highly successful novelist, has joined with Robert Reccord, who leads the most widely dispersed home missions organization in the world—the North American Mission Board—to write a book about workplace impact. *Made to Count* is the culmination of a deep conviction on the part of both men that, if the message of Christ is to change our world, it must escape the walls of the church and permeate the workplace. Because of the diversity of experience of the authors, what has resulted is a scintillating read brimful of information needed to involve your church and your people in the taking of the eternal message of the sav-ing Christ to the milling multitudes of the workplace. This book will change you and your church.

—PAIGE PATTERSON
Southwestern Baptist Theological Seminary
Fort Worth, Texas

At last, a book that demonstrates with unmistakable clarity the biblical principle that for the Christian all ground is holy ground and every bush is a burning bush! As a layman, my calling to do good works in the power of the Holy Spirit has absolutely no inferiority to the calling of "full-time" ministers. *Made to Count* shows with undisguised clarity that we are all "full-time," needing to seize every opportunity and to rededicate ourselves to joyful service of God. "Whether therefore ye eat or drink or whatsoever ye do, do all for the glory of God."

—STU EPPERSON
CEO, Salem Communications

Bob and Randy are more than qualified to write a book on making life count. They bring years of experience both in full-time ministry and in the workplace to bring a message of hope to those seeking to make a difference for Christ in our world.

—STEVE DOUGLASS
President, Campus Crusade for Christ

Made to Count is a must-read for every church leader, every church member, and all those wanting God to make a difference in their lives, and through their lives. This book will challenge you where you live and gets to the heart of what being *on mission* is all about!

—ADMIRAL VERN CLARK

The Spirit of God is moving across the workplace in an amazing way, and *Made to Count* shares exciting accounts of transformed lives making a lasting impact day in and day out. This great read will give you hope, purpose, and practical insights for making your life count right where you are. Its fast-moving pace will help light your passion and restore your joy. It's a page-turner—as the reader you can't wait to see the next ordinary person doing extraordinary things with God!

—KENT HUMPHREYS
President, Fellowship of Companies for Christ International

Boardrooms, living rooms, classrooms, and locker rooms seem to be full of mediocrity. If you are searching for that which is important, enduring, and substantial, *Made to Count* will propel you from your comfort zone to the end zone. This is a must-read for leaders of all ages who want to soar instead of settle.

—DR. JAY STRACK
President/Founder, StudentLeadership.net

From time to time, God chooses to move in churches and communities in such a powerful, transcending way that denominational boundaries and issues that too often divide us are blown away. We are on the verge of such a movement, as God captures the hearts of "pew people" across our land, charging them to make a difference in the workplace, schools, and neighborhoods. That's what *Made to Count* is all about. Read this book; then have your church study its principles. Then hold on as God uses His people to change their world!

—Dr. Ed Young
Pastor, Second Baptist Church, Houston, Texas

You don't have to be in a leadership position to be a leader, and you don't have to be a "minister" to share Christ. As Christians, God has equipped each of us with talents and gifts that we can use in a variety of ways. *Made to Count* reveilles captivating stories of ordinary people doing extraordinary things, and it challenges you to discover your own plan for success. This book can help you make it count!

—John C. Maxwell
Founder, INJOY Group

Ben Franklin looked at the flashing lightning and thought, *If I could only harness that power*. Bob Reccord and Randy Singer have looked at the modern church and told us how to harness, and at the same time unleash, the awesome power of the church. This is a book that inspires, but it does more than inspire—it informs us in practical and biblical terms how to do what we desperately need to do. I commend it fully.

—Adrian Rogers
Pastor, Bellevue Baptist Church, Memphis

When Bob Reccord and Randy Singer speak or write, I pay attention, because they are two of the top thinkers and communicators in North America. Their latest book, *Made to Count*, will force you out of your comfort zone and challenge you to live your life at the highest level possible.

—Pat Williams
Senior Vice President, Orlando Magic

When God's people truly surrender everything to Him, there's no limit to what He can and will accomplish in our homes, our churches, our workplaces, and our communities. The Lord is moving in a way that transcends denominational boundaries and anything else that might come between us. Read *Made to Count*, apply and share its message, and see what God will do!

—H. B. London Jr.
Vice President, Ministry Outreach/Pastoral Ministries
Focus on the Family

From time to time God has miraculously used people—yes, laypeople—in the workplace to bring about world-changing happenings. Is the church ready for this experience today? I believe it is! Bob Reccord and Randy Singer, in writing the book entitled *Made to Count*, have captured by way of testimony what God is doing in the hearts and lives of men and women who are committed to the mission of Christ's church in their world and traffic pattern of life. You'll be thrilled as you read these accounts and challenged to make that same commitment in your own life.

—THOMAS E. TRASK
General Superintendent, Assemblies of God

Pastors—read this book! Twice! Then have each of your lay leaders read it. These principles will transform your church, unleashing the people in the pews to exponentially increase their impact both inside and outside the church walls. This book shows what it means to be salt and light in today's world.

—JOHNNY HUNT
Pastor, First Baptist Church, Woodstock, Georgia

Made to Count is a great blend—it is both principle-based and practical. Applying these truths will help anyone who wants to discover and pursue their God-given purpose. It's never too late to make your life count. Start today!

—MARK MILLER
Vice President Training & Development, Chick-fil-A, Inc.

Bob Reccord and Randy Singer, two men whom I have gotten to know and admire greatly, have written a practical and challenging book for all of us. Both of them have left a successful business career to work with a large mission organization and, as such, have a unique perspective on the workplace. They are extraordinarily capable communicators and have written this book in a compelling way. You will be gripped from page one, and your life will be changed forever, no matter where you are in your spiritual walk after being challenged by this book. I am delighted to be able to recommend it unequivocally and whole-heartedly.

—RON BLUE
President, Christian Financial Professionals Network CFPN

For those who sometimes feel that finding God's calling and will seems like a search for the Holy Grail, this book is for you. It is the perfect follow-on to *The Purpose Driven Life*. Built around eight biblical principles of discovering God's calling, it focuses on answering, "What should I do with my life to make it count?" As part of the leadership of the Spiritual Discovery Class at a very large church (McLean Bible in McLean, Virginia) we feel *Made to Count* is the perfect blend of wise biblical insight, heartwarming and inspiring life stories, and practical tools and applications to enable anybody to change their world, right where they are. And after all, isn't that the way the Master planned it?

—PAM PRYOR
Former Chief of Staff for Congressman J.C. Watts

Made to Count!

Discovering What To Do with Your Life

Bob Reccord and Randy Singer

W Publishing Group
A Division of Thomas Nelson Publishers
Since 1798
www.wpublishinggroup.com

Published by W Publishing Group, a Division of Thomas Nelson, Inc., P.O. Box 141000, Nashville, Tennessee, 37214.

W Publishing Group books may be purchased in bulk for educational, business, fundraising, or sales promotional use. For information, please email SpecialMarkets@ThomasNelson.com.

The people interviewed for this book have graciously given us permission to include their stories.

All Scripture quotations, unless otherwise indicated, are taken from The Holy Bible, New International Version. Copyright © 1973, 1978, 1984. International Bible Society. Used by permission of Zondervan Bible Publishers.

Other Scripture references are from the following sources:

The New King James Version (NKJV), copyright © 1979, 1980, 1982, Thomas Nelson, Inc., Publishers.

THE AMPLIFIED BIBLE (Amp.), Old Testament copyright © 1965 1987 by the Zondervan Corporation. The Amplified New Testament Copyright © 1958, 1987 by the Lockman Foundation. Used by permission.

The Holy Bible, New Living Translation (NLT), copyright © 1996. Used by permission of Tyndale House Publishers, Inc., Wheaton, Illinois 60189. All rights reserved.

The Message (MSG), copyright © 1993. Used by permission of NavPress Publishing Group.

The New Revised Standard Version Bible (NRSV), copyright © 1989 by the Division of Christian Education of the National Council of the Churches of Christ in the USA.

The King James Version of the Bible (KJV).

Library of Congress Cataloging-in-Publication Data

Reccord, Robert E.
 Made to count / by Bob Reccord and Randy Singer.
  p. cm.

ISBN 0-8499-0891-4 (tradepaper)
ISBN 0-8499-1819-7 (hardcover)

1. Christian life. I. Singer, Randy B. II. Title.
BV4501.3.R43   2004
248.4—dc22   2004002635

Printed in the United States of America
05 06 07 08 09 BTY 5 4 3 2 1

In Honor of One of God's Great Pioneering Statesmen

A mentor to Bob and a friend to Randy, Bill Bright challenged every Christ-follower to fulfill the Great Commission in this generation. And that needs to start right where you are!

Shortly before his death, Bill Bright requested the opportunity to write a special endorsement for this book. His heart resonated with and overwhelmingly affirmed the principles of this book. For that we are humbled and deeply honored.

At last! A book that inspires us to make our lives count and affirms God's high calling to "secular" professions. My dear friends Bob Reccord and Randy Singer eloquently ask the tough questions we all need to face. There are too few entertainers, lawyers, politicians, businessmen and women who are faithful witnesses for Christ and His Kingdom. This captivating book will challenge your thinking on the call of God, help you discover the purpose for your life, and motivate you with stories of those used by God to make a difference. Ironically, it took two leaders of a mission board to show the power of secular professions as a platform for the gospel in new and exciting ways. Everyone serious about fulfilling the Great Commission in our lifetime must read this book.

— BILL BRIGHT
Founder, Campus Crusade for Christ

Contents

Contents

Foreword

When Bob Reccord asked me to consider writing the Foreword to his book *Made to Count*, coauthored with Randy Singer, I was apprehensive. I wondered what a business writer and consultant knew about discovering God's unique plan for our lives. But that was before I read the book. Once I picked it up, I couldn't put it down, because Bob and Randy are writing all about God's call to the workplace and how He wants us to make our lives count right where we're planted—in everyday life. I, like you perhaps, had always thought, when somebody was called by God, that meant you either went into church ministry or became a missionary. And the impression was, if you became a missionary, somehow you were going to be sent to the far regions of Africa and basically asked to sacrifice your life for those in need. In reading *Made to Count*, you'll find that's a narrow image of what it means to be called by God. In fact, you'll realize that He's calling us all to live lives alongside Him that really make a difference. That's certainly been my experience in recent years.

In this marvelous book you'll read a number of stories about people who love the Lord and were wondering what their calling was. As I learned from Richard Bowles—author of the perennial bestseller *What Color Is Your Parachute?*—you can't talk about calling without talking about the Caller. So the first part of fulfilling God's purpose in your life is to have a relationship with His Son, Jesus Christ. Once that relationship is clear, then you can begin to see where His energy is going in your life and work alongside Him.

According to Bowles, there are three aspects of your calling. Two of them we share with all mankind. The first is to get to know God more in our lives. The second is to make the world a better place for our having been here. And the third is unique to us. What are our talents and skills, and how can they be used to enhance the Kingdom?

Read this book! Enjoy this book. And realize that God wants you—just as He wanted me—to suit up and be on His team. He wants you to make your life count where you're planted in everyday life. Sure, some will be called to formal ministry, but as Reccord and Singer point out, His agenda is too big to be limited to those professional vocations. All of us have to play a part.

Real life stories are told of people in arenas ranging from politics to the media to the law to business and to education who have experienced God's call and are finding God doing extraordinary things through their lives. Some are household names; others are not. But the examples they give will be wonderful ways for you to understand that God has a calling for all of us.

Bob and Randy have been businessmen as well as ministers. They understand our issues and care about us. I'm so glad you asked me to write this foreword, Bob. Just reading this book has been a reinforcing and eye-opening experience for me. I'm glad I'm now suited up for God and on His team. The journey is fabulous—get aboard!

—KEN BLANCHARD
Co-author of *The One Minute Manager*®
and *Raving Fans*®

Introduction

What's your greatest fear? That's a question we've asked all across North America.

Mental health experts say that almost everyone has some type of phobia. A popular reality television show feeds on people's fears, pulling strong ratings by forcing contestants to do things that make their skin crawl and heart pound. It seems that fear is just a natural part of the fabric of life.

Many of us experience common fears, like snakes, being alone, a fear of heights, or speaking in front of an audience. There are the not-so-common fears with the impressive names: amathophobia, the fear of dust; blennophobia, the fear of slime; or catoptrophobia, the fear of mirrors (with good reason, for some of us). And how many of us remember fearing the dark, or what it held, as we were growing up? Some adults still see danger and risk lurking around the darkened corners of life's journey.

But none of these is the most common answer we've heard. Though the initial responses covered a broad range of concerns, by far the most voiced response strikes deep at the heart of all of us: *to come to life's end without having made a significant difference*. Atychiphobia. The fear of failure.

Most people want to leave an imprint. To leave things and people better than we found them. Yet we fear that the impact of our lives could more resemble a fist in the water than a handprint in cement. The handprint is there to stay. But the water ripples made by the fist soon settle and smooth as though the fist had never been there. And so we dread the notion that, in the end, our lives might not count for much.

This book goes straight to that fear. It will help you find your life's meaning, live your life's passion, and discover your life's purpose.

We believe that God still speaks and moves in mysterious and wonderful ways. And right now, the One who created you, who uniquely designed you for a special task, has plans for you—"plans to prosper and not to harm you, plans to give you hope and a future."[1]

We'll show you how to hear His call and discover that plan, using biblical principles that have revolutionized the lives of dozens of people we've interviewed and millions of others around the world. What's unique about this book is that you'll meet lots of incredible people who will share openly and honestly how they discovered God's plan for making their life count. Not just how they found their life's work, although many will tell you that story. And not just how they overcame adversity, although you'll read of those adventures too. You'll learn much more: how they advanced from just getting by to achieving success to *really* making their life count by fulfilling their God-given calling.

Some of these folks you've probably heard about before. People like J. C. Watts, a United States congressman whom God called back to his family; Dr. Phillip Johnson, a Berkeley professor who challenged the established worldview of evolution; and Janet Parshall, a mom whom God called into talk radio. Others are folks you've never heard about: a college sophomore who ran for mayor of his city, a couple called to Hollywood to start a prayer ministry, and an outrageous follower of Christ who spends his working hours cleaning port-a-johns. That's right, cleaning port-a-johns.

The details will fascinate you. And so will the common themes. In fact, the more people we interviewed, the more we discovered similar trends. We came to the conclusion that just like many fears are universal, there are universal principles that come into play with those seeking to discover God's plan and make life count. Not surprisingly, these principles are set forth in the ancient Scriptures, placed there for your benefit by the same God who created you for a special plan and life-changing purpose.

In the following pages, you'll see these biblical truths with flesh and bone on them. You'll discover:

1. God prepared a unique plan and calling for your life even before you were born.
2. God calls you to a life-changing relationship with Him through Jesus Christ.
3. God calls you to partner with Him in a mission that is bigger than you are.
4. God calls you to be *on mission* with Him right where you are—starting now.
5. God reveals His mission through His Word, His Spirit, wise counsel, and His work in circumstances around you.
6. God will repeatedly bring you to a crossroads of choice as He forges you for His mission.
7. God guides and provides for your mission one step at a time.
8. When you answer God's call, you will experience His pleasure and change your world.

These principles transcend time, cultures, and most notably, occupational pursuits. They're not just applicable to a subculture of "professional" ministers or missionaries but apply equally to those "called" to the workplace. We're passionate about serving God in the workplace—a secular environment—because we've been there ourselves. In fact, it might surprise you to know our journey, which is probably not what you would expect for two guys leading a major Christian missions agency.

Before becoming president of the North American Mission Board (NAMB), Bob served in a variety of ministry capacities, including church staff member, senior pastor at two churches, U. S. director of Leadership Training for Evangelism Explosion International, plus he led the major implementation of restructuring the Southern Baptist Convention for the twenty-first century. But tucked into his resume is a key part of his career that provided him with the experience and insight to relate to nonordained readers of this book. He was a business executive in Michigan, working in a corporate environment, dealing with business issues ranging from renovating a

Introduction

> *I thank God for my career changes.
> They've prepared me for coauthoring
> this book and for my position as presi-
> dent of NAMB. During an interview
> for this job, a member of the presidential
> search team put it this way: "In looking
> at your resume, Bob, either you've
> made some of the dumbest career moves
> I've ever seen, or God has been prepar-
> ing you for this role at every step of your
> journey." Our unpredictable twists and
> turns only make sense when viewed
> through the prism of God.*
>
> —Bob Reccord

manufacturing plant to dou-
bling sales revenues in a
recession. Yet, in each role in
his career, including those in
business and industry, Bob
was *on mission* with God—
frequently sharing the story
of how Christ found him,
redeemed him, and called
him away from a career path
that at first seemed to be
leading to medical school
but was then leading him in
a new direction of ministry.
As president of NAMB he
travels and speaks extensively
and has authored three
books, each designed to help Christians thrive in the middle of life's toughest trials and temptations.

Randy, a lawyer by profession, is executive vice president of NAMB. Before
practicing law, he taught and coached in high school. After five years of teaching he pursued his dream of attending law school, graduating second in his
class from William and Mary. For twelve years he practiced law at one of
Virginia's largest law firms, serving for two years as head of the litigation section of thirty lawyers. During that time, he tried the longest bench trial in
Virginia state court history—six solid months of testimony and argument—
and the first jury trial in Virginia to receive gavel-to-gavel television coverage.
During his time as a trial lawyer, Randy was also a law school professor.
Recently, Randy became an award-winning fiction author, tapping into his
courtroom experience to pen legal thrillers designed to entertain readers while
confronting them with biblical truths on controversial issues.

Because we are so grateful for the beautiful grace of God, both of us have
looked for natural opportunities throughout our careers to tell others about

our faith in Christ, what He's done in our lives, how He's changed us, and how we see Him working today. This sharing of our faith has been in two primary ways: *showing* Christ to others by striving for excellence in all we do, because we are doing it for the Lord (Colossians 3:16–17); and by *telling* others verbally about Christ. This sharing of our faith is what we call being *on mission*. To us it means recognizing that the Great Commission is the opportunity of all Christians, not just those in vocational ministry. It's a very personal awakening to a great truth of Scripture: Not only do people *in general* need to know Christ, but people *around us* need to be blessed by knowing Him and His marvelous grace as well. And so, as on-mission Christians, we stay alert for natural times and ways to share Christ's grace and love wherever we are, whenever we can, with whomever we can.

Before we embark on this journey, allow us one final caveat. The principles we've discovered are organic and pervasive, woven through the lives of people in a way that makes it impossible to organize everything into neat little categories. They should be viewed more like ingredients in a recipe than cookie-cutter solutions that force everyone into the same mold. We'll try to highlight these principles as they flow naturally from the pages of Scripture and the lives of those we profile. But life is complex and doesn't allow for artificial distinctions. So you won't find that type of rigid organization in this book. It may take several chapters to unpack a few of the principles and only one chapter to unpack another. We will frequently cross-reference principles as we see several of them converge together in one story. For

> *Nobody could make a bigger career change than going from a trial lawyer to a mission board employee! Some of my partners thought I was crazy for making the move, others said they already knew I was crazy but this just confirmed it. But the most puzzling reaction came from fellow Christians who congratulated me for stepping into the ministry. "I was already in the ministry," I would tell them. "God just changed my mission field." Then they'd give me that* Are you serious? *look—the wheels turning. The law practice, a ministry? Our courts, a mission field? You bet!*
>
> *—Randy Singer*

Introduction

those of you who want eight simple steps that guarantee a life of success, keep looking. For those who are interested in eight God-centered principles that will help make your life count for eternity, keep reading—this book's for you.

1

Made to Count!

Starting books is hard. So we sought some sage advice. Authors and editors, publishers and readers—they all told us basically the same thing: Start with something that draws the reader's attention, something unpredictable, something that makes a big stink.

"Are you sure?"

"Yep, we're sure."

Okay, you asked for it:

Andy was building a new home. As often happens, his construction crew was having an awful time with their subcontractors, suppliers, and schedule. Nothing was going right, the boss was frustrated, and the men were grouchy. The weather was hot and humid, smothering the men like a wet blanket. To add to the misery, the construction site's port-a-john reeked with odors that made the crew gag. The company that was charged with keeping it serviced hadn't been heard from for days.

Suddenly, blaring music pounded the air as a truck rolled down the street toward the site. The music seemed to fill the block with its rock beat, and everybody's attention shifted to the vehicle that slid to a stop in front of the partially completed house. They noticed that it wasn't the regular maintenance man who got out of the truck. Instead, it was a big, burly guy, covered with tattoos, flashing a huge smile, and singing at the top of his lungs. He greeted the entire crew with a contagious grin, grabbed his materials and headed—enthusiastically!—into the odiferous disaster. Just before stepping in, he yelled across the yard that the former man had quit, and he would be taking over. Then he disappeared into the four-by-six-foot cubicle. Rumblings began inside the port-a-john and grew louder and louder, as though he were attacking every inch of the relief station. It almost sounded like he was wrestling with a tiger in there.

The construction crew suspended work temporarily, their gazes drawn to the spectacle of the port-a-john. A few snickered. They knew that the only thing worse than the smell of a port-a-john that hadn't been maintained well was the smell of cleaning that same port-a-john on a hot and humid day. But this guy seemed to stay inside forever. Every man on the site wondered how he could stand it and thought of how quickly they would have raced in and out just to escape the stink.

After a while the crew noticed something radically different. An inviting smell drifted across the yard. Then Mr. Good-natured finally emerged with his smile still intact. "Hey," he said, "the guy taking care of this for you wasn't doing a very good job. From here on out, I guarantee this will be the best it can possibly be, because I'm here to serve you." With that, he hopped in his truck, grinned, waved, turned on the blaring music once again and began to back out of the driveway.

Dumbfounded, one man yelled to the driver, "How can you do that? More important, *why* did you do that?"

"Oh, it's simple," replied Mr. Good-natured. "You see, I work for the Lord. And I do every task as though I were doing it for Him. See you next week!" And with a smile, and singing at the top of his voice, he drove away leaving the awestruck crew with their mouths on the ground.

Making life count is not so much about what you do as *how* you do it. And *why*. And, most important, for *whom* you do it.

This book will outline some principles designed to make your life count. The temptation for those of us who want to make a difference is to jump right into the *what* or at least the *how*. But we started this book with our friend from the cleaning crew for one very critical reason. We can know the eight principles of this book by heart, backwards and forwards and in three different languages, but if we don't have the right motivation for doing what we do, our lives will never make an eternal impact.

> *Making life count is not so much about what you do as how you do it. And why. And, most important, for whom you do it.*

The ironic thing about the way God works is this: If you yearn for an important position, a major platform, a lot of fame, or massive power, *He won't use you*. We didn't really start with the port-a-john story because it made a "big stink"; we started with it because the cleaning guy illustrates a foundational issue about motivation. To make life count, we must first die to ourselves and be willing to do whatever God asks us to do. In the words of Paul, we must be "crucified with Christ."[1] For some that means doing for the glory of Christ a job that might make others turn up their noses. For others, it might mean following God's call into an arena of life they feel totally unequipped to handle.

Death to self. It sounds so hard. And if we're not careful, it brings about images of God as a big ogre in the sky, consigning each of us to a mission in life that will make us most miserable. But that's not the God of the Bible nor the God who caused our friend to have so much enthusiasm when he cleaned port-a-johns. When we trust God's plans even more than our own, we discover a level of contentment and impact that we never dreamed possible. It allows us to glory in the most menial tasks, and to attempt the most impossible ones. After all, shouldn't the same God who created us also know the most fulfilling mission for our life?

> "For I know the plans I have for you," declares the LORD, "plans to prosper you and not to harm you, plans to give you hope and a future.

Then you will call upon me and come and pray to me, and I will listen to you. You will seek me and find me when you seek me with all
your heart."[2]

These comforting words, spoken by God through the prophet Jeremiah thousands of years ago, still echo in our hearts today. And if you've ever wondered
whether they still have relevance in our hectic twenty-first century society,
we'd like you to meet someone. Her name is **Ruth Okediji.**

For some, an acceptance to Harvard Law School would be cause for celebration. But not for Ruth. She remembers being entirely underwhelmed. *That's
nice*, she thought. But it wasn't Ruth's first choice. She had her heart set on
becoming a full-time missionary. *Maybe I'll just get a law degree first*, thought the
Nigerian whiz kid. *Then, I can fulfill my dream and go to Bible college.*

Sound crazy? Well, you haven't heard the half of it. Welcome to Ruth's
world—a place where God speaks and moves in mysterious ways, just like in
Bible times.

Ruth was born in Nigeria to parents who'd been led to the Lord by missionaries. Her parents "paid a high price" for following Christ and eventually
moved the family to the United States. There, at age seven, Ruth also
became a Christ follower. The girl who seemed to do everything early graduated from high school three years ahead of schedule. The family moved back
to Nigeria where Ruth attended college, abiding by the Christian "dos and
don'ts" and generally living a godly life.

But Ruth wanted more. She would get up early in the morning and pray:
*Lord, I can be a good girl all my life, if that's all you want. But Lord, I've got a
hunger to do more.*

God answered with a persistent friend who dragged her to a Bible study
on the book of Jeremiah. It was through that study that Ruth discovered a
God who cares about every step of our lives. For eight weeks, she couldn't get
away from this challenge: "And you will seek Me and find Me, when you
search for Me with all your heart."[3]

At the end of the study, Ruth got down on her knees and took God at His
word. *I want to know if You have a specific plan for my life*, she prayed. *If not, I'll
just keep being a good girl. I know I can do that. But if there's more, show me what
it is, and I'll do all of it.* Her life would never be the same.

"It was like a love affair," Ruth says, the joy still in her voice. Even now you can tell that Ruth still hasn't gotten over it. "My life changed so radically that my parents, who were sold-out Christians themselves, wondered if I'd joined a cult." She chuckles at the memory.

Radical faith. A radical commitment. What could it mean? For Ruth, she was sure it would mean full-time ministry. "I wanted to be a missionary," she recalls. "I wanted to go to Bible school."

"So why didn't you?" we asked.

"Because I couldn't get any peace about it. I would wake up early, around three or four in the morning, and pray." (For this lady, early means *early*.) "I would beg God to let me go into full-time ministry. I wanted to be with Campus Crusade, but it was clear as day to me that He just kept saying no." It was, according to Ruth, one of the most difficult periods of her life. "I was crushed. I concluded that I just wasn't good enough to go into full-time Christian ministry."

And so, at the age of nineteen, as a recent college graduate not "good enough" for the ministry, Ruth decided to pursue Plan B. She "cast [her] bread on the waters"[4] and applied to a few graduate schools—the usual culprits from the American Ivy League: Columbia (her dad's alma mater), Harvard, and Cornell. Poor girl. No wonder she couldn't muster any excitement. "In the back of my mind, I still wanted to go to Bible school. I figured I would just go ahead and get a graduate degree first."

"I remember when the acceptance letter came from Harvard. It just didn't seem like a big deal, compared to my dreams."

Ruth tucked her acceptance letter away after showing it to her mom and dad (another "that's nice" reaction, but remember, he's a Columbia man). She also didn't give it much thought, because the family simply didn't have the funds to afford a Harvard education. Her father was a professor and couldn't afford the high tuition of an Ivy League school. Not to worry. Ruth's uncle had a brilliant idea.

"Harvard Law School is fine," said her uncle, who had business and academic connections in Toledo, Ohio, "but why don't you go to Toledo Business School, get an MBA, work a little, and save money for your Harvard Law School tuition?" Barely bothering to pray about it, Ruth set her face toward Toledo. She sent Harvard a letter deferring and went on with her life.

Months later, after hearing a Harvard alum speak, Ruth knew she had missed God's call. "I prayed hard about it later that night, and God convicted me. I just wept before the Lord and repented of my prayerlessness in the decision to turn down Harvard." Ruth immediately wrote Harvard asking to be reconsidered and then prayed for six weeks, watching the mailbox every day. Harvard did not respond.

As August crept along Ruth became more passionate in her prayers. Then one morning, just a few weeks before law school would convene, she heard God's answer. "It was like an audible voice in the room with me, telling me I would attend Harvard. Nothing in the natural realm had changed, but I knew beyond a doubt that this was what God had planned for me. I ran and woke up my roommate, shaking her out of bed and saying, 'God speaks! God speaks!' She, of course, thought I was crazy."

Ruth felt compelled to fast that day and tell others that she was now going to Harvard. When the mail came *that very day*, she received a letter from the Harvard admissions office, giving her details about the start of school, as if they had never even received her rejection letter. The letter from Harvard had an April postmark. Ruth received it in mid-August. A few weeks later, she started her law career at Harvard. God had spoken indeed! And it wouldn't be the last time.

For the next four years, Ruth saw God do some amazing things in the lives of her fellow students, many times using her in the process. She came to realize that Harvard was her mission field, but it was also just a temporary assignment. "I decided that if I couldn't be a missionary, I could at least go to Wall Street with one of the megafirms and make a lot of money to support missionaries."

God had other plans. During her final year of law school, Ruth received notice that she had been granted an interview for a job even though she hadn't planned to apply. The problem was that she didn't find out about her time slot until less than an hour before the interview. There was no time to clear up the mistake. So she threw on a dress and headed to the interview room to tell the prospective employer that it was all a big misunderstanding. The employer was the associate dean of the University of Oklahoma College of Law, interviewing Ruth for a teaching position.

Ruth felt impressed to go through with the interview, then committed the matter to prayer. "I didn't want to go to Oklahoma," she recalls. "First, I had never even been to Oklahoma, and I had all the East Coast snobbery going. Second, my parents had been in education their whole lives. I didn't want to do the same thing. And third, I was headed to Wall Street to fund missionaries!" But she didn't say no this time without praying it through. For days, she just told God all the reasons she didn't want to go to Oklahoma. "Then finally, one morning, I just gave up. 'If you want me to go to Oklahoma, I will go to Oklahoma.' I felt an immediate *pop* of relief."

At Oklahoma, Ruth discovered that she had a gift for teaching. We talked to students who studied under Ruth years ago and still rave about her teaching style and what a great role model she was. She taught for eleven years in Oklahoma, with stints as a visiting researcher at Harvard Law School and the Max Planck Institute in Germany, and as a consultant to the World Intellectual Property Organization in Geneva, Switzerland. She now teaches at the University of Minnesota.

> I have an open door policy. And a teacher gets lots of questions. This gives me a chance to give my testimony. If they want to know who I am, what makes me tick, I share from the Bible. I can't separate who I am from the words of Scripture. And if students have needs, I pray with them, and I share from Scripture. There is no situation in the lives of my students that the Word doesn't have something to say about. I tell my students: "I am interested in you!"

Ruth recognizes that students respond to authenticity and love. The approach has served her well. She shows them Christ—in the form of a law school professor.

"Two words that sound so easy," says Ruth: "Follow me." She hesitates. "But it's not just following Christ geographically. It's going where He would go and doing what He would do for the reasons He would do it."

Later in this book, you'll learn about others who God is using in surprising ways to redeem the dark corners of our culture. And in the next chapter, we'll begin looking at the first of eight Biblical principles about how God calls us to a mission that will change our world. For now, it's enough to know that God speaks. And to know that He is speaking *to you!* The same God who said He has a plan for us, makes it clear that we can hear His call and discover the plan: "Whether you turn to the right or to the left, your ears will hear a voice behind you, saying, 'This is the way; walk in it.'"[5]

That's the message of this book. Discover what God is saying to *you*. Learn how He's guiding you—not just in *what* you do, but *how* you do it. And most important, *why* you do it in the first place. For both Ruth and the man cleaning port-a-johns, making life count was not about status or power or positions. "I work for the Lord," said the port-a-john guy.

"It was like a love affair," said Ruth.

From port-a-johns to the ivy-covered walls of Harvard Law School, and everywhere in between, God is searching for those who love Him enough to trust His plans for us. Plans to prosper and not harm us. Plans to make our lives count.

PRINCIPLE 1

God prepared a unique plan and calling for your life even before you were born.

Key scriptures:

- "Before I formed you in the womb I knew you, before you were born I set you apart; I appointed you as a prophet to the nations" (Jeremiah 1:5).
- "God, who had set me apart before I was born and called me through his grace . . ." (Galatians 1:15 NRSV).
- "For we are His workmanship, created in Christ Jesus for good works, which God prepared beforehand that we should walk in them" (Ephesians 2:10 NKJV).

Key points:

- God designed you with your destiny in mind, creating you with every gift and resource necessary to perfectly accomplish His will.
- *Everyone* is designed with a unique plan and calling in mind, not just those in full-time ministry.
- It's time to let God "out of the box" as you search for His *unique* plan and calling for your life.

2

Designed for a Destiny

What will God think of next? That's what Jay Sekulow must have been wondering as he stood before the nine scowling judges of the U. S. Supreme Court. How he got there—a Jewish lawyer defending the rights of Christians to evangelize at airports—is an amazing story of how God prepares a unique destiny for us even before we are born.

Jay was born in Brooklyn on June 10, 1956, and soon after moved to Long Island with his family. There, he attended a Hebrew school, though religion was never a very important part of his life.

> Sometimes my father referred to the "Supreme Being," but he usually reserved such references for the holidays. I didn't think much about God either. I do remember that when I was thirteen years old, I'd exchange friendly insults with a Gentile friend of mine—a Catholic, I believe.[1]

As a teenager, Jay and his family moved to Atlanta, where he finished high school. After graduation, he decided to enroll in Mercer University, a Baptist college, so he could stay close to home.

"Dad," he asked, "will it bother you if I go to a school that calls itself a Baptist college?"

Fortunately for Jay, his dad was a pragmatic man.

"I'm just glad you decided on a four-year college," his dad replied. "Go ahead, get yourself a good education."

Jay enrolled at Mercer determined to outstudy and outsmart all the Christians. He especially looked forward to Bible class, where he would be able to prove that Jesus was not the Messiah.

But then he ran headlong into the prophesy of the suffering Messiah contained in Isaiah 53. It boggled his mind. *I have to be misreading the text*, thought Jay.

He realized with great relief that he was reading from a "Christian" Bible—and the King James Version at that. He grabbed the Jewish text, but the description of the suffering Messiah seemed just as clear. How did he resolve this new crisis of belief?

He did what any aspiring lawyer might do. He took out a sheet of paper and drew a line down the middle. He decided to make a list of why Jesus fit the description of the Messiah on the right side, and a list of why He did not on the left. The left side of the paper remained eerily blank.

> I kept looking for a traditional Jewish explanation that would satisfy, but found none. The only plausible explanation seemed to be Jesus . . .
>
> I'd never felt the need for the Messiah before, but now that I was studying the prophesies and reading about what the Messiah was supposed to do, it sounded pretty good. I'd always thought my cultural Judaism was sufficient, but in the course of studying about the Messiah who would die as a sin-bearer, I realized that I needed a Messiah to do that for me.

A few days later, Jay went to hear a Jews for Jesus singing group named the Liberated Wailing Wall. Jay felt enormous relief when he realized that other Jews believed in Christ as the Messiah. At the conclusion of the service, the group invited people to walk the aisle and join the group at the front if they wanted to give their life to Christ. Jay Sekulow walked the aisle and everything changed.

His first challenge as a new follower of Christ was breaking the news to his parents. He decided at first not to say anything for a while, but he found that he couldn't keep the good news to himself. This was a life-changing decision. He *had* to share it with those he loved.

> That night, I woke up about two o'clock. I couldn't go back to sleep, so what did I do? I went and woke up my father. I told him that I'd decided Jesus was our Messiah. His response was, *"You* decided?" And of course, he was implying, "Who are you to decide?" But he didn't elaborate. He just shook his head sleepily and said, "We'll talk about it in the morning."

But when morning came, Jay's dad never mentioned a word about the prior night. In fact, it would be three years before Jay had a real opportunity to discuss Christ with his parents. Though they didn't agree with Jay, they were never hostile. "I've always been grateful," Jay says, "that whatever my parents might think of my beliefs, they love me and respect me enough to prevent any disagreements from tearing us apart."

Now that God had this young law student's fervent heart, it was time to prepare his mind for the challenges ahead. In His omnipotence, God saw the day that Jay Sekulow would stand before the Supreme Court in case after case and defend the Constitutional rights of Christians. But to be successful, Jay would need a lot of trial experience and the ability to take firm stands for unpopular causes. In short, Jay needed a thick hide. And God had just the ticket—the IRS.

> I began my career at law as a prosecutor for the IRS. It was the best experience I could have had. In one sense, it's a miserable job; prosecuting people for fraud and tax evasion never won anybody a popularity contest. I even had a few death threats. What made it worthwhile was that I was trying as many as twelve cases per week. It was phenomenal. That kind of experience can really launch a person into a terrific career.

Jay Sekulow, tax collector. And a pretty good one, at that. But God wasn't finished with him yet. Jay had proven his faithfulness in the "little things." Now, God was ready to entrust him with "much."

Made to Count!

When the IRS requested that Jay relocate, he left government work and entered private practice. Jay's law firm flourished, as did a real estate development company that Jay started on the side, grossing over $20 million in its first year.

But the thing that motivated Jay the most was the work he was doing as a board member for Jews for Jesus, helping the organization that first introduced him to Christ. So when the chance came to work for them as general counsel, Jay immediately left the lucrative private practice of law. Before long, he was defending the rights of Jews to share the gospel in the airports, arguing before the highest court in the land at the age of thirty. He won the case with a rare unanimous ruling from the nine justices. He had come a long way from prosecuting tax cheats.

Did you ever consider the fact that God designed you for a unique mission in life?

Today, Jay heads one of the top public interest law firms in the country, the American Center for Law and Justice. He heads a large staff of lawyers who take on hundreds of cases a year. Jay himself has argued at the Supreme Court nine times, always defending the religious freedoms guaranteed by our Constitution.

In a 1990 case involving the constitutionality of Bible and prayer clubs on public school campuses, Jay cleared the way for generations of public school students to share the gospel with their classmates. Three years later, another case guaranteed the rights of churches and religious groups to use school facilities after hours.

It may sound like every lawyer's dream, but Jay will be the first to tell you it's not all fame and glory. Cases are still won or lost based on the briefs—lengthy written submissions that Jay and his team toil over for hours. Every new Supreme Court case means hundreds of hours of drafting, editing, and researching briefs, as well as massive amounts of time preparing and rehearsing oral arguments. Sleep becomes a rare commodity. As the day of oral argument approaches, the tension becomes nearly unbearable. But Jay Sekulow loves it. The law fascinates him and the tension energizes him. And in the midst of all the fevered activity, Jay never loses sight of the fact that God, not the court, is ultimately in control. That thought always calms him in the storm.

He would rather discuss the next big case than his own role in defending religious freedom. Talk to him for five minutes or listen to his daily radio talk show, and you'll be amazed at the passion and energy Jay brings to his quest. It's almost as if God looked out at the future on June 10, 1956, and knew He would one day need a good constitutional lawyer. So He created Jay Sekulow.

A Flawless Design

Did you ever consider the fact that, just like Jay Sekulow, God has perfectly designed you for a unique mission in life? You may think you're carrying around a design defect or two, that maybe God created you on a Friday afternoon or a Monday morning, but nothing could be further from the truth. God created you with a purpose in mind. And the master designer knew just what it would take for you to accomplish that purpose *in complete reliance on Him*.

Think about the many ways that God expresses this principle in Scripture. In the book of Jeremiah, we find these compelling words: "Before I formed you in the womb I knew you, before you were born I set you apart; I appointed you as a prophet to the nations."[2]

"That's just Jeremiah," we say. "Maybe God made Jeremiah perfectly suited to his task. But look at me, I'm no Jeremiah!"

Be careful, because God has some pretty strong words for that type of thinking. This time He speaks through another Old Testament prophet named Isaiah:

> Destruction is certain for those who argue with their Creator. Does a clay pot ever argue with its maker? Does the clay dispute with the one who shapes it, saying, "Stop, you are doing it wrong!" Does the pot exclaim, "How clumsy can you be!" How terrible it would be if a newborn baby said to its father and mother, "Why was I born? Why did you make me this way?" This is what the LORD, the Creator and Holy One of Israel, says: "Do you question what I do? Do you give me orders about the work of my hands? I am the one who made the earth and created people to live on it. With my hands I stretched out the heavens. All the millions of stars are at my command."[3]

God knows what He's doing. And lest we think that this was some special concept that just applied to Old Testament prophets, God placed this same thought—that He created us with a destiny in mind—on the heart of the apostle Paul. In his letter to the church at Galatia, Paul acknowledges this truth in his own life: "God . . . before I was born set me apart and called me through his grace."[4] Then, in his letter to the church at Ephesus, Paul makes it plain that this concept applies to *every* believer: "For we are His workmanship, created by Christ Jesus for good works, which God prepared beforehand that we should walk in them."[5]

That's a powerful verse, made even more so if we understand the sense of what Paul was really saying here. The word generally translated *workmanship* is the Greek word *poiema*, a word that literally means *masterpiece*. This awesome God, the One who created the majesty of the starry hosts and the intricacies of the mitochondria, says that we are His *masterpiece*, a work of art, specially created for a world-changing purpose. We are not God's Friday afternoon special, we are His crowning achievement, His display-case creation—His *masterpiece*.

But God does not create masterpieces just to put us on display. He creates us for a relationship with Him and to make a difference for Him. He creates us with all the tools and resources necessary to fulfill His calling on our lives.

THE FOUNDATIONAL CHARACTERISTICS OF GOD'S CALL

This unique plan for your life, the one that God prepared even before you were born, is your own individual "calling." Throughout history, God has always called people to make a difference for Him. That calling is primarily to *Someone* (Jesus Christ) and only then to do *something* that will take place *somewhere*. But it will always be in that order—the *Someone* will always be front and center. When one of the other two factors moves into first place everything else gets out of balance.

Throughout history, God's call has always been both *personal* and *purposeful*. The same God who calls you called Adam and Eve into a personal relationship with Him. He's the same Creator who called Noah to build a boat and save humanity and Abram to take his family at an advanced age and go to a brand new land where he would start the seed of a new nation and Moses to leave the backside of the desert and face down the most powerful leader in the world. He's also the same God who picked a shepherd boy named David out of the fields and made him the greatest king Israel ever had. He's the God who shaped the prophet Jeremiah even while he was in his mother's womb and set him apart as a clarion voice to his nation.

In the New Testament, that same God entered the world clothed in human flesh through His son Jesus. And the promised Messiah spoke to the masses, spending time among the crowds, deploying seventy for ministry and pouring His life into twelve to change the world. He would die on a cross, yet even there call a thief to follow Him to paradise. Following His resurrection, Jesus would use Peter to launch a new movement of people called to be world changers—the church (called-out ones). And the call of the resurrected Christ knew no socioeconomic barriers—from blind beggars to the Praetorian Guard in Rome. From slaves to merchants and rulers. From world leaders like President George W. Bush, Billy Graham, and the late Mother Teresa to everyday people like us.

And through each succeeding page of Scripture, we find person after person who God personally and purposely calls to the adventure of a lifetime in order to make a significant impact in changing their world. And that same God is still actively at work in your life today.

God's call is always personal, even when it takes place in the setting of the corporate. When God deals with people He calls them *by name*. After all, He is an intimate and personal God.

How different from the society in which we live where we all are known best by a Social Security number, an e-mail address, or simply as "resident." How many times have we all received blanket e-mails or envelopes with a computer-generated label entitled "resident" only to open the message and find it says, "We want to take this opportunity to bring you a *personal* message"?

That's never the way God operates. In Isaiah 43:1, He says, "Fear not, for I have redeemed you; I have summoned you *by name*; you are mine" (italics ours). Take a moment to recall a few of the biblical adventurers . . .

- When He called Noah to build a boat, *He called him by name.*
- When He called Abram to go to a new land and leave his comfort zone, *He called him by name.*
- When He spoke to Moses from the burning bush and placed a fire in his heart, *He called him by name.*

- When He spoke to Samuel in the middle of the night, *He called him by name.*
- When He chose David as the unexpected new king, *He called him by name.*
- When He heralded Zaccheus out of the sycamore tree, *He called him by name.*
- When a light as bright as the noonday sun broke forth on the road to Damascus and a voice called to Saul, *He called him by name.*

And God is still doing the same today. Jesus, in referring to Himself in John 10:3 as the Good Shepherd, says that the shepherd calls to his sheep, "and the sheep listen to his voice. He calls his own sheep *by name* and leads them out" (italics ours).

You will probably always remember where you were on that Saturday morning in February 2003 when the space shuttle Columbia disintegrated over Texas. All of our hearts stood still as we watched the sequence in stunned silence. Hurtling through space on reentry at over eighteen times the speed of sound, experiencing temperatures in excess of 3,000 degrees at more than 200,000 feet in altitude, the Columbia began to break apart.

Shortly afterward, President George W. Bush spoke to the nation to confirm the tragedy. Somberly, our president told us that all seven astronauts had been killed. As he described the circumstances he incorporated Isaiah 40:26 saying,

> Lift your eyes and look to the heavens:
> > Who created these?
> He who brings out the starry host one by one,
> > and calls them each by name.
> Because of His great power and mighty strength,
> > not one of them is missing.

In the same way that God knows the names of the stars, our president assured us, so also He knew each of the astronauts by name. And for those astronauts who knew Him personally, the work was more than just a mere job, it was a calling, a platform from which they lived their mission for their Lord.

Christian contemporary singer Steve Green affirmed that reality some days later. Rick Husband, commander of the Columbia, was one of Steve's closest friends. In an interview Green powerfully focused on this subject when he said:

> Rick recognized his calling absolutely to be an astronaut. Rick was a shining example of someone who understood his calling. He'd been gifted and called into an arena of service as an astronaut. He did it with everything inside of him. He was the best he could possibly be, and he did it to the glory of God.[6]

Rick Husband saw himself as *on mission*, but not just for NASA. He had an even higher calling. During his time at NASA, Rick pulled together other astronauts and aspiring astronauts into his own home for Bible study. He wanted those gifted and talented people to know the Creator into Whose heavens they would soar. That was his mission field, his platform for making a difference for the Savior Rick knew.

Wherever you are today and in whatever circumstances you find yourself, God is calling you by name to a special plan and an incredible adventure.

God also calls us *purposefully*. The exciting thing about God's message to us is that He has a purpose for each of our lives individually and for all of our lives corporately. God loves you and me enough to be intimately personal with us and to chart out a course for our lives to significantly impact our world. Jeremiah 29:11–13 says, "'I know the plans I have for you,' declares the LORD, 'plans to prosper you and not to harm you, plans to give you hope and a future. Then you will call upon me and come and pray to me, and I will listen to you. You will seek me and find me when you seek me with all your heart.'"

> **Whether life is going great or it's in a ditch, the characteristics of God's call in your life are always personal and purposeful.**

What a mind-blowing promise God made! And just in case you're going through a tough time and even feel God may have forgotten your address, let alone your name, you might note that this promise is made to Israel as they are being led away into captivity. God is not just a God of the good times, but

He's a God who's with you in the midst of the tough times, always planning a purpose of significance for your life and calling you to join Him in what He's doing. So whether life is going great or it's in a ditch, the characteristics of God's call in your life are always *personal* and *purposeful*.

And it's not a call that leaves us in the lurch about where to go and what to do. In the book of Hebrews in the New Testament God compares the living of our life with the running of a race. He talks about getting rid of issues that weigh us down in our life. God challenges us to keep our focus so we aren't distracted by circumstances, crowds, and other "contestants" but to stay the course. And notice a very important insight on the "course" we are called to run. The Scripture says it is "marked out for us."[7] God has gone to great lengths to chart a course for each of us to run as we follow Him.

So think about this concept and let it permeate your being. You were designed for a destiny. Before you were born, God looked into the future and planned an amazing mission that He wants you to complete. Oh sure, He can get it done without you, but instead, He wants you to experience the joy of being part of His redemptive work with mankind. Knowing exactly what would be needed, God created you, His masterpiece, as perfectly suited to your own calling as Jay Sekulow is to being a constitutional lawyer or Rick Husband was to being an astronaut. And now He waits patiently, calling you by name and inviting you to be part of the greatest adventure you'll ever experience.

3

God's Calling Is for Everyone, Not Just for Ministry Professionals

Amber, a willowy high school senior, sat next to her parents in the third pew. Church was their weekly ritual. Some Sundays she was totally tuned in to the service. But with college coming up Amber had a lot on her mind and had to admit she sometimes zoned out. *When will I hear from Tech? Will Brent call back? Does Jessica wanna go for coffee after church? Am I ready for biochem? Should I apply to one more school . . . just in case?* Halfway through the service, something unusual happened. Deep inside there seemed to be a still, small voice, almost a whisper. "Amber, are you listening? Today's message is for you!"

She resisted the urge to turn and see if the other teens in church had heard it too. Those who sat in the back would probably miss it. *Too busy passing notes.* Besides, the words seemed so soft, she realized if she hadn't been listening closely, she might have missed them. But what did it matter if the others heard? She'd always been a little different—a bit of a geek according to her classmates.

There it was again. She heard it even if no one else did, and that was enough.

She heard it first right after the pastor read the scripture for the service, Jeremiah 1:5 (NLT): "I knew you before I formed you in your mother's womb. Before you were born I set you apart and appointed you as my spokesman to the world." The quiet voice in her heart seemed to grow louder as he launched into his message.

Made to Count!

Pastor Wills had always been so encouraging in her life, but until today she'd never considered that God had anything special for her. Yet Pastor Wills was saying that *each* of us is created for a special purpose. "We are *created to count*. God has been preparing a unique plan and calling for your life since before you were born. If you feel a little different, even a little weird—that's great. God created you to experience His pleasure when you do that special thing that only you were created to do."

Was Amber hearing this right? The words resonated within her, penetrated her spirit, and spoke to her passion. *Yep, that's me . . . unique. In fact, some of the kids think I'm so unique I'm weird. And I know I feel His passion when I'm in the chemistry lab doing experiments. How weird is that?* But this message went beyond likes and dislikes, knowing our God-given abilities, our passion. It was about using those *for Him*. It was about why God created her the way He did, with a special plan in mind just for her!

The service was ending, and Amber felt electrified. She heard Pastor Wills extend an invitation to answer God's call to service. To come to the front of the church. That same inner voice prompted her to step out and move forward. *Put feet to my faith!* The next thing Amber knew, her feet were walking down the aisle, and her heart was answering the call.

"I think God's called me to be a biochemist," Amber whispered to Pastor Wills when she arrived at the head of the aisle, "to stand up for the sanctity of life in these new frontiers of biomolecular research."

"That's great, honey," said her loving pastor, patting her shoulder. Then he motioned for one of the deacons to come pray with her. The deacon led her to the empty front pew.

She felt a little awkward, not really knowing what to pray. The deacon didn't have a clue either. So they prayed something vague and then sat in silence while the pastor stood talking to others who had responded. And the still, small voice inside Amber's heart became a voice of doubt in her head.

At the end of the invitation, Pastor Wills brought the singing to a halt, said a final prayer, and made a special announcement. "Today," he said, "God has moved in the lives of several people. Kelly and Jessica have given their lives to Christ, inviting Him into their hearts as Savior and Lord!" The pastor beamed as he put his arms around the shoulders of the two teens while the congregation applauded.

Wow! thought Amber. *Cool!*

"In addition, Justin, one of our fine young adults, and his wife, Marty, are publicly sharing today that they sense God's call to go overseas to serve on the mission field. Jeff Rogers, one of our fine businessmen, has been grappling with God's call to vocational ministry for some time and today he's making public that he's leaving the workplace to head to seminary, then on to vocational ministry." The clapping rose to a swell for Justin, Marty, and Jeff.

"And there were several others," said Dr. Wills, "who made significant decisions as well."

Amber felt her face burn as she slumped in the front row where she'd been seated. *Made significant decisions? What did that mean? Was my decision just a "significant' decision?" Did I hear wrong? Miss God's call? Can God even use a Christian biochemist?* She felt foolish. Maybe she'd missed the whole point of the message. Amber couldn't remember a time when she'd felt more confused. *I should have listened more closely. Maybe I didn't hear the voice of God at all . . .*

Calling Out the Called

Though Amber is fictional, her experience is not. All too often, members of our churches who feel called to secular professions are treated like second-class citizens. It's almost as if we have taken this very first principle—that God prepared a unique plan and calling for our lives even before we were born—and added a caveat. If you're truly spiritual, that "unique plan and calling" will be to the mission field or ministry. How many times have we heard a pastor or a missionary leader talk about "calling out the called"? Or heard speakers plead with us to leave behind our secular pursuits and put it all on the altar for Christ? How many times have we been part of a "commissioning" service for those sent to the mission field? Or an "ordination" service for those surrendering to full-time Christian ministry?

Now, consider this: How many times have we been part of a commissioning service for people determined to make a difference for Christ *in some of the most challenging yet influential professions in America?* How many lawyers, politicians, entertainers, educators, journalists, and businessmen or businesswomen consider themselves "commissioned into the service of Christ"? It's no wonder Amber is confused. Rarely do we celebrate the decision of

Christians to join God in His work right where they are! In fact, like Amber's fictional pastor, sometimes we don't quite know what to do with such people. (The complete story of Amber, as well as her friends and pastor, is being told in a companion interactive Bible study workbook called the *Made to Count Life Planner*. It will walk you through these eight principles and help you achieve your life's mission.)

Don't get us wrong. God needs more, not fewer, Christians who will respond to His calling into full-time ministry and prepare to lead doctrinally-sound churches by seeking out the theological training available. Our pastors and their spouses have one of the toughest and most critical roles in the kingdom: equipping believers for the work of ministry. We would never want to denigrate that high calling. And then there are the dedicated missionaries. The authors of the book in your hands are leaders of a mission board. We love our jobs! And we're incredibly grateful for those who have responded to God's call on their lives to enter the mission field. They serve in the toughest places crossing cultural, socioeconomic, and geographic barriers to reach those who otherwise might never hear the gospel. They take the gospel to the inner cities, into the prisons of our country, and to remote locations that have no church.

> **Rarely do we celebrate the decision of Christians to join God in His work right where they are!**

We call these folks our missionary "heroes," and we rightly honor them for the sacrifices they make in sold-out service to the kingdom. We applaud and cheer for them when they step forward and announce their intention to follow God's call. We help them achieve the seminary training needed to maximize their impact. We pray for them and support them generously with our offerings. We study the mission fields to which they have moved. But the Ambers of the world sit slumped in their pews, feeling like second-class citizens, poor cousins to the real *on mission* Christians—the missionaries and the ministers.

As authors and leaders of the North American Mission Board, we believe we must warn the church not to send a message that elevates one type of calling over another. And we hear from our missionaries who know they can't reach this nation alone with concerns about an unhealthy message that has crept into the symbolism, terminology, and communications of the church. It's the church's own form of caste system, and it goes something like this:

- If you're *super*spiritual and *totally* surrendered to God, you'll go to the *international* mission field.

- If you're *fairly* spiritual and *somewhat* surrendered, you'll become a missionary right at *home* in your own country.

- If you're even *a little* spiritual, yet sensitive to God's calling, then you'll at least surrender to *full-time Christian ministry* or the *pastorate*.

- And then, for those who want to have their cake and eat it too, you can still try *to serve God in a secular arena* like the practice of law. (Oops . . . maybe not *that* secular of an arena!).

We hope you appreciate the tongue-in-cheek spirit in which we provide this list! But let's be honest; some folks in the church have these attitudes, and we must be careful not to let them take root. It's our position that the church today should embrace with joy, appreciation, respect, and support not only our missionary heroes but the *on mission* Christians who are taking a stand for Christ *right where they are*.

Maybe you are one of these. Maybe you are a teacher or a dentist or a homemaker, or maybe you work in a computer company or a lumber mill. Maybe you sense that God is calling you to serve Him by talking about Christ to neighbors in your cul-de-sac, to the guys in the break room at work or to the woman in the cubicle right across the office from you. Yet somewhere in the back of your mind, rattling around in your noggin, is the *false* message that if you were really answering God's call, you would be getting your passport and your shots, putting your house on the market, and heading to a place that requires you to cross an ocean.

After all, isn't this consistent with what Christ communicated? Consider the disciples—fishermen and tax collectors . . . *pagans*—until they met Christ. He immediately commanded that they drop their secular pursuits and become His disciples. "I will make you fishers of men," He told them.

Calling out the called. Isn't that the way that Christ worked?

CHRIST AND THE CALL

Sometimes that's how Christ worked. Like the apostles.[1] Blind Bartimaeus.[2] Paul.[3] All heard the call to follow Christ, then they immediately dropped what they were doing and never looked back.

For the rich young ruler, Christ was characteristically blunt: "Go your way, sell whatever you have and give to the poor, and you will have treasure in heaven; and come, take up the cross, and follow Me."[4] Sadly, the ruler rejected the adventure of a lifetime, clinging instead to the decaying riches he loved so dearly.

But have you ever thought about the Christ-followers whom He didn't "call out" into what today we would call full-time ministry? And have you ever wondered why? Take the Roman centurion, for example. Here is a man of great authority in the Roman army who desperately wanted to see his sick servant healed. The man came to Jesus, pleading for his servant. When Christ offered to go to the centurion's house and heal the servant, the centurion did an amazing thing. He begged Jesus *not* to come: "I am not worthy that You should come under my roof. But only speak a word, and my servant will be healed."[5]

Christ responded by healing the servant without even going to the centurion's house. And then He commended the centurion: "I have not found such great faith, not even in Israel!"[6] What a miracle! What humility by the centurion! What a commendation! But if we stop with what Christ said, we learn only half the lesson.

For the other half, let's focus on what Christ *didn't* say:

"Go your way, sell what you have and give to the poor, then I will heal your servant and you will follow me."

"Lay down your sword and pick up a cross; I will make you a soldier of the cross."

Or perhaps, a little more bluntly: "The Roman army?! Do you have any idea how corrupt and ungodly that organization is?"

After all, we are talking about the *Roman army*, an outfit that killed and oppressed the Jews. That enforced emperor worship. That used brute force to enslave entire nations and carry women and children into captivity. Could this man possibly be of any use to Jesus there? Could he really be a Christ-follower and stay in *that* job?

"Go your way," said Jesus, "and as you have believed, so let it be done for you."[7]

Can't you just see the disciples' jaws drop? The hand of Peter shooting up? "Hey, what about making *him* a 'fisher of men'?" Peter might want to ask. "How come *he* gets to keep his day job?"

But Jesus said not a word about changing careers. Not a whisper about the atrocities of being a military man. Not even a sideways twist of the head and a telltale wink that says, "Next time I come, be working for somebody respectable."

No. Christ simply commended this man's faith. And perhaps Christ didn't ask the centurion to leave the Roman army precisely *because* He needed a man of great faith right where Satan set up camp. Makes sense, doesn't it? Send the centurion to the place where the spiritual battle is raging the hottest.

And he's not the only one. There's Zaccheus, the tax collector.[8] And Joseph of Arimethea, who served Christ as a member of the corrupt Jewish religious establishment, the Sanhedrin.[9] And a man called "Legion," a demoniac healed by Christ who begged Jesus to let him tag along with the disciples. But Jesus wouldn't let him. "Go home to your friends, and tell them what great things the Lord has done for you, and how He has had compassion on you."[10]

And so it was with Christ. Some were "called out" to follow Him. Others were called to make a difference right where they were. Some were trained to be apostles, leaders of the New Testament church. Others were called to serve Christ in a secular field. And never is there a hint that one type of calling is more prized than the other.

In fact, according to Paul's letter to the Galatians, in Christ there is no "Jew nor Greek, slave nor free, male nor female, for you are all one in Christ Jesus."[11] To Paul's list we might add one more: in Christ, there is no professional or amateur. For we are all equally called to make a difference for Christ's kingdom.

THE ROLE OF THE LAITY IN THE GREAT COMMISSION

Any doubt that amateurs would play a pivotal role in fulfilling the Great Commission was eliminated early in the life of the church. With His parting words, Christ instructed His apostles to be His witnesses "in Jerusalem, and in all Judea and Samaria, and to the end of the earth."[12] But in typical apostle fashion, the gang got bogged down in Jerusalem.

The apostles, trained for nearly three and a half years by Christ Himself for church leadership, were overwhelmed by the explosive growth of the church. Disputes arose. (Sound familiar?) And the apostles found themselves spending more time playing referee than studying and preaching the Word of God. In particular, they had to preside over the daily distribution of food, because the Hellenistic widows claimed they were being neglected in favor of the Hebrew widows.

You can sense their frustration: "We didn't go to school for *this!*" Well, what they actually said sounded a *little* more dignified: "It is not desirable that we should leave the word of God and serve tables."[13] Their solution? They appointed seven men who were "full of the Holy Spirit and wisdom" to take care of the business of the church.[14] This freed the apostles to go back to prayer and the ministry of the Word.

It's amazing to watch what God accomplished through these seven men. Stephen was the first martyr of the church. A man who faced death without flinching, calling on God to forgive those who stoned him. And when the persecution intensified, it was these "laypeople" and other "amateurs" who took the gospel throughout Judea and Samaria. Revival broke out in Samaria through the preaching of Philip, another layperson who God used mightily. Scripture records that the multitudes with one accord heeded the things spoken by Phillip, "and there was great joy in that city."[15]

Then, in the midst of this astonishing city movement, (to understand the local impact, think of a Billy Graham revival without the stadium), God led Philip to a desert road to meet *one* guy. And the man didn't even have anything in common with Philip. He was from another continent, had different colored skin, dressed in a way that seemed strange to Philip, and spoke a different language—we're talking *big* barriers to cross. But because of Philip's availability and obedience to God's call, that man accepted Christ and took the Savior back to Africa. Over time others, such as St. Augustine and David Livingstone, were influential in that continent, and now statistics tell us that approximately twenty thousand people become Christ-followers every day in Africa alone.[16]

Where were the apostles during this great revival and critical step in the

Great Commission? On the bleeding edge of the mission field, helping take the gospel to Africa or other continents? Hardly. Not those guys. The apostles were still hunkered down in Jerusalem!

"At that time a great persecution arose against the church which was at Jerusalem; and they were all scattered throughout the regions of Judea and Samaria, *except the apostles.*"[17]

Don't misunderstand. We're not making fun of the apostles. They probably stayed where the heat was the hottest. They preached with great power and authority. And, according to legend, all but one died a martyr's death. But our point is simply this: From the beginning, God used the "amateurs" as well as the "pros" to fulfill the Great Commission. And He works no differently today.

When Christ issued the Great Commission, He didn't emphasize the training the apostles had received or the sermons they would preach or the church office they might hold. Instead, He focused on a power that's available to everyone, from brand new Christians to seminary presidents. "But you shall receive power," Christ emphasized, "when the Holy Spirit has come upon you; and you shall be witnesses . . ."[18]

> From the beginning, God used the "amateurs" as well as the "pros" to fulfill the Great Commission.

The power is *universally* available, and the call is *universally* applicable. It is also nonnegotiable. You can't hire a pastor to take your place. This is not a mercenary army. There are persons who will see Christ only through you and skills that only you bring to this great task. So, whether you are paid to be good (a full-time minister) or are good for nothing (the rest of us), you are called to be a vital part of the Great Commission.

A DIVERSE ARMY OF BELIEVERS

The key is to understand that God's unique plan and calling for your life is not bound by the man-made distinction between secular and sacred. If God has called you to do it, then it's sacred. Throughout history, God has called some of His followers *into* full-time ministry, some *out of* full-time ministry, and still others to stay *right where they are.*

In fact, we'd like to introduce you to three such followers of Christ. They lived in different eras and had very different experiences but shared one common thread. They all discovered the unique calling that God had prepared for them even before they were born, and they weren't deterred by man-made distinctions between the secular and the sacred.

Charles Finney. In the autumn of 1821, the jury was still out on the fate of Charles Graddison Finney. In all honesty, most of his friends and acquaintances had written him off a long time ago. Even the pastor in his small church in upstate New York, a man named George W. Gale, believed that Finney was a lost cause. Literally.

The problem with Finney, believed Gale and others, was that the same keen intellect that made him such a great lawyer also prevented Finney from taking the step of faith necessary to trust Christ. After all, why would someone as self-reliant, smart, and successful as the young Charles Finney even need God?

Finney would debate Gale for hours, stumping the Princeton-trained theologian with unanswerable questions. He would also cross-examine his neighbors with the simple yet deadly logic of a trained lawyer.

"If God answers prayers that are consistent with His will, then why has He withheld a great revival?" Finney would ask. "You have prayed enough since I have attended these meetings to have prayed the devil out of [town], if there is any virtue in your prayers. But here you are, praying on and complaining still."[19]

It's no wonder that George Gale, and most of the others, gave up on Charles Finney, saving their prayers for someone more reasonable.

But Finney the lawyer, and Gale the theologian, didn't know two significant facts. Not everyone in the congregation had thrown in the towel on Finney. Several younger members, including Finney's future wife, stubbornly refused to quit praying for him. More important, God had not given up on Finney. Though Finney was an outstanding lawyer, God had other plans.

And so the Hound of Heaven went to work, convicting the arrogant attorney day and night of his sin. It came to the point where Finney himself recognized that "my pride of heart [was] the great difficulty that stood in the way" of knowing Christ. On a particularly emotional autumn morning, when he was overcome with a sense of his own unworthiness, he resolved to go for a walk in the woods and accept the salvation of Christ "or die in the attempt."

Finney's conversion was so dramatic and complete that it turned the town upside down, ironically answering the very prayers for revival that Finney had mocked. On the first day after his conversion, Finney literally put down his lawyer's briefcase and picked up a preacher's Bible.

The first person he met that morning was Judge Wright, the senior partner in Finney's firm and his mentor in the law. Instead of the usual talk of cases or politics, Finney told about his conversion to Christ. The judge dropped his jaw in astonishment, then hung his head and left the office without saying a word. (A few days later, after he too found Christ in the same woods, the sophisticated judge returned to Finney shouting: "I've got it! I've got it!" Then he fell to his knees and praised God.)

The second man Finney met at his office that morning was a deacon from the church with an important case Finney was scheduled to argue that very day. "You'd better settle that case," Finney advised him.

"What do you mean?" asked the startled deacon. Finney had never mentioned settlement before.

"I have a retainer from the Lord Jesus Christ to plead His cause, and I can [no longer] plead yours," replied Finney.

The deacon settled his case. And Finney went on to become one of the greatest revival preachers this country has ever seen.

Wow! What an amazing story of God's amazing grace. If He can use a lawyer to preach revivals, than He can use anybody to do anything. But does it always work that way? We get saved one day and, if we're really serious about it, we stop our secular pursuits immediately and start preaching the very next day?

I have a retainer from the Lord Jesus Christ to plead His cause, and I can no longer plead yours.

CHARLES FINNEY, MEET MARK EARLEY

Mark Earley. In so many ways Mark Earley, the president of Prison Fellowship Ministries, is the opposite of Charles Finney. For starters, nobody ever thought Mark Earley was beyond hope. Even as a student, Mark was one of the "good" kids. "I attended a small church in Chesapeake, Virginia, every Sunday," Mark recalls. "I was working on my points, growing up with loving parents and a good church. I figured if I obeyed my parents, worked hard and racked up enough good points, then one day I would go to heaven."

Mark's theology seemed comfortable enough until his Sunday school teacher entered class claiming to be a changed man. "Gary Bradley just walked in, plopped Bibles on the table for every student in the class and said, 'This week I became a Christian.'"

Quite a shock to an impressionable high school senior who assumed everyone in his church was already a Christian. But Mark had a lot of respect for his Sunday school teacher, and so he agreed to join a Bible study on the Gospel of John. One day as they took turns reading Scripture, the lot fell to Mark to read John 3:16. He whizzed through the familiar verse, but then his teacher asked him to read it again. "This time," said Gary, "put your name in there."

"For God so loved Mark Earley," the young man read, "that He gave His only begotten Son. So that if Mark Earley believes in Him, Mark Earley will not perish but will have everlasting life."

"At that moment," says Mark, "the proverbial light bulb went on. Before that I knew God loved the world, but I didn't know He loved me personally. I understood that Christ had died for the world, but not for me personally. When I understood *that,* I couldn't run to Christ fast enough."

Unlike Finney's dramatic conversion, the soft-spoken student simply knelt by his bed and asked Christ into his heart. No blinding light. No angelic trumpets. Not even hot tears streaming down his cheeks. Just a quiet resolve to follow Christ wherever He might take him.

He attended William and Mary, majoring in religion and preparing for missions work. "I was serious about following Christ. To me, being 100 percent sold out meant full-time Christian ministry." That commitment took him to the mission field in the Philippines, working with The Navigators in campus ministry. While there, Mark felt God's stirring again. This time, it was not *toward* the international mission field, but *away* from it.

"So many Filipinos would ask me: 'What's it like to live in America?' I realized that most of the rest of the world would give anything to be in my country, to enjoy our freedoms and liberty. And I really started thinking about how indebted Americans are to our founders, people who risked their lives and gave their all—their entire working lives, their best efforts and best thoughts to those principles articulated in the Declaration of Independence."

The more God turned Mark's thoughts toward his homeland, the more Mark realized how fragile America's liberties and freedoms really are. "I had this deep sense that we can't rely on the commitment of our forefathers alone, that every generation has to make a fresh and new commitment to the democratic and religious principles of the founders. Each generation has its own responsibility. And I started to think I could make a difference."

Called from the mission field into politics? You've got to be kidding. What did others think about that?

"The advice I got was well-intentioned, but most people urged me to stay in full-time ministry rather than consider the public square as a mission field to which I was now being called," admits Mark. "I was actually breaking the mold.

"I think it's because the church has used the idea of *calling* as referring to geography, occupation, or people. So we struggle with the issues of where to live, what to do, whom to marry. But I discovered that God's calling is really to Himself. Paul says that 'God, who has called you into fellowship with His Son Jesus Christ our Lord, is faithful.'[19] I am called to fellowship with Jesus. In that context, God will place me wherever He wants me to be, and that pursuit will become holy."

Holiness and politics. It was this brash and idealistic notion that Mark brought back to America. He went to law school (don't all politicians?) and worked for a few years in the private practice of law. Then he made what appeared to be one of the dumbest political moves in the history of Virginia politics.

He became a political kamikaze pilot. He ran for state senator against a popular and powerful incumbent who had served in the senate for twelve years. Mark ran as a Republican in Chesapeake, a city that boasted no elected Republicans in any branch of government. Not one! Not even a city council member.

"Nobody thought we were going to win, including me at times. We were outspent three to one. I'd never raised money before in my life. People would say, 'He's a nice guy, but he doesn't stand a chance.'"

Mark's cutting-edge campaign strategy in the age of media-driven elections? Walking. "We wore out a few pairs of shoes. My wife and I just went door to door and talked about the issues people cared about."

And when the returns came in, walking beat television. Mark Earley became Chesapeake's only elected Republican, eeking out 50.1 percent of the votes, not counting hanging chads.

For ten years Mark served in the state senate, followed by a term as attorney general of Virginia. He forged a strange coalition for a Republican: school teachers, religious conservatives, and minority voters. "I spent a lot of time in the African-American community," Mark explains, "working hard on issues of racial reconciliation." He also developed a mentorship program for at-risk kids throughout the commonwealth and started a Bible study for Virginia legislators.

"I constantly remind myself," Mark told us during his interview for this book, "that Christ came to redeem and reign over every square inch of His creation." Including, according to Mark, that square inch in the dark and dirty corner of our world called politics.

But just because God leads you into something doesn't mean it will always be smooth sailing. Mark learned that painful lesson during what he calls "the hardest year of my life." In 2001, he accepted the Republican nomination for governor of the Commonwealth of Virginia. Like the first political race he entered, the odds were against him. But this time, all the shoe leather in the world couldn't get him elected.

The remarkable thing is not that Mark lost a tough election in a super-charged political climate. Nor that he would describe it as the toughest time in his political life. No, the remarkable thing is that early the next morning, Mark got right back to basics, reminding himself that God had a plan for his life, and that it was still a good plan. No pity party for this guy.

> I got up the next morning, had my quiet time and wrote at the top of my journal, "things I believe today." I listed ten things, including two pertaining to my understanding of God's sovereignty. First, losing the race for governor has to be part of God's plan and grace for my life, and I accept it as such. Second, I believe that God, having closed this door, will open another. Then I prayed: *Lord, I eagerly anticipate and wait for Your direction of where You want me to go and what You want me to do.* The list was important, and I needed to share it with my kids,

because they took it harder than I did. So we had our morning together, our family devotionals, and I shared that with them.

Two days later, God called with a new assignment. Well, not precisely God. It was actually Chuck Colson. But there was no doubt in Mark's mind that he was calling on God's behalf. "We've been praying for four years for the next Prison Fellowship president," Chuck said when Mark returned the call. "And God has led us to you. Would you consider praying about this with us?"

And even Mark Earley, a stoic Christian if ever there was one, a man who generally handles life's ups and downs without getting emotional, can hardly contain his enthusiasm and wonder at this part of God's plan. "Prison Fellowship," he says, "was an opportunity for me to be involved in all of the things I've ever had a passion about since I became a Christian: evangelism, disciple making, missions, public policy, the criminal justice system, and caring for those on the margins of life."[20]

From all accounts, Prison Fellowship is in good hands. And it's amazing how God groomed Mark from the very beginning to be an experienced leader for one of this nation's leading ministries. From Virginia to the Philippines and back. From ministry to politics and back. There's not much predictable about God's leading in Mark's life if you look at geography or occupation. But there is if you focus on obedience.

When God said "Go," Mark started walking. And he wore out some perfectly good shoes along the way.

Like Charles Finney, some of us will be called into full-time ministry. Others, like Mark Earley, will be called from the ministry to a whole new endeavor. But still others won't be called to go anywhere at all.

CHARLES FINNEY AND MARK EARLEY, MEET WILLIAM WILBERFORCE

But first, meet John Newton. Because in order to understand the driving passion of Wilberforce, you've got to know a few things about his mentor, John Newton.

John Newton had seen the worst of the British slave trade. He knew men who tried to get as many slave girls pregnant as possible on the voyages to the new world. He'd seen men so cynical that their whole mission on the slave ships was to find a Christian, ridicule him and try to talk him out of his faith. He'd seen men so cruel that they'd think nothing of whipping the skin off the back of a young deckhand for a minor infraction. And he was reminded of the worst of those offenders every morning when he looked in the mirror. John Newton, former slave trader, knew a thing or two about the slave trade.

But John Newton had also experienced God's amazing grace, heard the call to ministry and served as a pastor for more than twenty-five years. He also penned hymns. His burning passion was to find a way to abolish the evil that he once propagated.

His outspoken views won some converts—none more important than a twenty-seven-year-old member of Parliament who wrote a letter to Reverend Newton in 1785 requesting a *secret* meeting. To avoid anyone finding out, they met at the parsonage rather than the church.[21]

William Wilberforce. The strain showed on the face of young William Wilberforce. During their clandestine meeting, he told Reverend Newton that he had heard him preach when he was just a boy, but he "was afraid to surrender to Christ for fear of what others might say."

"And now?" asked Newton quietly.

"Now I have come to a crisis of my soul," answered the grim-faced member of Parliament. "I am afraid of turning my back on Christ. But I also fear losing face and prestige. If my constituents were to hear that I embraced . . . religion, my career would be over." Wilberforce paused and shifted in his seat, then gave Newton a determined half-smile. "But maybe that would not be so bad. You have always inspired me, Reverend Newton. When I used to go to Olney and hear your sermons I felt like jumping up and asking you to help me be a preacher like you.

"When I returned to London that enthusiasm cooled and I eventually got into politics. Still, as I read the Bible and Christian books, I am convinced that I must act on what I have read. I've come to see you about this before I go out of my mind."

For the next few hours, Reverend John Newton explained the way of the

Cross and total surrender to Christ. Wilberforce wept and gave his life to Christ. Now he was ready to follow Newton into the ministry and face the consequences.

But Newton wisely counseled against it: "If God can use an ex-slave trader for His work, imagine what He can do through a gifted member of Parliament. There's nothing in the Bible that says you cannot be both a Christian and a statesman. True, these two seldom are found in one person, but it happens."

Wilberforce accepted this advice and decided to remain where he was and serve God. He went public with his newfound faith, enduring ridicule and then winning grudging respect from his contemporaries. He turned his considerable energy toward abolishing the slave trade, a blight on the soul of the British Empire.

In 1788, after a stirring three-and-a-half hour oratory on the subject, Wilberforce made his first motion to abolish the slave trade. His impassioned speech had such an impact on the other members of Parliament that the local papers predicted sure passage of the Bill. "The House of Commons on Tuesday was crowded with Liverpool merchants who hung their heads in sorrow, for the African occupation of bolts and chains is no more," predicted the London paper.

The prediction, however, was premature. After delay tactics and other political maneuvering by his opponents, Wilberforce lost the first of many votes on this critical issue. But it would not be the last. Every single year, for the next seventeen years, Wilberforce would make a motion to abolish the British slave trade. Every year, for the next seventeen years, his motion would be defeated. But Wilberforce never forgot the words of Newton, and the conviction that he was called to fight for Christian principles in Parliament never left him. Often, in the years following the death of his mentor, Wilberforce would be motivated by the words of Newton's most famous song, set to the chant of an African folk melody.

> Amazing grace! How sweet the sound
> That saved a wretch like me!
> I once was lost, but now am found,
> Was blind, but now I see.

In 1806, after eighteen years of hard work, Wilberforce finally heard the "sweet sound" he had longed for. After they counted votes on his motion to abolish the slave trade, the ranking member of Parliament said very simply, "The ayes have it!" Wilberforce had won.

But he wasn't satisfied. Never flinching from his call, Wilberforce continued to work tirelessly against the entire institution of slavery. Eventually, just four days before his death in 1833, Parliament passed a vote to abolish slavery in all the British territories. Wilberforce *the Christian* had remained Wilberforce *the member of Parliament*. And God had used him mightily.

Sometimes, answering the call of God means being a Wilberforce, staying right where you are, enduring defeat after defeat, content in the knowledge that God is not mocked, and in *His* timing *His* cause will prevail.

Remember our first principle? God prepared a unique plan and calling for your life even before you were born. For Charles Finney, God provided training on how to plead a case, then turned Finney into a revival preacher. For Mark Earley, God combined a heart for missions with the real-world savvy of politics—all so Mark could be an effective president for Prison Fellowship. And for William Wilberforce, God placed him in the middle of the political arena and gave him a mentor determined to help Wilberforce eradicate slavery, then called Wilberforce to take a stand right where he was.

God's call is not limited by human traditions or preconceptions about full-time ministry. The same God who called Finney to preach, and Earley and Wilberforce into politics, is the same God calling you in surprising ways today. And just remember: If he can use a lawyer to preach, and turn a missionary into a politician, He can use anybody to do anything!

4

Finding God's Unique Plan
Outside the Box

Carpe diem! A life of adventure. A life of significance, not merely success.

That's what God calls us to. This amazing plan that God prepared for us even before we were born is always a plan to make a difference. It is a plan of high risk and high reward. It's what we all want deep inside our hearts. Why? Because God created us to make a difference in our world and to be dissatisfied until we start making that happen, even if the first part of our life has been a drive to succeed. Too often we have obtained what we sought only to ask later, "Is that all there is?" The accumulation of stuff—awards, promotions, high-tech toys, frequent flyer miles, and second homes—leaves a vacancy in our soul. The dreaded realization closes in around our hearts like strangling fingers as we gasp and grasp the reality: Stuff doesn't satisfy!

It's the lesson Robin Williams was teaching his students in the movie, *Dead Poets Society.* Playing the character of Professor Keating, he leads the boys across the campus of their prep school into an ivy-covered building where the memories of past generations line a heavy, glass trophy case. In a scene thick with musty tradition, he invites his students to gaze at the faces of athletic heroes posing with confidence and smiling back at them from photos now brown with age. He points to the awards and trophies that are lined up like proud sentinels but are merely gathering dust. The professor instructs a student to read a poem by Robert Herrick:

Made to Count!

Gather ye rosebuds while ye may,
Old time is still a' flying,
And this same flower that smiles today,
Tomorrow will be dying.

Professor Keating's teachable point? Seize the day—or, in Latin—*carpe diem!*

Directing the attention of his captivated students to the fading photos of these campus heroes from days gone by, the professor points out that they weren't so different. Full of hormones and feeling invincible, those boys from yesteryear were bursting with hope and life, yet now they were gone. "Did they wait until it was too late to make from their lives even one iota of what they were capable? Because you see, gentlemen, these boys are now fertilizing daffodils. But if you listen real close, you can hear them whisper their legacy to you." Placing his own ear tightly against the showcase, the professor challenges his charges: "Go on . . . lean in!"

As the boys lean in, mesmerized by the professor's ability to stir their imaginations, he whispers hoarsely: "*Carpe ... diem ...* Hear it? *Carpe diem!* Seize the day, boys; make your life extraordinary!"

It's one of those movie scenes that imbeds itself in your mind. A light suddenly comes on as you watch it, one that all of us need while groping in the darkness for life's significance and meaning. We want to make a difference. God hard-wired us to do that. We desire our life to be an adventure. We hunger for our lives to be extraordinary and not just run of the mill, merely ending up "fertilizing daffodils."

If that's our desire, then what derails that plan? Why do our lives sometimes feel so boxed in?

Life in a Box

It's staggering how it happens. Life starts out when we're children as an amazing journey, filled with adventure at every turn. It doesn't take us long to strive for the adventure of breaking free and running loose from the prison of our playpen. As our mom and dad try to keep their eye on us by cloistering us within their purview of safety, we're bent on forging new trails and exploring new horizons. The adventure begins with squirming, crawling, and yelling.

Meals are interspersed with our hands slapping into piles of mashed potatoes and applesauce as the new tactile experiences bring a smile of satisfaction to our faces. We conduct aesthetic experiments on the kitchen floor, creating new designs down there with the food from our plate.

Then we step out (literally) into the wonderful world of upright mobility. The first few adventurous steps often end with our face plastered to the floor. But, being resilient creatures, we bounce back up and take off for new territories once again. Later life's heartbeat quickens as we dare to tackle a bike ride without training wheels. New worlds await when we step into the academic jungles of school. Relationships blossom, social skills take root, cultural and racial barriers are crossed. Where before we have grown up forging our own direction, suddenly team sports and class activities mold us to be a contributor for the greater good, not merely a solo artist.

The journey picks up speed and, to the horror of our parents, we begin playing dodge 'em cars on those urban racetracks called freeways. And who can forget the perspiration-producing event of stepping out on our first date, hoping that a new pimple doesn't erupt before the special night. Finally, college brings our first major "solo flight," launching us out of the nest on our own, removed from the protective shadow of parents and home that guided us through that first eighteen-year obstacle course called growing up.

But somehow, as we journey into adulthood, our sense of adventure wanes, and the routine seeps into our lives, bringing with it an anesthetizing effect to our journey. The reckless abandon that characterized the early years of our journey settles into a predictability and comfortable cocoon of safety absent risk, niceness absent critical thinking, and uniformity absent diversity. We suddenly find ourselves in a secure but boring box.

For example, we become cautious as we navigate the employment maze, entering the rat race but being careful not to take too much risk lest we— heaven forbid!—make a mistake. We establish regular work hours. We get our first home, which leads to a bit larger home, a path that lays the foundation for wanting a still bigger home. And we get two cars, the requisite two and one-half children (though we're not sure what to do with the one-half child), and we take two weeks of vacation each year. We even try to start a savings account, though most of the time there's too much month at the end of the money. We adjust to the dress of whatever our workplace says is "appropriate," and we set out to make our way up the promotional ladder. Etc., etc., etc., ad infinitum, ad nauseum. And pretty soon we're wondering, *How do I get out of this box? What happened to all the fun and adventure I thought I was going to have?*

We don't just put *ourselves* in a box. We're not satisfied until we put God in a box, too. Some of us relegate God to His appropriate portion of our lives, Sundays (and now and again weddings and funerals). We want Him to help in the "between a rock and hard place" times of our lives, but we let Him know we can handle it the rest of the time, thank you very much. Others of us limit Him to specific expectations. Life becomes segmented, like a *Time* magazine. We have the business section, the entertainment section, the health and medical section, the domestic section, oh, and don't forget, the *religious* section. We feel if we can keep life separated that neatly we'll be in pretty good shape. And when it comes to our salvation or safety, we've still got what we think we need in a pinch—shazam!—God *in a box*. We believe in a religion built more on a god we create than the God of the Bible. Our "Christianity" is a matter of convenience rather than conviction.

> **God never intended to be confined to a box or for any of us to be in one either.**

Because we're so careful to keep control over our lives, we water down the Christian life to the point that there is actually very little *Christ* in it. In fact, if we're honest, we have to ask whether our life really reflects a commitment to a living biblical Christ, or a cultural Christianity. We learn to go through the religious motions, use the Christian lingo, attend Christian meetings and events, but we lack the evidence of a life transformed by Jesus Christ. We may even blame God for our lack of fun and adventure.

Yet God intended the adventure to continue, for life to be fully and holistically integrated. God never intended to be confined to a box or for any of us to be in one either. In God's view all of life is sacred; after all, He created it. The challenge is that too often we miss a vital truth of Scripture. When God created the world, He said, "It is good." He didn't say, "What is sacred is good, and what is secular is bad."

As we saw in the prior chapter, the "sacred" was never meant to be relegated strictly to the temple or the church. Instead, the sacredness of God's mission to bring everyone into a personal relationship with Him and to become involved in His life-changing ministry to the world was intended to penetrate *every* area of life, and to involve *everyone* answering His call. Even our Puritan forefathers got that right.

> There was for them no disjunction between the sacred and the secular; all creation, so far as they were concerned, was sacred, and all activities, of whatever kind, must be sanctified, that is, done to the glory of God. . . . Seeing life whole, they integrated contemplation with action, worship with work, labour with rest, love of God with love of neighbor and of self, personal with social identity, and the wide spectrum of relational responsibilities with each other, in a thoroughly conscientious and thought-out way. . . . They were eminently balanced."[1]

When we miss this great truth we miss out on some of the greatest opportunities for adventure life has to offer. And the Christian community, if we're not careful, lapses into a stained-glass subculture with its own music, lingo, clothing, entertainment, and business directories so that we can protect ourselves from the evils of the "world out there."

Within the Christian community are people who recognize only certain methods about the way God guides and when and where He operates. In the last chapter, we talked about the myth that God calls people only into vocational ministry, not secular pursuits. A related myth is the feeling that the church is the *only* place *real* ministry happens. According to this mythology, if we're going to change the world, we need to get the people of the world to come *into* the church, so we can get the change going! And, oh, by the way, we're happy for them to come as long as they don't come too fast and they don't arrive looking, acting, or thinking too different from the members we already have (those situations are so messy for us to deal with).

If you do venture outside the walls Monday through Saturday, many of our church friends have set views of "acceptable" careers and activities for those of the faith. It's not just the distinction between full-time ministry and secular fields that we mentioned in the last chapter, but it also goes to the *type* of secular career as well. For the very spiritual there is the expected call to vocational missions or ministry. Those who don't make it to the top rung might be fortunate enough to find themselves teaching—preferably in a Christian school. The next rung down is for those working in one of the *helping* professions (doctor, nurse, therapist, etc.) and striving to deliver a good chunk of time in service at the church as well. And by all means, be sure you avoid some professions like media (you'll become too cynical) or Hollywood and Broadway (you can't keep your Christianity there) or politics (now there's a profession you can't trust).

Peggy Wehmeyer. That's what happened to television reporter Peggy Wehmeyer as she journeyed through her college years. After accepting Christ as her Savior and Lord, she became active in a campus ministry that "focused her life." But she also loved the idea of touching her world and being involved in campus leadership outside the Christian circles. Moving from major to major, she finally landed in a journalism class and found that it fired her passion, maximized her strengths, and gave her a sense that God had planned something special for her in that arena. She had discovered the application of our first principle in her life: "I sensed this is what I was created to do. It was a fit for me! Not just my gifts but also my passions."[2]

Peggy also experienced firsthand the confining nature of a "box" created by the expectations of others:

> But I thought a committed Christian went into full-time vocational work. I was a little confused. So I became very involved in a campus ministry, but every time I wanted to get involved in campus politics, or the Journalism Department, it took me away from some of my ministry activities. I was chided by ministry leaders for spending too much time in activities that took me away from the ministry. But I kept asking, "Shouldn't we be active in the world outside the church?" I felt ashamed if I couldn't make it to ministry activities, because I was too busy with other campus events. I got the message very clearly that I should go into full-time ministry if I was really a dedicated Christian.

Peggy had to choose between following the plan that God had been preparing for her since before she was born, or staying in the box constructed by others. If Peggy had stayed in that box, she probably would not have become the first religion correspondent at ABC *World News Tonight,* reporting to Peter Jennings!

Bob had a similar frustration, but with a different twist. Having met Christ at Indiana University and the wonderful lady who would become his wife, he headed off to seminary wanting to make a difference for Christ. And what a ride it was! Three years of seminary, a staff position for three years at one of the largest churches in the denomination, an invitation to a key denominational position at age twenty-seven, and then serving as the U.S. coordinator for an exploding interdenominational parachurch ministry.

Then came an unexpected turn in the adventure. God opened a door for Bob to become the director of human resources for a business corporation in Michigan. His income would be in the workplace while he helped churches that were struggling or unable to afford leadership. This approach is often referred to as bivocational ministry. It's the model Paul set out in the New Testament as a tentmaker. It's a unique and powerful way to be *on mission* for Christ.

You might imagine how shell-shocked Bob became when he received letters and calls from friends and Christian leaders he respected saying things like, "Is there something we should know? Why is it you're leaving the *ministry?* Did you burnout or break down? What's wrong?"

The message was clear. Many were telling him, as others had Peggy: "If you're really committed to making a difference for Christ, the place to be is full-time vocational ministry or missions." But if he had listened, there would be many individuals Bob worked with who may not have come to know Jesus Christ personally. It was from the position of a businessman that Bob had the platform to introduce them to Christ. And he wouldn't have missed that for the world!

There's great joy in the journey of being called to vocational Christian work, but the reality is that only a relatively small percentage of those who know Christ will ever serve in those arenas. Where does that leave everyone else? Uncalled?

So Who Are the "Called" Anyway?

The word "calling" has long been thrown around in Christian circles. Most often the term has been used in reference to those vocationally employed in ministry or missions. Yet history doesn't substantiate such a narrow definition. From early in Scripture God called individuals to follow and serve Him from many walks of life. Some were prophets and priests, but many were shepherds, kings, carpenters, former prostitutes, builders, soldiers, teachers, and estate administrators. Take just a moment and read Hebrews 11, which the church often refers to as "The Faith Hall of Fame." How many priests and prophets do you find listed there?

Throughout the early church's history and into the seventeenth and eighteenth centuries the very term *calling* served as the base for the word *vocation*. Your employment was your vocation, derived from the Latin root that meant *calling*. Whatever job you did was to be viewed as a divine appointment from God.

If we look at the early history of our nation (that wasn't written by revisionists), we will find the fathers of our country talking about their "calling" and their "vocation" rather than their job. They frequently affirmed the fact that God called them to become involved in politics. Theirs was a conviction that God was busy in the affairs of men, placing them where He wanted, never being caught unaware by even the smallest issue or circumstance. We may have become more modern, sophisticated, and advanced, but have we lost a crucial part of our soul by not speaking in these terms in modern times? God hasn't changed. He's still active in the lives of men and women, calling them to purposes larger than themselves.

Even today *Webster's Dictionary* still carries that emphasis in its definition of *calling* . . .

- A strong inner impulse toward a peculiar course of action, esp. when accompanied by conviction of divine influence.
- The vocation or profession in which one customarily engages.

So, God has always called every follower, both in the Old and New Testaments, to join Him in His redemptive mission to the world to bring people into right relationship with Him and, as a result, with each other. In both Testaments followers are called to be a royal priesthood (Exodus 19:5–8, 1 Peter 2:5)—those charged with sharing God's message to the world, interceding for the world to God and ministering in His name to a hurting world. In the New Testament even the name of the new body of believers sent to take Christ to the world would reflects God's calling. The word "church" in the New Testament was *ecclesia*—the called-out ones. And it wasn't just the "preachers" of the church who were called to make a difference; it was *every member!*

Paul himself showed that the "called" were not an exclusive club. In Romans 1 he introduces himself as "Paul, a servant of Christ Jesus, called to be an apostle and set apart for the gospel of God." There was no question in Paul's mind that God had called him to make a significant difference for Christ in his world—not only knowing Him but making Him known. The Greek word Paul uses here is *kletos*, which could be translated "personally invited." God had personally beckoned Paul to enter into a relationship with Him and to be *on mission* for Him.

Yet only five verses later Paul addresses the entire constituency of the church at Rome—every member. Get a load of these words: "And you also are among those who are called to belong to Jesus Christ. To all in Rome who are loved by God and called to be his saints."[3] The word here is the same word he used for himself, *kletos*. Paul saw the members of the church just as called as himself—to different roles, without question, but all called to walk with Christ and be *on mission* for Christ. Paul, like ministers today, was gifted and specifically called to equip others for their mission in reaching their world for Christ. (Paul stresses the same reality again in 1 Corinthians 1:1–2) That same sense of *calling* was to significantly impact the life of every devoted follower of Christ.

Os Guiness, one of the most penetrating Christian thinkers of our day, points out that disciples of Jesus were referred to as "called ones" or "followers of the Way."[4] Later history would distinguish a *primary calling* and a *secondary calling*. The primary calling is *by* Christ, *to* Christ, and *for* Christ. The secondary calling is for everyone, everywhere, and in everything to think, speak, live, and act entirely for Christ.

Therefore, every Christian is called to be *on mission* for Christ. Guiness sums it up when he reminds us, "Answering the call of the Creator is 'the ultimate why' for living, the highest source of purpose in human existence."[5]And when you answer, Guiness affirms, you will "hear God whisper three things to you in a hundred intimate ways—'You are chosen; you are gifted; you are special.'"[5]

A Two-fold Call

Now here's the exciting part. God doesn't just call us so that He can chew us up, use our lives in some master plan, and then spit us out. God's call is much more personal than that. In fact, it's a two-fold call: first to a life-changing relationship with Him and then to a life-fulfilling mission alongside Him.

The God of all creation, who is powerful, mighty, just, holy, and altogether awesome is also a loving God. It is His love that reaches from every corner of existence to call you and me to a life-changing relationship with Him. The Bible proclaims that He has loved us with an everlasting love. With that unfailing love, He draws us to Himself.

It was that same love that compelled Him to bridge the huge gap that existed between Him and us due to our sinful nature. The Bible makes it clear that we come into this world separated from God because of a sinful, self-focused nature. We have a tendency to want to chart our own course and to do things our way. We want what we want, when we want it, and the way we want it. The Bible compares us to sheep, who have gone astray wandering away from the Shepherd.

The reality is that all of us have a heart condition. We may not be having heart attacks, and we may not have clogged arteries, but when we're not in a personal and intimate relationship with God the Creator, we have a terminal disease. Yet out of love, He sent the prescription and solution for our ruptured relationship with Him:

- For God so loved the world that he gave his one and only Son, that whoever believes in him shall not perish but have eternal life.[7]

- But God demonstrates his own love for us in this: While we were still sinners, Christ died for us.[8]
- God made him who had no sin to be sin for us, so that in him we might become the righteousness of God.[9]
- Salvation is found in no one else, for there is no other name under heaven given to men by which we must be saved.[10]

So, if we want a life filled with adventure, significance, and impact, we must first make sure that we are sure that we are in a personal, intimate relationship with the Creator of all life. Are you? For God's first call is by faith in the person and work of Jesus Christ to enter into a personal relationship with Him.

As we share the stories of those who have made such an impact in their world, you will see one common element. It forms the core of our second principle, which will be covered in detail in the next two chapters. Before God called them to make a difference, He called them to Himself. The ways in which they heard that call are as varied and unique as the personalities involved, but every one of them accepted God's call and first entered into a love relationship with Him before they attempted anything alongside Him.

Before we leave this point, we need to emphasize that such a relationship is a pure gift from God. It's God who takes the initiative to draw people to Himself and offer them the gift of eternal life. Each individual will respond—some receiving the free gift, and some rejecting it. Each will make a personal choice—a willful choice and an eternal choice.

However, to be authentic, "making a decision for Christ" is more than simply believing intellectually some facts about Christ. We think this is worth pondering. When Scripture says, "believe on the Lord Jesus, and you will be saved,"[11] it does not mean merely acknowledging that some facts about Christ are true. The word *believe* is taken from a Greek word *pisteuo,* which refers to faith. But since *faith* is not a verb in English, it has been translated *believe.* The gist is that we must give intellectual assent and place the full weight of our trust for a personal relationship with God in what Jesus Christ has accomplished in His death, burial, and resurrection *alone.* It cannot be Christ plus anything. It must be *Christ alone!*

The second part of the two-fold call is this: God calls us to a life-fulfilling mission alongside Him. This forms the core of the third principle we will be studying in this book—that God calls you to partner with Him in a mission that is bigger than you are. Notice the words *alongside* and *partner* in these sentences. Too often we speak of doing things "for God." Oh, we mean well. But we miss an important semantic nuance. When we do something *for* someone we tend to be the one in control. We come up with the idea, we create the plan, and we execute the strategy. But a careful reading of the Bible tell us that God says He will do the planning, guiding, and directing. And therein lies a BIG difference! God is not nearly as concerned about what we are going to do *for* Him as He is about whether we are willing to be obedient *alongside* Him in what He already is doing. Our mission is a partnership with God in absolute control of the planning process while we make ourselves available to execute His plan. Contrary to what we have heard, we are not called to live *for* Christ. We're called to live *in* Christ. The Christian life is not just one of imitation but habitation.

> People were changed in order to become change agents in the lives of others.

An amazing thing about God's call to people throughout Scripture, and throughout history for that matter, is that He always blessed them in order that they in turn might be a blessing. People were saved in order to be sent. They were changed in order to become change agents in the lives of others. And God is still working in people's lives that way today.

Salvation is a gift, but it's a gift that brings with it a responsibility. God has given to each one who places their full weight of trust in Him the ministry of reconciliation. Findley Edge says it well when he proclaims, "The call to salvation and the call to ministry are one and the same call."[12] Edge goes on to ask whether we can ever take on a relationship with Christ by authentic faith but decide not to come alongside Christ and be *on mission* with Him. Listen to the sobering answer.

> My response to this is a clear and resounding no! Salvation is a gift, wholly a gift, but this gift is given only on the basis of the quality of response which God Himself sets. The One who called us to this

mission and the fulfilling of it, who gifted us, who appointed some to equip us, and who empowers us and gives us His presence through the Holy Spirit expects us to fulfill this mission when we say to Him, "I give You my life." Authentic faith is a faith that fulfills that to which God has called us.[13]

God does not leave His mission for us to guesswork. He guarantees His guidance for all those who have entered into a personal relationship with Him.

> I will guide you along the best pathway for your life.
> I will advise you and watch over you.[14]

> Whether you turn to the right or to the left, your ears will hear a voice behind you, saying, "This is the way; walk in it."[15]

> Trust in the LORD with all your heart
>   and lean not on your own understanding;
> In all your ways acknowledge him,
>   and he will make your paths straight.[16]

Step by step, the God who designed us for a unique destiny then called us into a life-changing relationship with Himself also guides us into a life-changing mission alongside Him.

Our friend **Jeff** stepped out of the security of working for someone else in the health care industry eight years ago, when he sensed God calling him to launch out in a new direction. He started his own company in a tough business sector fraught with medical and governmental land mines. He asked us, as well as a few other close friends, to commit to pray for him and with him that he would honor God. Eight years down the road his company is listed on the New York Stock Exchange and is generating annual revenues of $1.4 billion.

Recently, Jeff's company acquired a major competitor. What started as a business deal turned into a divine appointment. The owner of the acquired health care system had made it big—elite sports cars, planes, boats, multiple homes, and huge bank accounts. But something was missing in his life.

The due diligence on the acquisition was complex, demanding, and tedious. At every step Jeff simply prayed, *If this is your will, Lord, lead it to completion. If not, stop it at any point.* After they consummated the deal, Jeff invited the former owner to a lunch. In the middle of lunch, the conversation took a serious turn.

"Tell me, Jeff," the man asked wistfully, "what gives you such peace? I've watched you as we've walked through this entire transaction, and you seemed to be at peace whether it worked or whether it didn't. I can't understand that. In fact, I can't understand deep peace, period. I've got it all but that. Yet it's what I want *more* than anything else."

Sitting in the restaurant, gazing out over a breathtaking seascape, Jeff began to share with his new friend how a relationship with Jesus Christ changed his entire life. The conversation grew deeper, more intense, and lasted longer than either man had expected. At the end of the lunch Jeff asked his friend if he had a desire to experience that peace personally and to invite the Prince of Peace into his heart. To Jeff's surprise, the man replied without hesitation, "More than anything." And there, in the midst of a fancy restaurant, that businessman first experienced the calmness that only Christ can bring. The experience of sharing Christ was far more satisfying to Jeff than any high-flying business deal he'd ever made.

We've got a feeling that changing the ownership of a company was not the primary transaction God had in mind for that business dealing. We think it was far more this: Jeff was called to be *on mission* and placed by God in the center of the business world; then the door swung open for him to practice what he believes by helping others find the good news he had found.

The fact that Jeff happened to be a CEO is not really relevant to what happened here. It's tempting for us to look at a guy like Jeff and start making excuses. "If only I were a CEO . . ." Or perhaps, "This job is a dead-end street and even God couldn't help me do something significant here . . ." Or even this, "Staying home with these kids isn't going to change anybody's world!" Before you utter any of these sentences, think about the very first story of calling that we told in this book. Remember our friend the port-a-john cleaner, who was full of confidence and good cheer? He knew who he served and was open about it. That's why he was so good-natured, even though his job could have made him sour on life. There's a reason we put the port-a-john cleaner first. Not everyone will obtain a position of power, but everyone already has a sphere of influence. Show those within your sphere how Christ wants you to do the job you've been given, then stand back and watch what happens.

Seize the Day . . . by Surrendering

We hope you're starting to grasp the magnitude of our first principle: God prepared a unique plan and calling for your life even before you were born. You were designed for a destiny. In the words of Paul to the church at Galatia, God "set [you] apart from birth, and called [you] by his grace."[17]

We've seen that this calling is not limited by profession. You can be just as called to be a biochemist as a pastor. And we've agreed not to try to box God in as we seek this unique plan and calling. In fact, His plan for our lives is often found way outside the box of what we might expect.

Most important, we've seen that this calling is first and foremost a calling to Christ, and only then a calling to complete a mission alongside Him. In that truth lies one of the great ironies of the kingdom of God. If we want to do what Professor Keating so eloquently suggested in *Dead Poets Society*—if we truly want to *seize the day* and avoid just fertilizing daffodils—then we've got to begin by surrendering.

If you're ready to raise the white flag on your own plans and ambitions, then it's time to dig deeper into this next principle: God calls you to a life-changing relationship with Him through Jesus Christ. You'll learn that we can only discover God's will for our lives when we have first surrendered our own.

PRINCIPLE 2

God calls you to a life-changing relationship with Him through Jesus Christ.

Key scripture:

- "Therefore, if anyone is in Christ, he is a new creation; the old has gone, the new has come!" (2 Corinthians 5:17).

Key points:

- Surrender to Christ radically changes our mission in life.
- The power to complete our mission comes not from ourselves, but from Christ at work in us.
- When we abide in Christ, even our weaknesses can be used for His glory.

"The Power Lies Within You" and Other Self-Help Lies

The self-help books practically scream at you when you visit your local bookstore, assaulting your psyche with their wisdom.

- *Can't never could.*
- *The best way to predict your future is to create it.*
- *It's not who you are that holds you back, it's who you think you're not.*
- *What lies before us and what lies behind us are tiny matters compared to what lies within us.*

And this gem, from Norman Vincent Peale himself: *Believe in yourself! Have faith in your abilities! Without a humble but reasonable confidence in your own powers you cannot be successful or happy.*

It's enough to fire you up, to try something outrageous, to test that power within you to the max, like trying the Hawaii Ironman Triathlon—a 2.4-mile ocean swim, a 112-mile bike ride, and a 26-mile marathon in the scorching heat of Kona. On second thought, let's not get carried away. We get tired just thinking about it.

So it's hard to imagine what **Ricky Hoyt** must have been thinking in the middle of that race. Disabled from birth, he trained for the 1989 Ironman with his father. He knew he would get lots of skeptical looks on the race course; people might shake their heads in wonder when they saw Ricky. He also knew the winners would probably cross the finish line hours ahead of him. His goal would be to finish, even if it took all day, even if he had to cross the finish line in the dark.

Words on paper can't come close to describing the events of that day. The grim look of determination on Ricky's face. The astonished looks of the spectators. The buzz that grew through the crowd as they wondered whether Ricky would finish. The loneliness of running by flashlight on the deserted roads of Kona, as Ricky *started* the final leg of the race well after the leaders had already *finished* the entire race. And the roar of approval as the crowd greeted Ricky at the finish line followed by an ear-to-ear smile on the face of the young man who refused to let a disability define his life. The tears and goose bumps on the spectators would have told you that something truly extraordinary had happened. This was well beyond sports history and the human will to succeed. It was impossible, really. They had just witnessed a young man who couldn't even walk finish his first Ironman triathlon!

Ricky Hoyt was born with cerebral palsy. He finished the race just one second ahead of his forty-nine-year old-father—the man who swam through 2.4 miles of ocean pulling Ricky behind him in a rubber raft, then pedaled an oversized fifty-eight-pound bike for 112 miles with Ricky sitting in a basket on the front, then pushed Ricky in a special cart for the 26.2-mile running marathon.

All the self-help books and motivational sayings in the world could not have carried Ricky through that race. It was the love and strength of a father that took Ricky where he could not go alone.

A Life-Changing Relationship

What an amazing metaphor of a life transformed by Christ. It's not like God helps us do a little better what we can do on our own. He doesn't call us to Him so that we can keep pursuing our own agenda and accomplish a mission we could have done by ourselves. When God calls us into a life-changing relationship with Him through Jesus Christ, He takes us places we could never go alone.

We become like Ricky Hoyt, totally dependent on our Father. And He changes *everything!*

Consider Saul of Tarsus. Before he met Christ, he was a Pharisee and a persecutor of the Christ-followers. He consented to the stoning of Stephen, an early martyr of the church. He wreaked havoc with the church, going house to house, arresting the Lord's disciples and dragging them off to prison. In the most literal sense of the word, Saul was a terrorist.

But Saul met Jesus Christ on the road to Damascus and everything changed. He didn't become a more accomplished Pharisee or a more intimidating terrorist. His heart changed. His priorities changed. And his mission changed. Saul, the terrorist of the church, became "Paul, an apostle of Jesus Christ by the will of God."[1]

Paul's mission changed from destroying the church to building it. God called him to do things Paul could never have done on his own. Paul the apostle became an advocate for the faith, rather than a persecutor of it. And he did such a great job that we tend to forget a fairly obvious truth: Paul was not particularly gifted as a speaker. Listen, for example, to Paul's own analysis of his skills:

> When I came to you, brothers, I did not come with eloquence or superior wisdom as I proclaimed to you the testimony about God. For I resolved to know nothing while I was with you except Jesus Christ and him crucified. I came to you in weakness and fear, and with much trembling.[2]

Lest we think that Paul was just engaging in some false modesty here, we might want to look quickly at the story of Paul when he preached at Troas. Luke tells us that Paul was a little long-winded that night, preaching straight through until midnight. And just to make sure that we don't get the impression that Paul was mesmerizing the crowd as time flew by, Luke describes this little tidbit: "Seated in a window was a young man named Eutychus, who was sinking into a deep sleep as Paul talked on and on."[3]

Now there's a verse that ought to be encouraging to pastors. Paul could lull people to sleep with the best of them! And not just dozing, but what Luke describes as a "deep sleep." You know the kind—the mouth hanging open, a little slobber dripping down the chin. A *deep* sleep. Does Paul sound like a captivating orator to you?

But watch what happens next. Poor slumbering Euthychus falls out the third floor window, smacking his body against the ground so hard that the men pick him up and assume he is dead. Then Paul comes on the scene, draws young Euthycus to himself, and the young man wakes up from the dead!

Listen to the way Luke understates this miracle. The people, says Luke, "were not [just] a little comforted."[4]

Don't you love the way God works? He takes Saul, the worst of sinners, and turns him into Paul, the best of missionaries. Then he calls Paul to preach, though Paul isn't particularly eloquent or wise. He does all this so there will be no mistake about who gets the glory or how it was possible in the first place. "My message and my preaching were not with wise and persuasive words," said Paul, "but with a demonstration of the Spirit's power, so that your faith might not rest on men's wisdom, but on God's power."[5]

And You?

Have you felt the power of God in your life? When was the last time you had something happen that could only be explained by the awesome work of the Holy Spirit? When was the last time the words of Scripture just jumped off the pages at you, and it felt like you were reading a personal love letter from God? When was the last time you found yourself in such deep and intimate prayer that time just flew by and you were surprised at how long it had been? When was the last time you worshipped with your whole being, almost feeling transported to the presence of God?

If it's been a while, or if the answer is never, then you really need to camp out on this principle before going any further. God called us to a life-changing *relationship* with Him through Jesus Christ. And this new *relationship* changes everything. "Therefore, if anyone is in Christ, he is a new creation; the old has gone, the new has come!"[6]

The key here is to understand the huge difference between religion and relationship. God doesn't call us to more religion, He calls us to an intimate relationship. *Religion is activity; relationship is intimacy. While religion is words and works, relationship is walk.* Trying to do God's will through being religious would be like Ricky Hoyt trying to finish the Ironman triathlon by training harder. The key to Ricky's inspiring feat was not activity, it was the awesome relationship and dependency he shared with his father.

Churches are filled with good people who live nice lives but fail to have a personal relationship with the One who designed them. Their lives are pleasant, and they're not rocking any boats. But God intended more. From the beginning of creation, God desired a personal and intimate relationship with His highest creation—*us!* When we go through the motions without any of the meaning, all we have is empty religious ritual. Jesus made it plain that He would never be satisfied with that kind of insipid existence nor would we. He declared, "I came that [you] may have and enjoy life, and have it in abundance (to the full, till it overflows)."[7]

As we shared in the last chapter, there's only one way for that to occur. It's the one entrance point in a relationship with God— personally inviting Jesus Christ into your life and making a commitment to live as a Christ-follower. The Bible tells us, "There is salvation in and through *no one else*, for there is no other name under heaven given among men by and in which we must be saved."[8]

So the first critical step in finding God's call and plan for your life is to be sure you've entered into a personal relationship with the One who created you for a purpose. Who could know the purpose for your life better than the One who designed you? It sounds simple, doesn't it? Yet so many people miss it. Jesus Himself knew that would be the case. Listen to what He said in the greatest message ever shared, the Sermon on the Mount:

> Enter through the narrow gate; for wide is the gate and spacious and broad is the way that leads away to destruction, and many are those who are entering through it. But the gate is narrow (contracted by pressure) and the way is straitened and compressed that leads away to life, and *few are those who find it*."[9]

Another version of Scripture in modern language says it this way:

> Don't look for shortcuts to God. The market is flooded with surefire, easygoing formulas for a successful life that can be practiced in your spare time. Don't fall for that stuff, even though crowds of people do. The way to life—to God!—is vigorous and requires total attention.[10]

Made to Count!

Did you catch that? The market is flooded with surefire, easygoing formulas for a successful life that can be practiced in your spare time. It almost seems like Jesus was frequenting the same bookstores that we do and getting bombarded with the same self-help nonsense.

Those surefire formulas that Christ referred to might make you a little better at doing the things you already can do, but they won't help you do what you can't do alone. They won't radically change your life. They won't bring you into a personal relationship with a heavenly Father who wants to help you go where you can't go alone. They can't change you from a terrorist to a missionary. Or even from an atheist sold-out to communism to an advocate sold-out to Christ.

Marvin Olasky grew up in a Jewish family in New England. "Followed the sad tradition of contemporary Judaism: Bar mitzvah at thirteen; atheist at fourteen."[11] And, says Olasky, "since Satan abhors a vacuum, I began worshipping idols made of paper: political writings on which I floated leftward." The young rebel with the high IQ attended Yale, where he was praised by liberal teachers for his radical ideas:

> What I remember most about college is that I could do and write the silliest things and receive plaudits, as long as my lunacy was leftward. I received honor grades for, among other things, cutting out pictures from old Red Sox yearbooks and interspersing them with commentary about baseball racism; describing my own atheism and then claiming that such belief was at the core of the American tradition; and taking a black cat in a bag to a course in the art museum, letting him out on the floor, and explaining that I had just created a work of art that showed how the Black Panthers were freeing themselves from the container in which American society had placed members of their race.

While in college, Olasky served an internship with the *Boston Globe*, where he says his leftist political views "fit right in." Then came graduation, and the rebel had to think of something properly radical to do. The answer? "I headed west from Boston on a bicycle and peddled to Oregon, where I became a reporter on a small town newspaper. Some physical toughness could now go along with my intellectual superiority, and I would proceed to write snotty articles and educate the residents of Deschutes County on the way things ought to be."

Alas, the unenlightened residents of Deschutes County took umbrage with Olasky's snotty articles, so he "grandiosely resigned." Within six months, Olasky had joined the Communist Party, USA.

> I had it all figured out intellectually. There was no God who could change people from the inside out, and ordinary individuals were unimportant anyway. Radical change could come only outside in, by shifting the socioeconomic environment . . . through dictatorial action by a wise collection of leaders who would act for the good of all—and I would be one of those leaders.

For this self-appointed Communist leader, his next order of business was a trip across his new "fatherland" on the trans-Siberian railroad and then back to the *Boston Globe.* Eventually, he landed in graduate school at the University of Michigan. It was here that God began to do a work in Marvin's life, starting not with a Christian friend, or a pastor, or even a great Christian writer. The first seeds of doubt, and eventually conviction, were triggered by Lenin himself.

> One day near the end of 1973, I was reading Lenin's famous essay, "Socialism and Religion." At that point God changed my worldview not through thunder or a whirlwind, but by means of a small whisper that became a repeated, resounding question in my brain: *What if Lenin is wrong? What if there is a God?*

Marvin eventually came to believe that God existed. And since his communism had been based on atheism, he also left the Communist Party. He still didn't turn to Christ—he would not go so easily—but he had at least started the journey. He took a second crucial step in 1974, when he needed to develop a reading knowledge of Russian for his doctoral program. Having nothing else handy in that language, he picked up a copy of a Russian New

Testament that had been given to him as a novelty item two years before and started reading. Cover to cover. To his surprise, it had "the ring of truth."

And God wasn't finished with him yet. The very next year, Marvin was assigned as a graduate assistant to teach a course in early American literature. The materials were inundated with Puritan sermons. As Marvin recounts it, "These dead white males from over three hundred years ago were preaching to me."

He started reading C. S. Lewis and Francis Shaeffer, but it would still be a few months before Marvin surrendered his life. He had moved to San Diego and began attending a conservative Baptist church. One night, this man with the soaring intellect, the scholar who had studied Lenin, Marx, Lewis, and Shaeffer, was confronted with an approach he simply couldn't resist.

> A very elderly deacon, the deacon of visitation, came over to our apartment. He and I sat outside on the patio, in the California sunshine. I don't know if he'd even graduated from high school, he wasn't going to go through a lot of arguments like that, he just said: "Well, you believe this stuff, right?" And I said, "I guess I do." Then he said, "Well, you better join up." And I said, "Well, I guess I'd better."

Marvin Olasky attacked his newfound faith with the fervor of . . . well, an evangelist. He eventually moved to Austin, Texas, and started teaching journalism at the University of Texas. He came to believe that the problem with modern charities and welfare programs was that they didn't impose any responsibilities on the poor and totally neglected the spiritual element. He researched the history of poverty for a year at the Library of Congress and, to test his assumptions, dressing up like a beggar and visiting homeless shelters in Washington, D.C. For two days he received plenty of food, but nobody asked why he had become homeless. Nobody provided him with a Bible, despite his repeated requests.

He wrote about his research in a book called *The Tragedy of American Compassion*. The book was panned by liberal critics as the work of a "crank." But former secretary of education William Bennett called it "the most important book on welfare and social policy in a decade."[11] And eventually, George W. Bush became aware of the book and adopted Olasky's premise of a need for "compassionate conservatism"—social help that does not exclude the spiritual component.

Olasky doesn't just preach this stuff. He helped set-up New Start and City School (faith-based antipoverty and educational programs), helped his wife with a crisis pregnancy center, and adopted a three-week-old, at-risk African-American baby. He walks the walk.

But he does preach it as well. Recently, he has been doing so as editor-in-chief of *World* magazine, America's fourth largest weekly magazine. Unlike the other market leaders, *World* looks at current events from a biblical perspective.

The transformation continues. From atheist to Christian. From arrogant intellectual to humble servant. From Communism to conservatism.

"It's time to join up," said the visitation deacon. And join up Marvin did.

Professor Marvin Olasky. Proof positive that in any language, the Word of God does not return void.

Being About the Father's Business

The key to Marvin Olasky's transformation had nothing to do with finding the power deep within himself to do those things he wanted to do. The truth is, Olasky was doing a pretty good job of being an atheist and Communist all by himself. The key to Olasky's life is the same as any Christ-follower. When we invite Christ in, He does some serious housecleaning. Old desires, hangouts, and philosophies that focus on *us* are carried out to the trash. New desires, hangouts, and philosophies that focus on *Him* are carried in. We become, in the words of Paul, an entirely "new creation." The old has gone. The new has come!

This fresh start with Christ has two inevitable impacts on the mission for our life. First, we will dare to do those things we could never do alone. And second, we won't do *anything* or go *anywhere* unless we know that God has called us to it and will go with us through it.

Are you willing to go anywhere God calls you and do anything He asks you to do? Or do you want to leave some room for those self-help formulas, ready to run your own race if the call of God gets too intense?

Remember the father/son triathlon team? It may interest you to know that the Hoyts have competed in more than sixty-two marathons (including twenty straight years of the Boston marathon) as well as 185 triathlons. In 2003, their streak of consecutive Boston marathons was interrupted when the father, Dick Hoyt, had to undergo surgery a few weeks before the race and the doctors recommended that he not run. Many runners volunteered to push his son so that the streak would not be broken. But his son refused.

"I only want to do it with my father," Ricky said.

"It's All About My Strengths," Another Self-Help Lie

In the last chapter, we saw the difference between the philosophies of the self-help gurus and the biblical view of calling. The self-help principles are me-focused. The power is within *me*. If *I* can dream it, *I* can achieve it. *I* must believe in *myself*, have faith in *my* abilities! But Christ-followers are called to die to self and to abide in Christ. The focus is not on *me*, but on *Him*.

That's why this second principle is so important: God calls you to a life-changing relationship with Him through Jesus Christ. It is only when we abide in Christ that we realize the full potential of our calling and avoid the me-centered philosophy that robs us of our destiny. The "power" lies not within us, but within our relationship with Christ.

> Abide in Me, and I in you. As the branch cannot bear fruit of itself,
> unless it abides in the vine, neither can you, unless you abide in Me.
> I am the vine, you are the branches. He who abides in Me, and I in
> him, bears much fruit; for without Me you can do nothing.[1]

There is a corollary to this distinction between the self-help philosophies and the biblical view of calling, and we think it's an important concept for every Christ-follower to grasp. The self-help philosophy tells you to focus almost exclusively on your strengths—unlock their full potential, and you will change your world. Not surprisingly, the Bible takes a different view. "When I am weak, then I am strong,"[2] said Paul. "[God's] power is made perfect in [my] weakness."[3]

Though this concept seems counterintuitive, it's absolutely key to realizing the full potential of your calling. God shares His glory with no man. When He works through our weaknesses, in the most improbable ways, then there can be no question about who should get the credit. And that's why, if we focus exclusively on our strengths, we may miss a major part of what God wants to do in our lives.

> **We should evaluate both our strengths and our weaknesses with a focus on *God*, not on *us*.**

Of course, we're not saying that we just turn a blind eye to our God-given strengths and try to operate exclusively in our areas of weakness. That would be foolish. But we *are* saying that we should evaluate both our strengths and weaknesses with a focus on *God*, not on *us*. Through this prism, our strengths are seen as gifts and talents that God hard-wired into us. Discovering what we do best, and giving our Creator the glory for it, is an important part of our calling. But an equally important part is honestly acknowledging our weaknesses. We must manage those weaknesses that might lead us into sin, and also leave room for God to work in spite of—no, because of—the weaknesses in our lives.

Abiding in Christ means that we allow Him to both maximize our strengths and work powerfully through our weaknesses. And when He does, heads will shake in disbelief at what God alone has accomplished. "That, as it is written, 'He who glories, let him glory in the LORD.'"[4]

Maximize God-Given Strengths

Into every life, God has hard-wired strengths that help each of us become unique individuals. You can see it all throughout Scripture.

- For Noah there was the tenacity that kept him building an ark for 120 years amidst the ridicule of his neighbors and despite the fact that, as far as we know, it had never rained before.
- Abraham displayed a willingness to risk it all when he left the comfort

zone of one of the most advanced regions of the world to take his family to a destination he did not know.

- Moses had great courage, whether interceding for an abused fellow Hebrew in captivity or telling Pharaoh to "Let my people go!"
- David's innate charisma caused men to follow his leadership even in the toughest circumstances.
- Solomon exercised God-given wisdom in executing decisions that left all those around him marveling at his insight.
- Esther displayed with gentle steel the power of conviction that saved her own people from disaster.
- Paul had a rapier mind that could dissect the philosophies of his day while defending the gospel of Christ.

Each of these discovered significant God-given strengths that they used to impact their world. And we are similarly blessed with varying degrees of talent, intellectual capacity, physical prowess, personality skills, temperaments, and so much more—each individually crafted by our Creator for the unique mission He prepared for us even before we were born. That's exactly what David meant when he said in the book of Psalms:

> Oh yes, you shape me first inside, then out;
> > you formed me in my mother's womb.
> I thank you, High God—you're breathtaking!
> > Body and soul, I am marvelously made!
> > I worship in adoration—what a creation!
> You know me inside out,
> > you know every bone in my body;
> You know exactly how I was made, bit by bit,
> > how I was sculpted from nothing into something.
> Like an open book, you watched me grow from conception to birth;
> > all the stages of my life were spread out before you,
> The days of my life all prepared
> > before I even lived one day.[5]

Did you notice the phrase David used when he talked about how God fashioned us "bit by bit" and "sculpted from nothing into something"? It's almost as if David could look out at our twenty-first century and envision God as the master computer programmer, writing the program for our lives byte by byte, hard-wiring us with everything necessary to get the job done.

In chapter 11, we'll be exploring this concept in more detail, helping you discover exactly how God hard-wired you and what that might be saying about His plans for you. We'll ask you a number of questions designed to uncover those talents and strengths that God wants you to use in the furtherance of His kingdom. We'll also provide you with access to an Internet-based tool that will help you understand your Personality Temperament Profile, so that you can see how God designed your personality and the way you relate to others.

But we don't want you to wait until then to begin thinking in general terms about the strengths that God entrusted to you. After all, you are the stewards of these talents, and God expects you to maximize them for His glory. Your strengths and talents are God's gifts to you; what you do with them are your gifts to Him.

In their insightful book, *Soar with Your Strengths*, Donald Clifton and Paula Nelson list five characteristics that aid us in discovering our strengths. To their thoughts, we've added a few comments of our own in parentheses.

Listen for yearnings. Yearnings are characterized as things that naturally attract your interests, passions, and enjoyments. They are an indication of what "makes your soul sing" and gives you a sense of significance and accomplishment. (What do you think about in your leisure moments? What activities draw you in?)

Watch for satisfactions. It's in satisfactions that contentment is most often found. When God-given strengths are exercised profitably, there is an innate satisfaction that settles within the soul, a feeling of contentment that you are using the strengths God has given you to productively and effectively contribute to life and the world around you.

That satisfaction also builds a sense of significance deep within as you feel yourself growing and maturing. (Internally there is a sense of jubilance, an *All right!* that makes you feel like you are "on your game" in exercising your competencies.)

Watch for rapid learning. Where yearnings and satisfaction intersect, rapid learning is an inevitable result. In an arena of strength, learning is most often exponential rather than incremental. It seems to come easily, almost like it's second nature.

Glimpses of excellence. When strengths are exercised, excellence is a by-product. There is a desire from deep within to not only do something well, but also to be the best you can be at doing it. (We have a strong desire to go from good to great. And we seem to be able to achieve it.)

Total performance of excellence. This varies extensively from exercising excellence in a given event or time frame. Rather, this type of excellence is a continuum. (It means that every time we exercise strengths that have been built into our lives, and then sharpened, excellence results.)[6]

Strengths surface when we do almost effortlessly what seems to be challenging to those around us. The fact that these types of strengths are different in everybody is what makes life interesting and complementary at the same time. One person may be strong in public speaking but absolutely despise detail planning and administration. At the same time, someone close to him may love the intricacies of strategic planning and detailed questions but be dumbfounded at how anyone can stand up and speak or teach extemporaneously. Put them together, and you will have a well-planned and orchestrated conference featuring a gifted and talented speaker. It's for that reason secure leaders learn to lead with their strength and staff to their weakness. They allow those around them to exercise their own strengths without being intimidated or threatened. The synergy of the group becomes far stronger than the sum of the individual members.

But always remember this: God gives us strengths not so we can glory in our gifts and giftedness but so we can glory in the Giver. "Every good gift and every perfect gift is from above, and comes down from the Father of lights, with whom there is no variation or shadow of turning."[7] And He gives us gifts in order that we might complete the mission He has planned for our life.

But There's Another Side

It's easy to become focused on our strengths and forget the flipside of the coin: God uses our weaknesses for His glory. Weaknesses come from internal qualities and external circumstances. But regardless of their origin, they are powerful tools in the hands of a God who has no limitations on what He can do.

Made to Count!

When things happen despite our weaknesses, God alone gets the glory. It's one of the great paradoxes in Scripture: His power made perfect in our weakness.

There are really three different types of weaknesses, each with its unique blend of challenges and opportunities.

- First, there are those weaknesses that result from an unrestrained extension of our strengths. We can safeguard against these weaknesses by being aware of our tendencies and exercising moderation.
- Second, there are personal weaknesses that arise from shortcomings in our personalities, physical abilities, intellect, or emotional makeup. These must be managed and controlled to keep us from sin and to allow us to become everything God wants us to be.
- Third, there are those personal and circumstantial weaknesses that we really can't do anything about. For these weaknesses—here's the tough part!—we should actually learn to *thank* God and expect Him to use these weaknesses for His glory.

Weaknesses that are the "other side" of our strengths. Strengths are a wonderful gift from God, but their excess inevitably becomes our weakness. It's critical for us to face the fact that any strength left unrestrained becomes an unavoidable weakness. Part of "maximizing" your strengths, as we talked about in the last section, is learning to control them. Master your strengths, or they will master you.

Think of Moses's courage. When exercised outside God's plan, it led to murder and exile. Or what about Abraham's risk tolerance? When he became impatient with God's timing, he took matters into his own hands and had a child with Hagar, thus forming the seed of the historic Arab/Israeli conflict. David's charisma led to his downfall by an inability to control his passions.

None of us is immune. When we rely too much on our strengths, we inevitably become weak. Like the gifted Christian speaker who gets so wrapped up in what he's saying, or how he's saying it, that he loses focus on the message itself. Or a diligent worker who, due to an amazing work ethic, doesn't know when to quit and becomes a workaholic. Or someone with intuitive wisdom who begins to think she knows it all and has the answer to everything.

Andy Horner. By his own admission, Andy is a perfect example of this trap. Born in Ireland, Andy was one of thirteen children. He grew up attending church every time the doors were open. "It seemed like we went every night of the week plus three times on Sunday. We walked about a mile and a half, so I figured I'd walked about 4,000 miles for Jesus by the time I was seventeen, and I was getting sick and tired of it."

He made a commitment to Christ at age eleven, but by age seventeen he'd had enough of the disciplines of home, the regiment of church, and the expectations of the family. So he joined the navy and turned his back on his faith for ten years. "But God never left me. He was so faithful, and my mother prayed so much, there wasn't a night of my life in those ten years that I didn't know something was wrong and missing inside of me." Years later he would reconnect with the church.

Andy left the service, got married, and launched a career of all-out service at Johnson Wax and later at Xerox. He focused on doing a job, doing it well, and giving everything he had. After eighteen years, he had given so much that he was "fried" emotionally and physically.

He decided he needed a career change and jumped at the opportunity to become COO of a home decorating empire called Home Interiors. Moving his family to Dallas, he attacked this new job like he had the others—full bore, 180 miles an hour, holding nothing back.

Though time was at a premium, Andy made time for church. He served as a deacon at First Baptist Church of Dallas, taught Bible study, and was part of church visitation. His childhood pattern, which he had rebelled against, was now being repeated in his own family. "Looking back on it, I was awesome. I would have won an Academy Award *outwardly*. But inside I'd lost my joy, my peace and, being Irish, I was filled with ego. I was doing a lot of things *for* Jesus, but I could never really get any peace that I was in His will."

Andy left Home Interiors after another eighteen years of exhausting devotion.

When I left, I was totally burned out, very depressed, and very unhappy. I was just struggling in every relationship possible. That's when I discovered something important about myself. I discovered that Andy Horner was what you might call 'impacted by horizontal relationships.' In other words, my greatest desire was to impress those around me. I wanted to let the church know how great I was working for Jesus. And frankly, I did a great job at that, but I became an empty shell.

Struggling with whether to go to the mission field, the ministry, or someplace else where he could make a radical difference for Christ, Andy found himself on a mission trip with a friend, Dr. David Wyrtzen.

Andy told him, "I wish God would call me into ministry. I've been waiting all my years for Him to call me. As a kid I used to pray and I would even put out a wet towel and ask God to make it dry by morning, just like Gideon. And I'm still waiting."

After a long pause, David turned to Andy and asked, "Do you think that God would put you through all He has in the business world just for you to get into something brand new and go to the mission field at age sixty? Why don't you become a minister in the workplace?"

"It wasn't long after that I was lying in bed and came to a crisis. I told God, 'I'm not going back into sales. I'm just not going to go there. Lord, I just can't do it.'"

And in the quiet stillness of his bedroom, Andy heard God saying, "Andrew, I've been waiting forty years for you to tell Me you can't do something. Now let Me do it for you."

As Andy describes it today, it was at this moment—as a sixty-year-old man—that he discovered God's will and call for his life. He went back into direct sales, but this time things were different. He decided to abide in Christ, leaving the results to his Lord, and safeguard against his own frantic work habits and self-reliance.

Andy launched Premier Designs, Inc. a jewelry business based on taking high fashion jewelry to neighborhood home shows. "We're a corporation built on biblical principles," Andy explains. "We started this company so moms could stay at home with their children and yet have a job and income that pays the bills."

Andy's company is built on the servant model. Every distributor understands that although she is in jewelry sales, she is sent to practice the love of Christ, loving people as they are and serving people every chance she gets. And God has blessed Andy as he focused on the ministry first, and left the results to God.

This year sixteen thousand plus independent distributors will be in more than one hundred thousand homes, sharing Christ as they show their wares. Premier Designs has become a financial success. Yet Andy realizes his job is to abide peacefully in Christ rather than dwell on the bottom line of his business. "I was sixty years old, I think, before God could trust me. There was just too much of me and not enough of Him in my life. I realized my strength had become my weakness. I admitted I couldn't do it, but He could, and He simply responded with the words I'll never forget: *Then let Me do it!* And God has."

So strengths are great as far as they go, but when they are left unchecked they become a weakness. Then, with loving discipline, God will use that weakness to break us, stripping away our reliance on our own strengths, until there is nothing left but to abide in Him.

Personal weaknesses. These do not necessarily arise out of our strengths, but arise out of shortcomings in our personalities, physical abilities, intellect, or emotional makeup. We generally respond with one of two extremes to these types of weaknesses. We either ignore them or we try to build them into strengths.

The first reaction is simple to address. Ignore your weaknesses and they will trip you up. A wise person is aware of his or her weaknesses and learns how to manage them. Donald Clifton and Paula Nelson remind us: "Excellence can be achieved only by *focusing* on strengths and *managing* weaknesses, not through the elimination of weaknesses (or ignoring them)."[8]

But notice the advice is to *manage* our weaknesses, not to try to turn them into strengths. While there's nothing wrong with wanting to improve any point of our life, we waste a significant amount of emotional energy when we try to make a weakness into a strength. While incremental improvements may be made, real success is usually limited. After all, we're working against the way God created us.

The wise decision is learning to *manage* our weaknesses. The key is creating a healthy awareness of the weakness and a need for help and constant vigilance in that area. While the weakness may remain present, it doesn't become a tripping point.

Circumstantial weaknesses. Sometimes these weaknesses come from *innate disabilities* we have or from *circumstances beyond our control*. The temptation in our society is to write another person off when he or she is encumbered by a circumstantial weakness. But our perspective is not God's perspective.

In God's economy all weaknesses, including innate disabilities and circumstantial weaknesses, can be a great source of strength. The apostle Paul experienced this firsthand when he talked about one of his innate weaknesses:

> So I wouldn't get a big head, I was given the gift of a handicap to keep me in constant touch with my limitations. Satan's angel did his best to get me down; what he in fact did was push me to my knees. No danger then of walking around high and mighty! At first I didn't think of it as a gift, and begged God to remove it. Three times I did that, and then He told me that,
>
> > My grace is enough; it's all you need.
> > My strength comes into its own in your weakness.
>
> Once I heard that, I was glad to let it happen. I quit focusing on the handicap and began appreciating the gift. It was a case of Christ's strength moving in on my weakness. Now I take limitations in stride, and with good cheer, these limitations they cut me down to size—abuse, accidents, opposition, bad breaks. I just let Christ take over! And so the weaker I get, the stronger I become.[9]

Paul learned what all of us need to grasp: "The weaker I get, the stronger I become!" Sometimes these weaknesses will be illness or physical limitations. Other times they will be vocational and job-related. Still others will be relational. Regardless of the reason, when these weaknesses are seen in a Biblical light, you can be assured that God is busily at work putting in you the qualities and mettle that He knows you will need to deal with them.[10]

Sometimes, an innate weakness will crop up in an area that used to be a strength, causing us to totally rely on God for things we used to take for granted. Both of us have examples from our own lives.

Randy, lean and in excellent physical shape, runs several miles each day. His life has been filled with athletics and outdoor activity. He's been called "the iron man."

He thought he was in good physical shape until a year ago when a medical exam revealed an alarming health condition. An Electron Beam Tomography (EBT) scan showed extensive calcification of the arteries that place him in the very top category for risk of heart attack—sobering news for someone in his forties. Randy's heart condition became his own thorn in the flesh, giving him a new appreciation for the words of the apostle Paul and the way God works through our weaknesses. This "thorn" helped his prayer life come alive, and allowed him to minister better to others with physical challenges. It also gave him a whole new passion for life. He senses the increased power of prayer at work in his own life, and praises God for this catalytic "weakness" that helped spur him to a deeper relationship with Christ.

Bob was known for years for his vibrant speaking voice. In the seventh grade, Bob had such a strong voice that he was invited by his school to begin hosting and serving as master of ceremonies for the school assemblies. Little did he know that God was preparing him for a life of speaking and preaching.

But recently, he too got a bad medical report. A precarious cyst was found on Bob's left vocal chord. Due to the positioning of the cyst, surgery could not guarantee success. In fact, surgeons say his voice could actually be worse after surgery rather than better. As a result, Bob has simply had to live with his "thorn in the flesh," constantly reminding him that the ability to communicate God's truth is as much a gift as God's truth itself. No longer does he take the strength of timbre and resonance in his voice for granted.

Both of us have come to realize just how fragile life and strengths are. Now we are more dependent on God than on our supposed strengths. And we both realize just how critical that dependence has become to effectiveness in ministry.

Achieving a Biblical Balance

Like most everything else in life, effectiveness comes from balance. Regardless of what self-help books may say, simply maximizing strengths is a lopsided answer. Nothing in life is quite that simple. Instead, it's more of a dialectic and constant tension.

God often uses unexpected circumstances to help us keep the balance intact or to improve the balance and its effect.

Made to Count!

Dan Cathy. President of the renowned Chick-fil-A restaurant corporation, Dan is a man with many natural strengths. He's a prominent business leader, a skilled professional musician, and a man with a warm and engaging personality. But God used a recent tragedy, not these strengths, to help Dan achieve greater balance in his life and become more like Christ.

On an April afternoon, Dan was working with his son, Ross, clearing some ground that the family owned. The Bobcat and front-end loader had done their work and pushed the brush, trees, and old fence lines into several seven-foot-high piles. Deciding to burn the piles, the men soaked each stack with diesel fuel to aid the ignition.

"When I pulled out some matches and lit the first of the three piles, they gradually caught fire because the gas had slowly soaked in for thirty minutes," Dan recalls. "Most of the fumes had evaporated. When I reached the fourth pile, Ross got up on the top of the pile and poured five gallons of gasoline on it. As soon as he finished pouring the gas, he jumped down and I lit the match. I was about an arm's length from the pile. As I lit the match the whole thing went *whavooom*. In a split second, I saw the flames erupt and felt this incredible wall of heat."

Dan immediately knew he was in trouble, having been virtually consumed by the blast. His son ran for the pickup, loaded his father in, and drove him to an intersection where LifeFlight, a helicopter rescue operation, would take Dan to Grady Memorial Hospital's burn unit. Dan's face and arms were covered with first- and second-degree burns. Thankfully, there were no third-degree burns. But the days following were excruciating, as he had to go through rehabilitation, including the washing, rubbing, and scraping of the burned areas. Doctors say this is one of the most painful recoveries of any kind, as the dead skin is literally peeled and scraped from the body, exposing raw nerves.

The recovery has been slow, but thorough, and Dan is the first to express his thanksgiving for God's faithful protection and for the impact it had on the priorities of his life.

> One of the things that has really helped me through this experience is to become much more focused in my one-on-one conversations with people. I don't allow 50 percent of my attention to be on them

and the other 50 percent of my mind to be thinking what I'm supposed to do next or where I'm headed. I feel myself much more zeroed in on people than on plans.

In addition, I've become convinced that one of the least talked about elements of leadership for business leaders is the area of *pastoral ministry*. You don't read that in management books, but it's something I'm trying to learn. We naturally tend to think about things like strategic responsibility, strategic planning and visioneering, and all the other roles of leaders that are very important. From my experience I learned that a key role is pastoral ministry—making hospital visits to employees, congratulatory calls on the birth of family members, attending funerals, and one-on-one counsel when people take the opportunity to ask. Also, as leaders we have the responsibility of being prepared to share with employees our personal testimony, hopefully even leading someone to Christ, having prayer with him or her or whatever else is needed. I'm becoming convinced that's all part of effective Christian leadership in the workplace today.

Since the accident, I've kept a little New Testament with me all the time. I'm not trying to be a Bible-thumping, right-wing zealot. But from a very practical standpoint I'm keeping that Bible in my left pocket and just hoping and praying that God will keep me flexible and alert to the opportunities that I have during the day to read a verse of Scripture and, where possible, to share it.

Today, Dan's whole perspective on life has changed, the value of every moment and opportunity deepened. He has changed his leadership style, from someone focused on the strengths of strategic planning and vision casting, to someone equally concerned about pastoral ministry. Every encounter is now precious and valuable because Dan learned firsthand just how fragile life can be and how quickly one can move from walking in strength to recovering in weakness.

Sometimes weaknesses brought on by circumstances beyond our control teach us some great truths about God's faithfulness and His work in our lives. As we read in the Psalms, "It was *good* for me to be afflicted so that I might learn your decrees."[11]

ABIDING IN CHRIST

It's amazing how God uses our strengths and weaknesses to mold us like clay in His hands into the vessels He wants us to be. It's not one or the other, but both that make the mix unique, special, and priceless.

The balance between strengths and weaknesses is best achieved when we learn to live out the picture found in John 15 of a branch abiding in the vine. It is from the vine that the branch draws its life, and because of the vine that the branch bears its fruit. In the same way, as we learn to abide in the sufficiency of Christ we bear fruit that lasts and has significant impact in life.

A key part of abiding in Christ, with our mix of strengths and weaknesses, is a willingness to humble ourselves before Him, surrendering the strengths and acknowledging the weaknesses. God tells us in His Owner's Manual that we are to submit ourselves into His hands . . . come near to Him, and in return He will come near to us.[12] And a major part of submission is humbling ourselves in God's mighty hands that He, in His time, will lift us up and lead us out to make an impact for Him.

But before you read by this too fast, take a moment and notice that He tells us to humble ourselves. It's not His job, but ours. It's a call to readily admit how desperately we need His love, grace, strength, and wisdom.

Stan Thomas found the truth of this principle in the toughest of times. Stan is one of the largest real estate developers in the United States. He grew up working in his dad's restaurant, then he attended the University of South Carolina for a year and a half before having to return home to help his family run the restaurant during his father's illness. Stan completed college by going to night school at Georgia State University. After graduation, he continued to help the family with the restaurant. Then, in 1987, he launched a development business, where his can-do spirit, competency, and vision shot him to quick success.

Then the bottom fell out. Over a period of three to four years, Stan lost almost everything and found his checkbook had collapsed from a positive net value to more than twenty million dollars in debt. "I remember the night when I pulled my family around me and told them that the next day we were going to lose our house. I can remember how sobered everyone was and all I could say was, 'We've still got each other and we'll come back.' It was one of the hardest times of my life."

Through that experience, Stan learned that regardless of how many strengths one might have, unexpected circumstances, turns in the economy, disappointing people, and other issues can quickly bring you down. But in those points of weakness, you have a choice to become better or bitter. And Stan chose "better." Working his way back to the positive side of the ledger, Stan made up his mind to repay every debt he had incurred. It wasn't because he had to—those debts had been written off by the individuals and companies—it was because he felt obligated to. That's what a Christ-follower would do, regardless.

> I worked hard to go back to every single institution that I owed to pay back the debts we'd incurred. I specifically remember going into one company to pay the money back and them telling me I didn't have to do it, because they'd written it off the previous year. I just looked at them and said, "You don't understand, I have to do this because that's the right thing to do." And then I paid them back.
>
> But I could hardly believe the results that came out of that. I remember one woman who worked in the office pulling me aside sometime later. With tears in her eyes she said, "You'll never know what your actions did to my husband. He's never seen this Christian-thing as a viable reality in life. He always thought it was a fake and something only weak people did. But seeing you grapple through such financial setbacks and then evidence such strength out of weakness, has changed his life." I still can't believe what happens when, even in the weak moments of life, we do what's right, and inevitably you see that God rewards us for that!

Stan has amazing strengths, has learned to manage his weaknesses, and constantly humbles himself before the Lord. In fact, he has one of the most gentle, humble spirits we've ever seen in a leader, though he'll be the last to admit it (a sign of true humility). And Stan summed up our point to this whole chapter when he said, "The thing I've learned is that strengths make you a better leader and weaknesses make you a better follower and servant. And both are critical in the eyes of Christ."

PRINCIPLE 3

God calls you to partner with Him in a mission that is bigger than you are.

Key scriptures:

- "So do not be ashamed to testify about our Lord, or ashamed of me his prisoner. But join with me in suffering for the gospel, by the power of God, who has saved us and called us to a holy life— not because of anything we have done but because of his own purpose and grace. . . . And of this gospel I was appointed a herald and an apostle and a teacher" (2 Timothy 1:8–9, 11).
- "On this rock I will build My church, and the gates of Hades shall not prevail against it" (Matthew 16:18 NKJV).

Key points:

- God's mission for our life is bigger than anything we could do on our own.
- God calls each of us to be part of an institution that will outlast us—the local church.
- God calls each of us to be part of a cause far greater than us— the Great Commission.

A Life-Changing Mission Bigger Than You

Sometimes you attend a day-long meeting where you swear somebody messed with the clock and made its gears go slower or put it in reverse. One of those meetings where you cram thirty minutes' worth of stuff into eight hours.

But this meeting was different. Ideas about college evangelism—how to reach the next generation—flew around the room. We had gathered the experts—campus ministers, youth group leaders, popular youth speakers. And they didn't disappoint.

Everyone was engaged. Well, most everyone. Popular youth speaker Louie Giglio, a dynamic speaker and Pied Piper for the next generation, was conspicuously quiet. He didn't seem to laugh when several of us joked about getting fired from our jobs if we implemented some of the cutting-edge stuff being tossed about the room. "I'd try this," someone might say, "except I don't have a death wish."

Finally, at Bob's urging, Louie spoke. "I've just been listening and learning," he said. "This has been great—a ton of good ideas."

"What do you think it will take to reach the next generation?" Bob prodded.

Louie became pensive. And then he nailed all of us. "Well," he said at last, "we've talked about some ideas that we like, but then we've jokingly said that we didn't like them enough to die for them. My read of the next generation is that they're looking for precisely that—something important enough to die for—and they're willing to follow someone who will put their life on the line for that cause."

Ouch!

We knew immediately Louie was right. And not just about the *next* generation. Men and women everywhere, of all ages, have longed to be part of something bigger than themselves. Something permanent. Something that matters. And in their best moments, they're willing to lay down their lives for that cause.

It's almost as though God created us that way, which, of course, He did!

It's this passion to be part of something truly significant that John Eldredge addresses in his best-selling book *Wild at Heart*. Though he writes primarily to men, a desire to be God's *intimate ally* is not limited to men:

> A man must have a battle to fight, a great mission to his life that involves and yet transcends even home and family. He must have a cause to which he is devoted even unto death, for this is written into the fabric of his being. Listen carefully now: *You do*. That is why God created you—to be his intimate *ally*, to join him in the Great Battle. You have a specific place in the line, a mission God made you for.
>
> Above all else, a warrior has a *vision*, he has a transcendence to his life, a cause greater than self-preservation. The root of all our woes and our false self was this: We were seeking to save and lost it. Christ calls a man beyond that, "but whoever loses his life for me and for the gospel will save it."
>
> [My life] was wasted away either striving or indulging. I was a mercenary. A mercenary fights for pay, for his own benefit, his life is devoted to himself. "The quality of a true warrior," says Bly, "is that he is in service to a purpose greater than himself; that is, to a transcendent cause."[1]

At another point, Eldredge makes it clear that we do not fight by ourselves: "Don't even think about going into battle alone."[2] He quotes from a speech made by Henry V at Agincourt, as the king rallies his small band of tired and wounded men for one last battle. Though they are outnumbered five to one, Henry appeals to their sense of destiny as a "band of brothers":

> We few, we happy few, we band of brothers;
> For he today that sheds his blood with me
> Shall be my brother . . .
> And gentlemen in England, now a-bed
> Shall think themselves accursed they were not here;
> And hold their manhoods cheap while any speaks
> That fought with us.[3]

If what Eldredge says is true, and instinctively we know that it is, then a few critical questions immediately spring to mind. *What in my life is worth dying for? Who is my "band of brothers"? And what is my transcendent cause?*

Fortunately, God did not leave the answers to guesswork.

"I will build my church," said Jesus. "And the gates of Hades will not overcome it."[4]

The church, *a band of brothers—and sisters!*

"[Christ] said to them, 'Go into all the world and preach the good news to all creation.'"[5]

The Great Commission, *a transcendent cause.*

Is there anything more worth dying for?

God will give you a specific mission in life that you cannot accomplish alone. It will be a mission so overwhelming that to even attempt it without Christ would be unthinkable. In fact, we have devised a quick test to help you determine if a particular mission is really what God is calling you to do: Can you accomplish it alone, without the help of God and other people? If so, then it is not God's mission for your life. God calls us to God-sized tasks, things we could never do on our own.

> **God will give you a specific mission in life that you cannot accomplish alone.**

But here's another important caveat about our mission—God's mission for our lives will ultimately help build His church and accomplish His Great Commission. He does not ask us to work independently of these great causes, nor does He tolerate those who work against them.

Some Christians say they can pursue Christ's call on their life without being involved in the local church and the Great Commission. Don't believe them. Every excuse to avoid the responsibilities of the local church and the Great Commission is a cop-out. You can be a brain surgeon. The best brain surgeon on the face of the planet. And you can cure thousands from brain cancer. But if you're not part of a local church, and if you're not committed to reaching those without Christ, then you're a brain surgeon selling yourself short and living in disobedience to Christ's commands. God gifted you to be a brain surgeon so that you can represent Christ, the ultimate physician, to your patients and to those you work with. His desire is not just to see people healed physically, but to see them healed spiritually as well. And he has placed you at an incredible point of need to help bring full healing in their lives, and to shepherd them into the care of a local New Testament church.

The Local Church—A Permanent Institution

The Berlin Wall. Enron. The Soviet Empire. WorldCom. The list goes on. Companies, institutions, and nations come and go. But the church remains. It transcends. It is the heir to His great promise. "I will build my church, and all the powers of hell will not conquer it. "[6]

The church is the bride of Christ.

Now imagine, just for a moment, that somebody really wants to be your friend and has pledged to be loyal to you. You spend hours talking, hanging out, sharing secrets, doing things together. You know each other's likes and dislikes and what this person is thinking when an eyebrow is raised.

There's only one problem. Your friend really doesn't like your spouse and makes fun of your spouse behind his or her back. When your spouse comes into the room, before long your friend gets up and moves out of the room. Your spouse and your friend have a personality conflict. Oil and water.

"I like you," your friend says. "But I can't stand your spouse."

We think we know what you might say. "If you want to be my friend, you'll learn to like my spouse."

Why? Because you love your spouse. And anyone who is truly your friend will not hate what you love, especially something as personal as your spouse.

Jesus Christ loves His bride, the church. If we claim to love Christ, then we will love the things that Christ loves. We cannot truly love Christ and lightly esteem the church. Now, most of us would never admit that we lightly esteem the church. We just don't really get involved. We ignore this crucial part of our calling for reasons that seem sufficient and just at the time. Here is an analysis of some of our more common rationalizations.

"I Just Don't Have Time"

It's undeniably true that church involvement absorbs a certain amount of time. Corporate worship and a small group Bible study are a must. Service of some type in the church is essential. If you do your job well, you get assigned more tasks. The 80/20 rule applies: 20 percent of the people do 80 percent of the work. In some churches, it's more like the 90/10 rule.

But in reality, we all "have time" for the church. We all have 52 weeks per year; 24 hours per day; 10,080 minutes per week; 25,986,400 seconds per month. It's not really a question of whether we "have time"; it's really a question of whether we will "make time." And that becomes a matter of priorities. We will squeeze in those things that matter most to us. The real issue is not whether we "have time," but whether our bedrock beliefs about what is really important dictate that we make this a priority.

Compare time spent helping to build Christ's church with all the other things during the week that you spend time on. Little league with the kids, reading, mentoring, work, exercise, television, walks, time with friends, etc. Now, add up all the time you spend on just plain wasteful activities. Still not enough time? Then ask yourself this: Which of these activities will outlast the church? Which of these activities bring people to Christ?

Long after your favorite television show has been taken off the air, or your sports team has been disbanded or moved, or the corporation you've worked for has become bankrupt, Christ will still be building His church. And He wants you to be a part of it.

We must realize that Christ is Lord of not just our time but of time in general. If your life is way too busy, and you feel out of control, could it be that you need to reprioritize your time? We recognize how this works in the financial arena. Many of us have been taught that if we tithe first, God can make the remaining 90 percent of our income go further than 100 percent would have gone otherwise. That's because we recognize Christ as Lord of our finances. Don't the same concepts apply with the far more precious resource of our time? Hasn't God numbered our days? Doesn't the same God who owns the cattle on a thousand hills also own each second of a thousand days?

We must be careful, however, that we don't fall into the notion that the only time that "counts" is time spent serving inside the four walls of the church. Christ wants our time and energy spent building His church, and we can't accomplish this by just spending time at church activities and programs.

Renowned African-American pastor S. M. Lockeridge used to make a clear distinction between the things done *in* and *for* the church and the ministry and mission that take place *outside* the church walls. Telling of an old farmer who had his grandson visiting on the farm for a week, Lockeridge painted a poignant picture of the farmer waking his grandson for chores long before the sun rose. Sleepy, groggy, and aching for the security of the bed's warm covers, the boy worked with his grandfather to feed the chickens, slop the pigs, water the flowers, milk the cows, and collect the eggs. He finally arrived at the kitchen where the aromas of a home-cooked farm breakfast saturated the air and greeted him.

Finishing breakfast with a slight burp the lad felt his grandfather's hand on his shoulder and heard the words, "Let's go, boy, we've got work to do!"

Surely, I must be dreaming, the boy thought. *Work to do! I thought that's what we've been doing!*

"No, my boy. We did chores. Anything done in the house, for the house, or around the house—them's the chores. The work is what happens in the field."

Perhaps in church life, we too often confuse the chores with the work! Ministry in the church—those are the chores. Activities at the church (ceramics classes, aerobics, fellowship times) those are not work or chores. They're something we want to do because those activities help us, relax us, or encourage us. But ministry and relationship building outside the church— that's the real work of a kingdom-minded body of believers!

We want to challenge you to bring some balance into this area of your life. Some of you are leaving the work of the church to others. Some of you are so busy with chores inside the church that you have no time to build relationships with those who need Christ. The key to balance is to be both a *min-*

ister *in the church* and *a missionary to the culture*. Our experience shows that it's hard to achieve this balance if you're involved in more than two ministries in the church. On the other hand, pastors have confirmed that if everyone in their church did just two ministries, all the work of the church would get done *and then some*. So, find two ministries in the church that fit your strengths and passions. Do them *very well*. And leave time to build bridges with neighbors, friends, and work associates outside the church. After all, that's the work of the church as well.

God is a God of efficiency. Trust Him. Turn your time over to Him and every thing that needs to be done *will be* done. "See then that you walk circumspectly, not as fools but as wise, redeeming the time, because the days are evil."[7]

"I Can't Find a Good Fit"

Recent polls show a dramatic increase in "church hoppers"—those who flit from one church to the next like a water bug, never fully landing and immersing themselves into a local body of believers. Something is never quite right. The pastor preaches too long, the members are not very friendly, the music is not "my style." There's got to be another church that will better meet my needs. And so the water bug goes, from one church to the next, landing for a flicker here, a moment there, constantly in search of the perfect fit and missing a vital part of their calling. They need to understand an important truth about the church. The church does not exist to serve them. That mindset—consumer Christianity or "McChurch" as some call it—is simply not scriptural. We exist to build Christ's kingdom by building Christ's church. The church does not exist to build our ego, our business, or even our circle of friends.

Drop in on a typical conversation at a restaurant where church members are eating after a service. You will probably hear something like:

"How'd you like the service today?"

"Not bad. I loved the music, but Pastor Goforth's got to get some new stuff."

"Yeah. I mean, how many times is he going to tell that story about the port-a-john cleaner, anyway?"

It's almost as if you had just dropped in on a few students discussing a movie they'd just seen.

"Did you like it?"

"Not bad. The acting was pretty good, but the story line was like so predictable."

"Yeah. And I'm getting so tired of those *Matrix*-style special effects. I mean . . . hello! You think we haven't seen that before?"

The church as theater—is that really what God intended? Maybe. But not the way we think of theater today. And certainly not with the role confusion that exists among some church members. Theater, of course, began in earnest with the Greeks. They popularized the idea of theater, drawing huge audiences and turning their plays into poignant commentaries on life. Classic Greek theater revolved around three different components. The *prompters* played a critical role in these live performances. They stayed down in front of the *actors* in an area that would later become the orchestra pit, coaching and directing the actors throughout the play. The actors, of course, developed the drama on the stage all for the benefit and pleasure of the attending *audience*, hoping that the audience would leave pleased with the performance.

For many in today's church, those roles translate neatly into the way they view worship:

- The *actors* are the pastors, choir, and praise team—those on stage.
- The *prompter* would, of course, be God Himself, orchestrating the leaders as the worship unfolds.
- The *audience* would be the congregation, watching and waiting to be blessed.

Scripture teaches differently. We are told that whatever we do, we are to do it with all our hearts, as for the Lord, and not for men.[8] Certainly, this includes worship and every other activity we do associated with church. God, and only God, is the audience.

The members are the actors, with the pastor and other leaders serving as prompters. After all, the job of the leaders is not to perform, but to equip the members for the work of ministry.[9] So Scripture would have us structure this analogy quite differently:

- The *actors* are the church members, each one a minister.
- The *prompters* are the pastors and other leaders.
- The *audience* is God alone.

This scriptural blueprint takes the members out of the role of critic and puts them into the role of participant. Worship is no longer viewed as a performance we judge but as an act we perform. Our question at the end of a church service should not be whether we thought the service was "good," but whether we thought that God was well pleased.

We take responsibility for the church, *our* church, with all its faults and blemishes. And we realize that the church will never be perfect, but it is still Christ's bride.

"The Church is Full of Hypocrites"

This is perhaps the most common condemnation of the church. "They dress up on Sunday and say all these sweet things *to* each other, then they say nasty things *about* each other the rest of the week." What makes this excuse difficult is the fact that there are some hypocrites in the church, just like there are some hypocrites in every other institution in our sin-marred society.

Again, it helps to look at the example of Christ. He died for an imperfect church, not a perfect one. By doing so, He set apart the true church (those who are followers of Christ) so that one day the church might be holy and without blemish:

> Christ also loved the church and gave Himself for her, that He might sanctify and cleanse her with the washing of water by the word, that He might present her to Himself a glorious church, not having spot or wrinkle or any such thing, but that she should be holy and without blemish.[10]

It may help to remind ourselves that the church is not a building or non-profit organization. The church is the body of Christ—His followers from across the ages. Sometimes those we accuse of being hypocrites in the church are not really part of the true church at all; they are simply unsaved members of a local congregation. Dr. Billy Graham has said that he fears as many as 50 percent of the members of American churches may not know Christ but are just going through the religious motions. But even those who are true followers of Christ are not perfect. The apostle Paul said, "For what I do is not the good I want to do; no, the evil I do not want to do—this I keep on doing."[11]

Christ's desire for us to be part of a local New Testament congregation of believers is not conditional. Scripture does not tell us to find a perfect church and join it. Scripture does not tell us to find a church that is a perfect fit. And it's a good thing. Perfect churches do not exist this side of eternity.

Think about the logic of people who use hypocrisy as an excuse not to join the church. They do not demand perfection in other areas of their life as a prerequisite to their participation. WorldCom was not a perfect company, but they still use telecommunications. Enron was not perfect, but they still invest on Wall Street and use utilities. Arthur Anderson was not perfect, but they still use accountants.

Do we refuse to get medical treatment when we hear about a medical malpractice claim? Do we stop using banks if a banker goes to jail? Of course not. We realize that one bad person or one bad company does not mean that we should never use those services. There may still be something incredibly valuable for us.

One of the primary reasons we gather is not to celebrate our perfection, but to encourage each other amidst our imperfection and to follow the One who is perfection.

> And let us consider how we may spur one another on toward love and good deeds. Let us not give up meeting together, as some are in the habit of doing, but let us encourage one another—and all the more as you see the Day approaching.[12]

Sure, you'll meet hypocrites in church. Pray for them. Love them. And spur them on toward love and good deeds. But don't quit meeting with other committed Christians because of them. If you do, the hypocrites will win, and you will lose. To say we follow Scripture, and to ignore the clear mandate that we regularly meet and grow together, would be to say one thing and do another. And that, friends, is the definition of hypocrisy.

The Great Commission—A Cause That Outlasts Us

There are few spiritual things on earth that we can do better here than we will in heaven. Fellowship is not one of them. Nor is worship. Neither one of us authors can sing a lick here on earth (yet God has a sense of humor since He gave us these grating singing voices and names like Reccord and Singer). But in heaven we'll sing with the best of you.

One thing we can do now that we won't be able to do then is to lead others to a personal relationship with Christ. Evangelism. Sharing the best thing that ever happened to us. Making disciples. It's the most important cause we'll ever embrace.

> Go therefore and make disciples of all the nations, baptizing them in the name of the Father and of the Son and of the Holy Spirit, teaching them to observe all things that I have commanded you; and lo, I am with you always, even to the end of the age.[13]

In the original Greek, the word for "go" in these verses literally means "as you are going." Jesus commanded His disciples to make other disciples "as they were going." He took it for granted that if they were serious about following, they would be serious about going. If we're truly following, we'll be fishers of men. And on the contrary, if we aren't fishers of men, then we're not fully following.

Sometimes, we confuse church activity—music, athletics, socials—with intentional evangelism. Even more frequently, we confuse church growth with intentional evangelism. But so much church growth has little to do with reaching those who don't know Christ. Listen to the way Myron Augsberger phrases it in his book *Invitation to Discipleship:*

> Far too often the evangelistic activities of the church are simply a stirring over again of the same people. Instead of being fishers of men we are keepers of aquariums, and flatter ourselves when we have "stolen fish" from someone else's bowl.[14]

Leading others to Christ—not stealing fish from someone's fish bowl—is the one reason that God leaves us on this earth after we come to know Christ. He wants us to walk into eternity with others at our side. But for too many of us, we've forgotten about the Great Cause, and we've become distracted with smaller, less significant stuff.

This book is primarily about discovering our vocational calling and mission in life. But there is more to being *on mission* than just knowing what God has called us to do vocationally. Being *on mission* is not just about having the right occupation; it's about having the right lifestyle. That's why, before we talk about being *on mission* at work, the next chapter in this book will deal with being *on mission* at home. And that's also why we've included this chapter on building the local church and advancing the Great Commission. Every *on mission* Christian is called to be part of those great causes and to adopt a lifestyle where sharing Christ and serving the church are priorities.

A Personal Mission Bigger Than You

So, the local church and the Great Commission, causes that are far bigger than any one of us, are part of the calling of every Christian. But within that context, God also honors each of us with a specific mission as our role in advancing His kingdom. And again, this mission is bigger than we are in the sense that we could never accomplish it alone. In fact, God often reveals this mission one step at a time so that we won't be blown away by the sheer magnitude of it, defeated by our own lack of faith before we even begin.

Think about the "impossible" missions that God assigned to the men and women in Scripture.

- For Abraham, ninety-nine years old and childless, it was to be the father of many nations.[15]
- For Moses, a man "slow of speech and tongue," it was an assignment to be the spokesperson before Pharaoh, demanding the release of the Israelites from slavery.[16]
- For Gideon, the self-confessed lowest member in the weakest clan in Israel, it was God's call to lead the entire nation against the Midianites.[17]
- For Esther, a political novice, it was God's call to plead with mighty King Xerxes of Persia to spare the Jews from annihilation.[18]
- For Paul, a man who claimed no eloquence or superior wisdom, it was God's call for him to be a vessel to bear the name of Christ to the Gentiles and their kings."[19]

- For Mary, a teenage virgin, it was God's call to bear and mother the Christ-child.[20]

The people featured in this book are no different. Each of them was blown away by God's assignment for their lives. And none of them tried doing it in their own power. They have lived out our third principle, step by step and day by day: God calls us to partner with Him in a mission that is bigger than you are.

Our temptation is to write this principle off as the lot of a privileged few. Maybe God has called them to a gargantuan mission. But the rest of us are consigned to labor on the small things in life, never really making much of a difference in our paltry arenas. To think this way is to entirely miss the way God works. He starts right where we are, calling us to be faithful in those "little things" that He's already entrusted to us. The next few chapters will focus on this, our fourth principle: God calls you to be *on mission* right where you are—in your home, in your neighborhood, at your workplace, in your school—starting now.

Then, as we demonstrate our faithfulness right where we are, God reveals the next phase of His mission for us through His Word, His Spirit, wise counsel, and His work in circumstances around us (our fifth principle). He typically brings us to a crossroads of choice as He forges and equips us for His mission (principle six). If we choose the road that honors God, regardless of the cost, He will then guide us one step at a time as He reveals the larger mission for our lives (principle seven).

Our advice at this point is simple. Be ready for God to call you to become part of something big. Real big. Far bigger than anything you can accomplish alone. And remember, that call always begins by making a difference right where you are and by honoring God at each crossroads of choice. Step by step, He will reveal your mission and provide the means for you to carry it out. By pursuing this mission, you will be doing your part in carrying out the Great Commission, the only cause worthy of total passion and unyielding devotion. And yes, Louie Giglio, it's a cause worth dying for.

Jesus Christ Himself has already proven that.

PRINCIPLE 4

God calls you to be on mission with Him right where you are—starting now.

Key scriptures:

- "As Jesus was getting into the boat, the man who had been demon-possessed begged to go with him. Jesus did not let him, but said, 'Go home to your family and tell them how much the Lord has done for you, and how he has had mercy on you.' So the man went away and began to tell in the Decapolis how much Jesus had done for him. And all the people were amazed" (Mark 5:18–20).
- "Whatever you do, work at it with all your heart, as working for the Lord, not for men" (Colossians 3:23).

Key points:

- You are called to make your family a top priority. Family responsibilities cannot be delegated to others or relegated to less than first place.
- Your home should be a nerve center for ministry as you reach out to your friends and neighbors.
- You should be "on call" at work, looking for creative opportunities to share the gospel with those around you.
- Your gospel witness at work will only be as credible as the quality of your work.

8

On Mission at Home

J. C. Watts. From football hero to eight years as a high-powered congressman, J. C. Watts seemed to be the embodiment of the American dream. As an outstanding college quarterback, J. C. led the University of Oklahoma to two Orange Bowl victories and was twice named Most Valuable Player. During his pro career, he was named Most Valuable Player of the Grey Cup, Canada's Super Bowl. Then, after he hung up his cleats, J. C. made a seamless transition into politics, gaining election to the House of Representatives from his native Oklahoma in 1994. At the time, he was the only African-American Republican in the House. Fellow congressmen quickly recognized his leadership qualities and elected him to serve as chairman of the House Republican Committee, a position he held for four years.

Like one of J. C.'s former offensive linemen, God cleared the way for J. C. to make an impact, both politically and spiritually. Shortly after arriving in Washington, J. C. was asked to speak at a prayer breakfast for members of Congress. He shared his testimony and talked about his salvation experience. After the breakfast, a House member from Arkansas told J. C. that another member he'd been talking to for three years was now ready to be 100 percent sure about his salvation. "I think when those things happen, it's confirmation that I'm where God wants me to be. That was encouraging to me."

J. C. also had opportunities to minister to his constituents back home during times of crisis. "At times like the Oklahoma City bombing of 1995 or the tornadoes of 1999, what can you say that's going to help? I was their congressman, but during that time I was also a Christian friend there to love them and care for them and cry with them. That was my mission."[1]

Like every other part of his life, it was not a mission J. C. took lightly. In our interview, he shared with us this valuable insight of what it really means to seek God's will:

> When you are sensitive to God's will for your life and you are honest and naked before God, there are some things that you're going to want to do and God's not going to want you to do them. But if you say to God, "I'm willing to accept *whatever* your will is," that's when you see God move mountains. That's when you see divine intervention. The trouble people get in is that they want to do things so badly and get so emotionally involved. When the Lord says, "No, J. C., that's not where I want you, that's not what I want you to do," that's when I'm tempted to take out the spiritual crowbar and try to pry the door open. And when we walk through those doors we see that God had nothing to do with it. But if you're open and sensitive to God's will for your life and you're willing to accept God's saying yes or no, mighty things happen when God is in the process.

And then, though we had been talking with him about his time in Congress, J. C. added this critical piece of advice: "Always consider your family. Will it be a hardship for them? Because God will never call you to anything that will wreck your family."

That last point, the needs of his family, became increasingly pivotal in J. C.'s life. And it finally drove him to a decision that left a lot of Washington insiders shaking their heads. At the peak of his political power, he felt God calling him to walk away from Washington. Even many Christians couldn't believe that God would enable J. C. Watts to become the rising star of the Republican Party, just to send him home. You can be called to Washington, they seemed to imply, but can you really be called away? J. C. had a different perspective:

The hard part as an elected official is not hanging on; it's letting go. The ego gets tied up in building empires, playing the games. And once you're satisfied with your contribution, with the Lord speaking to your heart to move on, you even have Christian people saying, "There's got to be something wrong. There's some scandal." I've heard all sorts of things. The bottom line is I'm doing what the Lord is telling me to do.

The greatest calling on a man's life is to be a dad. I don't think God gives us our families so we can go and do things that hurt our families. I got to that point where I can finally say, "I'm not going to keep missing parent-teacher conferences. I'm not going to keep missing Little League ball games." When you're seeking God's will, especially about public service, it's a family thing. You have to be open to say it's time for me to pass the torch. It's time for me to go home and be a husband and a dad again. My faith validates me, not my political office.

First Things First

While many thought J. C. was walking away from his political calling, he knew better. He realized that he was actually walking *toward* the greatest responsibility of a man's life—being a husband and a dad. Scripture teaches that anyone who does not provide for his own family is an "infidel."[2] And J. C. recognized this means more than just material provision. Our families deserve the highest priority of our time, energy, attention, and emotional investment. In our culture, the family is under attack. Recent court decisions jeopardize the sanctity of marriage. Traditional family values are scorned. Plus, our society tends to value us more for contributions made outside the family than those within the home. J. C. Watts is a good case in point. Star football player, political powerbroker, amazing public speaker. But God calls us first to our family priorities, and only then to these other platforms.

God isn't nearly as concerned about the plaudits and applause we receive as we might be. We can imagine a day when our calling takes us to dizzying heights, as we do God's bidding in the white-hot spotlight of the national media. Yes, God may have big plans for us. But He's also calling us to the here and now, asking us to be *on mission* right where we are. It may not be glamorous, but He wants us to start by being servants to those we spend time with on a daily basis, in our homes, neighborhoods, schools, and workplaces, showing them the love of Christ. And He begins by asking us a few simple questions: Do those who know you best also know Christ? Do they love Him? Are they following Him? Are you helping them understand *His* love for them by the way *you* act toward them?

This is the core of our fourth principle: God calls you to be *on mission* right where you are—starting now. For some, your full-time calling right now is to the home, raising your children in the fear and admonition of the Lord. We want you to realize that this calling is "highly esteemed" in God's eyes. And we will introduce you to others with this same calling, ordinary moms and dads who are using their home as a nerve center for ministry. But even if you work outside the home, your family is still a *priority* calling. That's why in this chapter and the next we will focus on being *on mission* at home, and only then we will turn to the issue of being *on mission* at work. This is consistent with the emphasis placed on the family and home throughout Scripture.

God declared Adam and Even to be "one flesh," establishing the first family. He called Abraham to be the "father" of many nations, promising him a family line that would be more numerous than the stars in the sky. The story of Ruth is the story of extended family, the loyalty of a daughter-in-law and restoration by a kinsman-redeemer. God promised David that his "lineage" would be established forever. God carefully chose the mother of the Christ-child, calling her blessed among women. Paul affirmed Timothy by noting that he had the same sincere faith as his mother and grandmother. And he disqualified from spiritual leadership any man who failed to manage his own home well.

From the pages of both the Old Testament and New, the message is uniform and crystal clear: *family matters!*

Christ and the Demoniac

They called him "Legion" because he was possessed by a multitude of demons. He would run around naked, living among the tombs, crying out and cutting himself with stones.[3] He was so strong that nobody could bind him, "not even with chains."[4] A WWF wrestler, without the spandex. Or the Incredible Hulk on steroids.

But when he met Jesus, the legions of demons left him, commanded by Christ to depart into a herd of swine. And suddenly, this bizarre man was healed both physically and spiritually. As Mark tells it, the people came out and saw "the one who had been demon-possessed and had the legion, sitting and clothed and in his right mind. And they were afraid."[5]

Now, here's where it *really* gets interesting. The people in that area (called the Gadarenes) begged Jesus to leave. And Legion begged Jesus to let him tag along. But Jesus said no. What on earth was He thinking? What evangelist wouldn't want a guy like Legion hanging around as Exhibit A?

"Ladies and gentlemen, here's a guy we used to call 'Legion.'" (Legion enters stage left, hands and ankles bound with plastic chains that look real. He's wearing spandex shorts.) "He was demon-possessed, out of control, living naked among the graves." (Legion grunts.) "Not even the chains could bind him! Then one day . . ." (Legion screams and breaks the plastic chains, the audience applauds on cue, and Legion gives his testimony of how Jesus healed him.)

But that's not the way Christ works! He wasn't about to let Legion become a traveling road show. In fact, Christ didn't even let Legion become a "foreign missionary." Christ sent him home! To one of the toughest mission fields of all.

The Bible says, "As Jesus was getting into the boat, the man who had been demon-possessed begged to go with him. Jesus did not let him, but said, 'Go home to your family and tell them how much the Lord has done for you, and how he has had mercy on you.'"[5]

It's the same thing that Christ is telling each of us today. First things first. Tell your family how much the Lord has done for you. Bless your children by helping them pursue their calling. Help your spouse become all that God wants him or her to be. Honor your parents in all you do.

The Power of a Praying Parent

Nobody had to convince **Susannah Wesley** of the importance of family. This prolific lady mothered nineteen children, though ten of them died before reaching the age of two. She lived during tumultuous times in eighteenth-century England, suffering for her faith along with her "nonconformist" husband, a clergyman who refused to obey the English law requiring the use of the Book of Common Prayer. Her home was burned by angry parishioners, and she raised her family in perpetual poverty. Her husband, Samuel, was confined to debtor's prison, reviled by many parishioners, and a constant source of controversy. But through the turmoil and poverty, Susannah taught her children to fear and trust the Lord. She gave each of her children a classical education, teaching them Greek and Latin at an early age. She expected each child to be able to read the entire book of Genesis by the age of six. And each week, she would take each child aside for a full hour to discuss spiritual matters affecting that child's life. But her most important contribution was not in the area of education and counseling. This incredibly busy mother would start each day on her knees, devoting a full hour of that time to pray for her children. She also prayed throughout the day with each child, believing that the children should be praying as soon as they could speak.

The results? All of her children developed a deep and abiding walk with Christ. Her son John Wesley, the founder of the Methodist church, became one of the greatest communicators of the gospel the world has ever seen. Another son named Charles penned hundreds of great hymns, including *Hark! The Herald Angels Sing* and *O for a Thousand Tongues to Sing*. Each of Susannah's children grew into powerful Christians, multiplying this godly woman's impact for Christ.

Are you praying fervently for your children? Are you too busy to devote time to this critical task? Think about Susannah Wesley with all those kids running around the house, lesson plans to prepare, chores to do, all kinds of responsibilities. Still, she managed to find an hour at the start of each day to pray specifically for her kids. What could be more important? Do you realize that the most critical calling in your life may be as a prayer warrior for your own children?

Even if you don't have children yet, it's not too early to start. Both of us began praying with our wives for our children even before they born. We prayed that our children would come to Christ early in their lives. We prayed that they would live obediently to Christ and follow His call. We prayed that they might find a godly spouse and raise a Christ-centered family. We knew then, and we know now, that nothing is more rewarding in life than seeing your own children make an impact for Christ. And we knew then, as we know even better now, that it all begins with prayer.

The Power of a Parent's Blessing

LaRue Coleman. Every father has a dream for his child. Tragedy occurs, however, when a father attempts to live his dream through his child's life. But when a father can let go and allow the child to fulfill his own dream, miracles happen!

LaRue Coleman grew up in an outstanding Christian home with a tremendously supportive dad. Money wasn't easy to come by in their home, but LaRue's father was committed to do everything he could to help his son through college and to a better life than he had been able to attain. When LaRue headed off to college, his dad gave him seventy-five dollars—all he had. The student loan office was LaRue's next stop, but it didn't take long to realize that, even with a loan, he needed extra income. That's when LaRue's opportunity came to wash windows.

He found that he was good—very good—at washing windows and serving others. Eight months later, while still washing windows and working hard to get through school, LaRue decided to take a leave of absence from college and launch into business. When he shared his plans with his dad, LaRue's father got in his car and drove to his son's apartment. LaRue sensed that his dad had come to talk him out of his business venture; he would try to encourage his son to finish his college education. But to LaRue's amazement, his dad sat quietly and listened while LaRue explained his decision. When LaRue was finished, his dad looked pensively at his son, and then a gentle smile spread across his face. He said, "I think you know what you want to do, son. God bless you." And with that he stood, shook his son's hand, got in his car, and drove back home.

"That may be the most significant moment I ever had with my father," LaRue reflects today. "To think that he would bless me, and my decision, even though it didn't fit the dream he had for my life. I'll never forget that. As a result, I was determined not to fail." And LaRue didn't fail. For the next eight years, he built a solid company. The windows he found himself washing were not those of homes but of major office buildings in Houston. Cleaning windows expanded to other lines of business, and LaRue was succeeding financially.

But doubts soon followed. And again, it would be the affirmation of a father that allowed LaRue to stay focused on God's mission.

At age twenty-four, I visited my sister in Louisiana. My parents were also there. My sister lived in a little shotgun house in south Louisiana. You could hardly turn around without bumping into the other wall. She needed something from the store so my dad and I volunteered to go. It was a dark and drizzly evening. We drove to the store and bought what was needed. We walked back to my beautiful sports car, got in, closed the doors, and I put my hands and head on the steering wheel and began to weep. To this very day, I don't know where it came from. I don't know where all the emotion had been hiding, but it suddenly poured out. Leaving my sister's little house in my expensive sports car I realized I had it all and she had nothing, yet she was happy and fulfilled and I was totally empty.

My dad just sat there and looked at me and finally asked me what was wrong. I responded, "Dad, I don't understand. How can I have all the things that I have? How can God bless me in the way that He has, and not bless my sister? And how can she be so happy and I'm so empty?"[7]

After a long silence LaRue's dad responded, "Son, I can't tell you why God blesses you and doesn't bless your sister *in the same way*, but I can tell you this: He has blessed you financially because He wants you to use those blessings in the lives of others to further His kingdom."

In the stillness of that sports car, symbolic of this world's wealth and success, I learned the most significant lesson of my business career. I learned that God's blessing is a trust of stewardship to those on whom He bestows it. While He may give it to a person, it is not primarily for that person, but rather for others and for kingdom work.

It began to dawn on me that this was a unique calling and He had placed me right in the middle of one of the biggest mission fields in the world—the workplace. Today, I love working behind the scenes, helping people out and changing people's circumstances, meeting people's needs, because that's what God has called me to do. I pray that the day comes when, as people look back over my life, they are able to say, "He was a great businessman, he had great integrity, he worked hard even though he made a lot of mistakes. But God also had a lot of grace and mercy on his life, and he loved the Lord and was obedient to everything he understood God to be saying." If they can say that, then my life will have been a success.

The point, of course, is not that LaRue's father encouraged him to stay in business, but that he gave LaRue the freedom to follow God's calling for his life, whatever that might be. For **Dan,** a law school student we met recently, the calling couldn't have been more different, but the result of a parent's blessing was the same.

I grew up in a traditional Korean home with a father I loved and respected. But we would go through a routine every night. He would come into my room and give me The Speech: "You're my only son. Your father is so proud of you. [Dan's father liked to talk about himself in the third person.] You are the family's only hope for success and wealth. You need to work hard and make enough money so that someday you can provide for your family and make your father proud."

Dan's acceptance to law school became a point of celebration and an opportunity to revise the speech. "You're my only son. Your father is so proud that you've made it into law school. When you graduate you need to go into corporate law, become successful, and make your family even more proud."

God started working in Dan's heart, giving him a passion not for corporate law, but for helping the down and out. Dan started dreading the periodic speeches from his father, knowing that one day he would end up disappointing the man who meant so much to him. Dan knew there wasn't much money in helping the disadvantaged, but he also knew he wouldn't be happy doing anything else.

Made to Count!

A few months ago, Dan's father asked if he could meet with Dan and Dan's girlfriend for lunch on Sunday. "Sure," said Dan. *Oh no,* he thought. *Here comes another speech about success.* Right on cue, toward the end of lunch, Dan's father said he had a few things he wanted to say. Dan was ready to mouth the speech by heart. It's a good thing he didn't try.

"You're my only son," said Dan's dad. "Soon you'll be graduating from law school, and your father has some advice for you." Dan nudged his girlfriend, bracing for the next words. "Do what makes you happy," said his dad. "More than anything, I only want to see you happy." His dad paused, then asked "What makes you happy, son?"

Dan's jaw dropped, not sure he had heard right. It takes a lot to make a second-year law student speechless, but this did it. Now, it was Dan's girlfriend nudging him. "Answer your dad," she whispered.

Dan wanted to say that his passion was to help people who really couldn't afford it. Corporate law was not going to happen. But first, he had a few questions.

"Are you okay, Dad? You've always wanted me to go into corporate law. Where did this come from?"

His father, not usually an emotional man, began to tear up. He locked his gaze on Dan and spoke slowly. "Your father is growing old son. He has buried a lot of friends. But this past week, he experienced something far sadder. He watched a friend bury his own daughter. She was successful, worked hard, and died young. It's not right for a parent to carry their child to the grave." Dan's father paused, swallowing hard as he found the next words. "Your father never wants to do that with you. He only wants you to be happy and to outlive him. Promise me, son, that you won't go into corporate law."

With that, the young law student started sharing his dream, secure in the power of a parent's blessing.

Your Turn

If you're a mom or a dad, have you ever given your children the freedom to know that you will support their dreams and passions for their lives? Moms, do you truly appreciate the importance of an encouraging mother in the lives of her children? Remember Susannah Wesley? It's no stretch to say that the nurturing of a mother altered the course of history.

But dads, don't think for a moment that your role is any less important. Our experience has shown that fathers are the ones most likely to create molds of success for their children, subtly defining the "acceptable" and "unacceptable" callings for them. The tricky part is that you might not even realize that you've done this. It usually isn't quite as explicit as Dan's father. Instead, the implicit message is found in hundreds of little hints and actions, all adding up to expectations that confine our children and cause a gut-wrenching dilemma: Do I follow God's call on my life or try to honor what my parents want me to do?

> **Have you ever given your children the freedom to know that you will support their dreams?**

The best way to combat these expectations is to address the issue head-on. Moms and dads, sit down with your children and let them know that the only thing you want for their lives is God's will. Ask them what they believe God is calling them to do. Affirm this sense of calling in their lives, let them know how proud you are of them, and allow them to experience the power of a parent's blessing.

Or maybe for you, the shoe is on the other foot. You've chosen to follow God's call but you sense that you've disappointed your parents in the process. Our advice to you is the same: address the issue head-on. Ask your parents if you can talk to them about it. Let them know how much they mean to you and how much you desire to honor them. Then share your sense of calling and ask for their prayers and support. Give them a little time and make them as much a part of your calling as you possibly can. You'll be amazed at how God works in the hearts of parents when they realize that their children are doing exactly what God called them to do.

9

Your Home as a
Nerve Center for Ministry

But being *on mission* at home is more than just helping family members fulfill their calling. It also includes being *on mission* together as a family, and using your home as a nerve center for ministry. It's about reaching out to your neighbors and friends, viewing your own cul-de-sac or apartment complex as the first concentric circle of your mission field. Otherwise, you can have a house full of believers, each individually pursuing God's call on his or her life, but none making a difference to those who live right next door.

Being *on mission* right where you are means reaching your friends and neighbors. It's a concept we all embrace in theory, but often have a hard time implementing. That's why we wanted to give you a few concrete examples from those who have implemented this concept in ways that we all could duplicate.

Thomas and Kerri Hammond. This Dacula, Georgia, couple was committed to making a difference for Christ. But with two little girls who were the love of her life and the focus of her energies, Kerri wondered just how much energy she would have left to be *on mission* in her new neighborhood. That's when a friend recommended that she and Thomas start praying for their new cul-de-sac.

When the Hammonds moved in there were already two families living there. Daily, Thomas and Kerri made the rounds of their cul-de-sac, praying for each neighbor by name and stopping at each lot or house under construction to pray for the families who eventually would move in. They asked God for opportunities to share Christ and to make a difference in every home surrounding theirs.

For eighteen months they demonstrated love to their neighbors and spent plenty of time working in the yards on every beautiful day. They knew that opportunities to build bridges to their neighbors couldn't be accomplished sitting on the couch. Relationships meant they had to go to where the neighbors were, and that was outside!

One by one the neighbors began to open up. Relationships developed when the Hammonds could minister to a neighbor who lost a family member, or listen to those with job concerns or invite their neighbors for a backyard cookout. But the first *major* break came when Kerri decided they should plan and promote a Friend-Packed-Cul-De-Sac Party. The whole cul-de-sac would be invited. Everybody would be fed through a cookout, and she would put Thomas in charge of organizing some crazy games.

Thomas was a little slow to catch the vision. "What!? Do you know how much it would cost to feed all our neighbors? We aren't rich!" But Kerri was resolute. She believed God had given her this plan and would take care of the needs. She wasn't sure how, but she was sure He would.

So the invitations went out. The responses came in. And *everybody* accepted! Kerri was elated. Thomas was worried. He looked at the checkbook. Kerri focused on the opportunity.

When the big day came, and everybody gathered around the food, Thomas announced he wanted to offer a blessing before they ate. He thanked God for every neighbor and asked God to bless every home. Thomas's prayer seemed to surprise the neighbors and to open their hearts for further ministry.

Two weeks later a neighbor named Laura paid them a visit. "I've got to talk with you. And it's got to be now. I've been watching you both for two years, and I keep telling my husband that you have something we don't. I need to know what it is! My husband finally told me, 'Just go ask them.' So here I am." And that day, with the door thrown wide open, Thomas and Kerri shared about their personal relationship with Christ. Laura received

Christ into her life, and her husband David responded to the Lord's invitation a few days after.

Two months later, Tim and Bridgette attended a church-based event with Thomas and Kerri. That night Bridgette encountered Jesus Christ and it changed everything about her. Within a few weeks, having watched his neighbors and his wife being transformed before his eyes, Tim said, "Hey, I want some of that!" And with those simple words, and the prayer of acceptance that followed, Tim's life took on a whole new meaning as well.

Not all responses were so amazing. Alan and Ann had come to America from England and were older than most of their neighbors. While generally friendly, Alan would shut down a conversation if anyone raised "that religion stuff." But then his mother died. She had been a special and integral part of Alan's life and her passing left a crater-sized hole in his heart. Thomas and the neighborhood guys decided to do something special for Alan. Knowing Alan's love for horticulture and gardens, Kerri recommended a new tree for the yard, in honor of Alan's mother.

Quietly the men organized. Two would go get the tree. Several others would get a wheel barrow and shovels. And a few hours later Alan opened his door to a semi-circle of neighbors ready to present and plant a tree in memory of the first woman in his life. "Alan we know you loved your mother, and we want this to remind you of her. Where would you like us to plant it?"

Overcome with emotion as he watched this random act of kindness, the door of Alan's heart cracked open. By the next morning Alan had planted flowers around the entire base of the tree. Alan is now open to things of Christ in a way he never was before.

Amazingly, by the end of four years every couple on the Hammonds' cul-de-sac except one had come to know Christ as Savior and started attending a local church.

So what do you do when you've reached your neighborhood mission field? Thomas and Kerri put their house up for sale and moved to a different street and a new mission field! And already, neighbors from all directions in the new subdivision are wanting to know what makes Thomas and Kerri different. The Hammonds are probably planning another Friend-Packed-Cul-De-Sac party right now!

Made to Count!

It's Amazing What a Bible Study May Turn Up

Cheryl Reccord. When she moved from Chesapeake, Virginia, to Alpharetta, Georgia, Cheryl was determined that she would address her neighborhood mission field. Why the conviction? Because in Chesapeake, she had been asked if she knew a neighbor who lived three doors down. When she looked puzzled, the person asking the question seemed surprised. "Surely you know her, Cheryl," came the reply. "She only lives three doors from you, and she's dying of cancer." Stunned, Cheryl realized she lived so close but at the same time was so far away. She made a commitment to go visit the neighbor in the next few days. But three days later she looked up early in the morning to see the cars flooding the street in front of the neighbor's house. Her neighbor had died, and now the door of opportunity was closed forever.

Cheryl decided that it would never happen again. So, after arriving in Alpharetta she and her friend Rhonda planned a Bible study for people throughout the neighborhood. The first one would be held in the Reccords' home. On the night of the Bible study, which was to begin at 7:00, Bob arrived home weary and hungry from five days on the road. Setting his suitcase down, with a wry smile on his face and his tongue planted firmly in his cheek, he said, "I'm so tired all I want to do is sit down and be brain dead. You know, if we turn out the lights, nobody will even know we're home."

A few minutes later, as Bob sat down for his first bite of dinner, there was a knock at the front door. Bob groaned and Cheryl ran to get it. When she opened the door, an attractive young woman stood there. With a cracking voice and a Brooklyn accent she introduced herself. Then, in typical Brooklyn style, she got right to the point of why she had come. "I need God. I've been to a number of churches and didn't really find Him there. I played tennis with you, Cheryl, in our neighborhood tennis league. So when I got the invitation to your house I thought it would be a safe place to come. And I thought maybe I'd find God here. If I don't, I may just quit looking."

Over the next twenty-four hours, Cheryl and those involved in the Bible study were able to minister to Toni Ann who invited Christ into her heart. But it didn't stop there. In the weeks and months that followed, her eight-year-old son and her brother-in-law accepted Christ. Her Jewish husband began to ask a lot of questions. Her Jewish mother-in-law got involved in a Bible study on the book of Romans in another state because of the change she saw in Toni Ann's life. Toni Ann's sister made a commitment to Christ and proved to be a great encouragement. Toni Ann's father, who was going through some very difficult times, began a Bible study of his own. And when she attended the Bat Mitzvah of a niece, the young girl's mother came running to Toni Ann exclaiming, "Toni Ann, you're not the same person anymore! What in the world has happened to you? I've got to know!" So Toni Ann, a fast talking, vivacious, and energetic New Yorker who couldn't keep good news to herself, shared what had happened.

A few months later Toni Ann's tennis partner was very ill, and Toni Ann requested that Cheryl visit her. "Please share with her the wonderful news about Jesus and His desire to have a personal relationship with each of us."

Hesitant, Cheryl explained to Toni Ann that she didn't know the lady well and didn't want to impose. "Oh, you won't be," Toni Ann assured her, "I told her you would be coming and that you had something great to share with her."

Walking to the neighbor's house with uncertainty, Cheryl knocked on the door. As it slowly opened, it was obvious the owner was feeling anything but well. But seeing Cheryl, her eyes lit up and she quickly ushered her inside the house where they soon found themselves in deep discussion about what is *really* important in life. Over the next few minutes, the neighbor reached the conclusion that a relationship with Christ was exactly what she needed.

It's astonishing to watch the chain reactions from one simple step like launching a home-based Bible study. What if Cheryl had focused on all the reasons why it wouldn't have been convenient to open her home, or how tired she and Bob might be, or how someone else could do it so much better? Tragically, they would have missed being a blessing—and receiving so many more.

USING YOUR HOME AS A SAFE HAVEN FOR CHILDREN

Gary and Lynette Frost. The Frosts have been married for twenty-eight years. Gary, a college football star known for his broken field running and powerful throwing arm, says the best running he ever did was after Lynette.

And like most men, years later Gary realizes that in marrying his dream girl, he "truly outran my punt coverage!" After graduation from seminary, Gary became a leading African-American pastor in the Midwest and the father of four. The kids were growing and life seemed settled and secure. It was the picture of a family suitable for framing.

God, however, doesn't call us to comfort zones. And He was preparing to kick the Frosts right out of theirs.

Lynette's sister was a caseworker for foster children in the county where the Frosts lived. The more she talked about the kids in trauma and difficulty, the more Lynette and Gary's hearts were stirred to reach out and help. Gary and Lynette had four children of their own all under age ten. How could they think about adding another? So they didn't think about it long; they just did it! Lynette threw open her home as a shelter for kids who needed a second chance. The first was a teenage girl who had never had the opportunity to be in a foster home. Transformed by the love she experienced in the Frosts' home, she begged Lynette to let her brother join her, and soon there were two!

Those two were the beginning of forty-eight (that's right, it's not a typo!) young lives that Lynette and Gary would touch. While many families keep foster children just a short while, Lynette and Gary would keep children for one to two years until they could be safely returned to their family or adopted into an approved and waiting home.

But it wasn't easy. "You have to be in it not for what you will get out of it," Lynette explains, "but for what you will give to it. It can be a thankless job at times. We would call it an effort in delayed gratification. Even Christ experienced that. When He healed the ten lepers, only one came back and said, 'Thanks.' It's inconvenient to reach out to kids from tough backgrounds, but love is often inconvenient. That's why it's love."

After a long season of having foster child after foster child grace their home, Lynette heard Gary say one morning, "God means for us to have another child, and his name's going to be Benjamin. I just don't know when we'll find him or how he'll come."

It wasn't much later that Lynette, who now worked as a foster and adoption recruitment coordinator, ran into a forlorn worker at her office. When Lynette asked what was wrong, the troubled worker sighed deeply and said, "I just don't know what we're going to do with that little baby!"

"What baby?" Lynette said.

"The baby who has been left at the hospital. We can't keep him more than one more day. He has no name and, what's worse, he has no home."

Before she could think, the words leaped out of Lynette's mouth, "That's Benjamin!"

"No, I told you he doesn't have a name," answered the coworker.

"No, you don't understand," replied Lynette. "It's Benjamin. It's God's Benjamin for us. Benjamin is supposed to be in our home."

And so little Benjamin became the forty-eighth foster child and a part of Gary and Lynette's home for good.

Lynette and Gary now have the rare privilege of watching many of their foster children mature, get married, and have families of their own. Those former foster children are now willing to give their lives away because someone reached out to them—for to whom much is given, much is required![1]

And Lynette and Gary? They're still reaching out to anybody in need, changing their world right where they are!

How about you? Are you willing to risk? You could investigate by calling your local foster care agency to see what the opportunities are for you. Your very own Benjamin just might be waiting.

Even the Tough Times Can Be *On Mission* Times

Jeanine Allen lives with her husband and two daughters in Lawrenceville, Georgia. Five years ago Jeanine learned she had breast cancer. Going through one mastectomy she thought she had found health and a new lease on life. And she had—for a year. That's when the cancer came back with a rage. Another mastectomy was followed by cancer discovered in the spine, tumor counts that resembled a roller coaster in tracking, and untold chemo and radiation treatments. But several years later, Jeanine is still valiantly fighting the battle. Her spirit is an encouragement to everyone she knows.

Her commitment to make a difference for Christ even during the tough times led Jeanine to ask her husband, Chuck, not to accompany her when she went for her cancer treatments. When Chuck tried to resist, Jeanine would have none of it. She believed that other women receiving cancer treatments would be much more open to talk with her if her husband wasn't there.

She told him, "I love you, honey. And I really appreciate your wanting to go with me and support me. But maybe God's allowing me to have this difficult time so that I can help someone else who's going through the same thing. And who knows, maybe God has a divine appointment for me while I'm sitting in a chemo-treatment chair!"

With a spirit like that, Jeanine leaves a wake of blessing everywhere she goes. And the people she's impacting the most? Her own family. As her girls watch their mom handle the toughest circumstances life can throw at her, they are learning how to be *on mission* in the face of adversity. They are also learning firsthand how to make a home a ministry center.

It makes you stop and think, doesn't it? *If Jeanine could make a difference like that even in the tough days she's walking through, what could God do with me?*

10

On Mission
at Work

A Gallup poll recently found that 50 percent of those interviewed in the for-profit world and 51 percent in the not-for-profit world said they were not engaged in their jobs *at all*. According to Gallup's definition, "not engaged" meant they may be productive but not psychologically connected to the organization. They show up, do their work, perform their duties, but they have absolutely no passion for their job.

But, wait, it gets worse. Twenty-two percent of the for-profit and not-for-profit-employees said they were beyond "not engaged"—they were actively disengaged! While they were physically present they were totally absent psychologically *and* not being productive. They take the paycheck but are a quiet cancer metastasizing throughout the organization. This leaves only 29 percent of people in the workplace who feel engaged in their work.[1]

Why? Is it because for too long we've considered our jobs as merely a position to fill? A way to put food on the table and pay the bills? Or, more cynically, as society's expectation of us and a necessary evil in life?

Perhaps we've forgotten that the first two institutions God established for productivity, fulfillment, and influence were home and work. That's why, when we fully understand this fourth principle—that God calls you to be *on mission* with Him right were you are, starting now—we will understand its application to our home life *and* work life.

As we discussed in chapter 4, work was originally referred to in Christian circles as a "calling" or "vocation." The very term vocation comes from the Latin *vocare* and *vocatio*, both of which carry, in the original intent, the idea of "to call." *Webster's Dictionary* lists as the first definition of call . . .

> A summons or strong inclination to a particular state or course of action; especially a divine call to the religious life.

Somewhere along the line, we lost the sense of one's work as a calling from God. We cheapened work by allowing it to become merely a means to earn money, acquire material goods, meet life's needs, and climb a corporate ladder. In profession after profession, job after job, workplace after workplace, men and women seem more focused on their "climb" than their "call."

As a result, we've lost the idea of work as a *divine opportunity* fleshed out in the everyday patterns of life. Divine opportunities became reserved for Sundays, religious holidays, church work, or mission trips, especially for people *called* to religious service such as vocational ministry and missions.

But God never meant it that way. God meant our vocation to be our *holy calling* where we would make an impact for Him in the world in which He has placed us. It's not an accident that He's taken His people and scattered them like seeds across society's soil to take root, spring up, and produce abiding fruit that will remain (see John 15).

When we see our job as a holy calling, it will transform the way we work at it. The apostle Paul reminds us that "Whatever you do, work at it with all your heart, as working for the Lord, not for men."[2] This attitude—doing our work for the audience of One—will lead to excellence in how we do it. For without excellence, we can scatter all the seed we want, but it will fall on the ground of hearts that have been hardened by the sloppy way we carry out our duties.

Once we have established a platform of excellence, we need to be "on call" for the divine opportunities that God sends our way. Sometimes, we will have opportunities to witness to a coworker, customer, or vendor. And our witness will be all the more effective because they've seen the difference that Christ made in our work lives. Other times, we will have opportunities to meet a need and then watch God work His transforming power. But the point is this: We need to stand ready, to be "on call," the same way that an emergency room doctor is "on call" to meet the needs of those who are wheeled through the doors of an emergency room.

We are to be the spiritual emergency room doctors at our workplace, ready to bring healing at that critical juncture where need meets opportunity.

It All Starts with Excellence.

Victorya Rogers. Hollywood: an unrivaled influence on American culture and a tough place to live for Christ. Just ask Victorya Rogers, who has worked there for eighteen years, eleven of those as a leading talent agent in the land filled with big dreams, big money, big temptations, big breaks, and too often, big falls. It all adds up to an arena with enormous impact, for those who can make the cut. But if you want to influence Hollywood, you'd better bring your "A game." Early on, Victorya discovered that *excellence in her profession* was her entry door to a credible hearing for sharing the gospel. A fast-paced, high-tech, arts-oriented culture like Hollywood doesn't put up with mediocrity. And credibility is given only to those who are excellent in their craft. So Victorya determined to be just that.

> My husband and I both firmly believe that everywhere we are God desires to use us as we honor Him in the way we do our work. There are too many "Sunday Christians" who think what you do Monday through Friday really doesn't matter. We're shocked at the business behavior of some people we find out later are Christians. Do they think they can get away with it? *Who* are they really living their life for? When Christians realize their vocation is also their calling, it changes the way they do business every day![3]

It certainly changed the way Victorya performed her calling, even when nobody else was looking. Her career started with a brief internship at *Entertainment Tonight* while she was in college. "I was committed to be a great typist and to work harder, faster, and better than anyone around me."

The effort paid off when she landed a temporary job as a receptionist at a talent agency. She was given the responsibility of answering six phones at once but felt that she could do more. Recognizing that the office's 150-page client roster was a mess, she launched into retyping and rearranging the entire book. She didn't know that the president of the company was observing this self-initiated project. Impressed with the results, the president took Victorya under his wing, mentoring her as she became one of the most successful talent agents in Hollywood.

> I learned that being faithful in the little things can lead to greater things. Even if people mistreat you and offer you little or no respect, job security comes when you do your work for God. If you're good at what you do, somebody will eventually recognize it.
>
> Whether it's Hollywood or anywhere else in North America, an employee's number one responsibility is to do her job well. We're not paid to be missionaries; we're paid to do a job. Even dynamic Christians can be confused on this issue. Too many try to preach on the job rather than do their job. Businesses don't need preachers; they need team members. But when the opportunity arises to naturally share Christ with those around you, even in the workplace, always be ready to give an answer for the hope that lies within you. Believe me, every person who does not know Jesus is searching for answers, and he or she is watching you, whether you realize it or not.
>
> I always felt that as believers we need to also be witnesses. And the bottom line is you're either a good witness or a bad witness. As a talent agent, I soon discovered that 98 percent of the people in my business were without Christ. But along the way I found that whether I was a secretary, a receptionist, a mailroom worker, or a talent agent, I was a missionary in Hollywood in each of those positions. The power of your witness is not found in the position you hold, but in the Person you serve.

Workplace leaders tell us that when they look for people to join them, they're not just looking for people who will do enough to *get by,* or whose main focus is watching the clock, or those who don't plan to exercise any more effort than the person working next to them. They want people who will treat the job as though the company was their own, for in reality it is.

These leaders know instinctively that no chain is stronger than its weakest link. How tragic if the weakest link claims to be a follower of Christ!

Famed founder and chairman of Chick-fil-A International, **Truett Cathy,** captures it well when he counsels:

- Save 10 percent
- Give 10 percent
- Work 10 percent harder.[4]

If you don't believe he means it, just hang around any Chick-fil-A restaurant and watch how the work is done. Strike up a conversation with the workers and notice how polite they are. Ask for special help and see how fast it's given. They personify Truett Cathy's attitude that if you learn to love your work, you'll never have to "work" again.[5]

> The power of your witness is not found in the position you hold, but in the Person you serve.

Chick-fil-A's standard for excellence is working. The private company has risen from one small restaurant a few decades ago to a privately held corporation that exceeds a billion dollars in annual revenue. Imagine how much more Chick-fil-A would earn if their happy customers could buy their chicken sandwiches seven days a week. Yet Chick-fil-A chooses to make a deliberate public statement of Christian faith by closing on Sunday.

IT STARTS WHERE YOU ARE

Not long ago Bob was pulled aside by a businessman. The man had risen to a very strategic and influential position in his company, yet seemed restless and discontent. He asked Bob to pray that God might open a new door of opportunity in another company. "I've got to find something different," said the man.

"Why?" Bob asked. "It seems like God's placed you in a strategic position in an expanding company surrounded by all kinds of people."

"That's just it. The people around me are all messed up. I don't know of one other Christian in the entire company. I get so frustrated dealing with nonbelievers all the time. I've got to get someplace where there are at least a few people who can understand my perspective. This can't possibly be God's call for me."

Bob took a deep breath. Not wanting to offend but determined to be direct, he measured his words carefully. "Thanks for asking me to pray for you. I think Christians praying for one another is essential and a key part of our strength. However, I'm sorry that I won't be able to pray for that request."

The businessman stared back in disbelief. "Why not?"

"Because I believe I'd be praying against God's will."

A puzzled look prompted Bob to continue.

"I believe God has loved you enough to entrust you with an unbelievable mission. Do you realize that He's placed you as possibly the sole Christ-follower in the entire company? How in the world could I pray against that? Somebody's entire future, their eternal destiny may well depend on your staying right where you are. Maybe you should start seeing the glass half full rather than half empty. Why don't you begin praying by name for those who work closest to you? Find some creative ways to begin to build bridges with them. Discover their interests and get involved with them even if it may be a little awkward at first. But whatever you do, don't give up on the most strategic assignment God may have put before you."

It would have been easy for Bob to go along and offer up a quick prayer for the man, but he knew that's not really what this man needed most. Sometimes, we have to be willing to shake up the thinking of those around us. Encourage them to look at things from a little different perspective, perhaps a biblical worldview.

Could it be that you've experienced some of the same feelings this vice president was expressing? Do you think that it would be easier to work in a more "Christian environment" than the one you're in? Don't be fooled. Often the challenges in one are just as significant as they are in the other. They just take on different shapes, forms, and expectations.

Why don't you just stop and thank God for exactly where He's placed you? Ask Him to open your eyes for the opportunities around you, and to show you some divine appointments before the week is over.

Be on the Lookout for Divine Appointments

Jim and Karen Covell. Like Victorya Rogers, the Covells found their calling in Hollywood. Jim is a composer for television and films, while Karen is a producer, and both are *on mission* for the Lord in a place that other Christians condemn.

> For a long time we never thought of it as a *calling*. We thought of it as something we simply were passionate about doing. Being working professionals in Hollywood was all we knew. And when we looked at our gifts and our talents, as well as our interests, they all led us to this place. Suddenly, we realized *this is our mission field!*[6]

For Jim and Karen, the journey has been an adventure. But the dreams of glamour wore off a long time ago. Karen says:

> There are a lot of people who come to Hollywood saying that they are *called* here, but too often, what they're really called to is the glamour, the glitz, the money, the attention, and the lifestyle.
>
> Those who are truly called of God understand that they are entering a mission field. They really care about the people here and not just the lifestyle. Their driving force is to see the people around them changed as they fulfill being Christ's ambassadors to the seat of influence.

Jim adds,

> People who are truly called to make a difference here have an amazing tenacity. Hollywood is a tough place, and its successes come and go quickly. The person who is truly called to Hollywood will say, "I'm here to be faithful and if that includes success—great. If that doesn't include success—great." Success isn't the issue, faithfulness is!

Explaining the fickleness of the Hollywood community, Jim puts it all in perspective as a composer when he describes how Hollywood works.

> Your career in Hollywood usually goes something like this:
> - Who is Jim Covell?
> - Get me Jim Covell for this job!

- Get me someone *like* Jim Covell.
- Get me anybody but Jim Covell.
- Whatever happened to Jim Covell?
- Who is Jim Covell?

It takes a strong constitution and tenacity, grounded in a divine call to handle that. There are no long-term jobs as a composer or a freelance producer here. The odds are greater that you would be elected a U.S. senator than that you would be a composer in a nighttime dramatic television series; there are one hundred senators and there are only about twelve composers for nighttime dramatic television shows. In feature films, there are probably only forty guys who work on a regular basis. So your odds are much better to be in some other profession. To survive in this place and make a difference for Christ, you have to be deeply rooted and committed in your calling!

But I don't want to make it sound like it's all hopeless, by any means. I hear a lot of people talk about dead-end jobs in Hollywood. I want to correct that. If there are people around you, there is no such thing as a dead-end job. I believe that the only dead-end job would be if everyone around you had become a Christian and there was no one else to share Christ with. Then it is time to move to a new arena for a job.

Both Jim and Karen have learned that you begin to look at people differently when you're *on mission* for Christ in a challenging environment like Hollywood. You see what people can become through Christ, not just what they are now. And you see spiritual needs where once you saw arrogance and pride.

Karen experienced this firsthand when she received a call from a West-Coast producer to be an associate producer for *Headliners and Legends with Matt Lauer*, a one-hour celebrity profile show on MSNBC.

I was so excited about being invited because I knew there were already a couple of Christians in that office doing a great job, and I love documentary work. At the first meeting, people sat around the table and brought ideas of those they would love to see profiled. I had a list of people and on the top of my list was Billy Graham. I felt like he was the most famous man in the world, and it would be an amazing profile.

But, as you might imagine, Karen's idea was shot down. Their arguments? He was too old! So the discussion continued in other directions, and then finally the decision was made. Hugh Hefner would be the first profile. And he's almost as old as Billy Graham!

Karen was devastated. What should she do? Surely she couldn't support anything about Hugh Hefner's life.

> It was really disturbing, and I came home to Jim and said, "I don't want to do this. We're going to spend the whole time just listing his successes as he's been destroying our country."
>
> "Wait a minute," Jim responded. "That's why we're here. We're here to reach people who need to hear about Jesus, not just the ones who already have. You've got to go there. Just be different from everybody else. Start praying for Hugh Hefner right now. Go to that mansion and make a difference!"

Karen felt like she'd been hit by a ton of bricks—in a positive way, of course. (Is there such a thing as a "positive" ton of bricks hitting you?) How could she have missed it? After all, Paul went to Athens and Corinth, the seats of pagan influence and sexuality in his day. Why should she run from the Playboy Mansion?

The next day, while talking to her producer, Karen took the risk of sharing the conversation she and her husband had the night before. Knowing he might not understand or support her perspective, her jaw dropped when he responded, "I've struggled with it as well. In fact, I went home and called my pastor to get some counsel. My pastor told me, 'If you don't cover this episode, somebody else will. And if they do it, they'll use their worldview. You have the opportunity to determine, as a producer, what exactly comes out of this story.'"

Together, as producer and associate producer, Rick and Karen decided to develop a different slant for the story. They would focus not simply on Hefner's successes and renown, but on why he became who he did. After all, everybody has a story. As they began researching, Karen hired a cameraman and sound-man who were also Christians. They all began to pray together. When the day of the interview arrived, they sat down with Hugh Hefner, and the producer asked questions based on their research. What were Hefner's parents like? What was his upbringing? What characterized the early years of his life?

Imagine the shocked crew listening as Hefner began to pour out how he'd been raised in a puritan home of religious tradition. His parents believed in God, but not a God of grace, love, and compassion. Theirs had been a rigid religion. They never told Hefner nor his brother that they loved them, and his mother never kissed him because she wanted to avoid germs. And so, Hefner set out to find love wherever he could.

With dry eyes, Hefner recalled how his parents had given him a blanket when he was a child—his "security blanket." He painted a vivid picture of a little boy going to bed at night hugging his blanket, the only thing he had to hug, the only thing that returned any warmth. The blanket was bordered with bunny rabbits; it became his "bunny blanket."

Hefner recounted how, as a boy, he always wanted a puppy, but his parents, especially his mother, said that dogs spread germs, so there couldn't be one in their house. It was only after they discovered a tumor in his ear, one that could be detrimental to his hearing, that his parents broke down and bought Hefner a dog. No one could have predicted, however, that the dog would unexpectedly die after just five days. Hugh Hefner recalled how he wrapped the dying dog in his bunny blanket as a means to comfort the puppy. But when the puppy died, his mother buried the dog and burned the blanket. Both sources of his deepest comfort were suddenly gone. He said very matter-of-factly, "I guess I'm still just that little boy trying to find love."

> The room was hushed in silence as we all sat and listened to the man pour out his story. Tears formed in my eyes. We realized the gaping void that existed deep in the man's soul. He went on to tell us that every Friday night he gets together with close friends and watches old romantic movies because he's still searching for what love is all about. And I realized that this man had confused sex with love, and he had turned a desperate need into a way to make money and become famous.

Suddenly, I couldn't hate the man any longer. I still don't agree with what he's done, but he's just someone who got twisted in a way that made him who he is today. At the end of the interview there was silence, and it was as though no one could move. There were "bunnies" standing around as well as his PR person and the rest of his entourage. Suddenly, his PR person, who had worked with Hefner for fifteen years, broke the silence by exclaiming, "This wasn't an interview. This was a therapy session!"

It was after the interview that I had the privilege of writing Mr. Hefner a letter. I thanked him for the oppportunity to tell his story. I thanked him for the time he allowed us to get to know him better. I told him that, in spite of all he has accomplished, I believed there was one thing he had not yet done; he had not acknowledged God as a loving God and did not know Him personally. I challenged him to seek out that loving God and sent him a copy of Ravi Zacharias's book *Can Man Live Without God?*

I was amazed two weeks later when he wrote back to me. He thanked me for the book and said that he'd enjoyed the interview very much. One sentence in his letter really stood out: "My spiritual values are very real and deeply felt and they don't have much to do with other people's views on God or religion, but thanks for writing."

I know I didn't change his life; I didn't see him get down on his knees and pray, but I did take the opportunity to open a door for him to understand that God loves him right where he is, but loves him way too much to let him stay there. That following Christmas after running into him again, I sent him a beautiful Bible with his name on the front.

Witnessing to Hugh Hefner—there's an assignment that was bigger than Karen. Just trying to see him as a human being with needs was hard enough, but reaching out to him with the love of Christ was ten times more difficult—until she heard his story. Karen took it one step at a time, knowing that the same God who saved her loved Hugh Hefner. And He happens to be a God who specializes in the impossible.

Take a moment and read Acts chapter 8. Notice how God, Who called

Philip as a deacon from the church in Jerusalem and therefore "a man from the pew," orchestrated his path and set before him a divine appointment with an Ethiopian eunuch. Has God done that for you? Maybe he did it, and you ignored it? Maybe you don't have many Hugh Hefners or Ethiopian eunuchs floating around your workplace, but the notoriety or stature of the person is not what's important. Is there somebody at work—anybody—with whom God could be orchestrating a divine appointment for you this week? How will you ensure that you don't miss it? Are you ready to "give an answer . . . for the hope that you have"?[7] That's what it means to be *on mission* at work.

Learn to Be Creatively Intentional

Okay. So you're ready for some divine appointments, but your spiritual day timer seems to stay empty. Are you praying for it to happen? Are you living in such a way that people see something different in you? How can they ask about "the hope that lies within you" if all they see is pessimism and despair? Are you performing your job with excellence, giving your testimony credibility among your coworkers? Equally important, are you sharing your faith discreetly, keeping in mind that you were hired to work, not to turn your office into a church? You may be faced with some intolerance of Christianity among your coworkers. Some feel like you're wasting time if you talk about faith on company time. Trying to keep it all in balance can be maddening.

A key is learning how to be creatively intentional in your approach to carrying out your mission. All employees are ethically responsible to carry out their work and fulfill the expectations of their employer, so they should do their work without allowing anything to divert them from their responsibilities. But creativity can overcome many hurdles!

Jonathan Stoudenmire is a construction manager for strip mall developments throughout the Southeast. He found early on that a busy construction site could be a tough place for trying to share the gospel. But he also learned that construction workers let down their guard when they gather around the table to eat. So Jonathan and his wife came up with a plan. Once a month she would put together a large lunch and deliver it to the construction site.

On that day lunch would be free for everyone, and it would be an absolute feast.

Jonathan would relax with the men over lunch. He worked hard to gain their respect by treating them like he knew he wanted to be treated. His affirmation was quick, his smile ready, his encouragement strong, and his support total. Jonathan would look for a chance to be vulnerable and let down his guard. And the men didn't miss that temperament. After all, it wasn't the temperament they expected on construction sites. Especially from the boss.

The result? Inevitably, Jonathan would get a chance to share his faith over lunch. No three-point sermons and tons of memorized Scripture. Just a humble and authentic explanation of how much Christ had changed his life. Often, some of the men would respond to his vulnerability with an openness of their own. Many men came to know Jesus Christ as Savior, because one man and his wife creatively and intentionally found a nonthreatening way to share the most important aspect of their lives.

> In your hearts set apart Christ as Lord. Always be prepared . . . to give the reason for the hope that you have. But do this with gentleness and respect.[8]

Make the Most of Small Opportunities

It's amazing how most of us have a sense of timing that's radically different from God's. We want things to happen instantly, but God looks at things from an eternal perspective. In our split-second society we become impatient waiting for food to cook in a microwave oven. We're impatient with our high-speed modems while forgetting that only a few years ago all we had was the U.S. Postal Service. We drive through fast-food restaurants only to complain that the food is not fast enough (except, of course, at Chick-fil-A).

Domino's Pizza became a fast-food empire by promising to deliver any pizza to your house in thirty minutes or less. Owner and founder, Tom Monaghan, claimed, "We don't sell pizza, we sell delivery." And they must, since most Domino Pizza delivery personnel can outrun any ambulance in any city on any day of the week! Now Domino's no longer makes that guarantee, because of lawsuits—a result of our impatient (and litigious!) society.

Their drivers could outrun the ambulance, but not the ambulance chasers.

Even when we pray for patience, we plead, "Lord, give me patience, and give it to me *now!*" But God's ways (and timing) have never been synonymous with ours:

> "For My thoughts are not your thoughts, neither are your ways My ways," says the Lord. "For as the heavens are higher than the earth, so are My ways higher than your ways, and My thoughts than your thoughts."[9]

God's working with His chosen nation, Israel, is an excellent example of this critical truth. After promising to give them the land of Canaan as far back as Abraham, God continually had to remind them that it was His timing that was essential, not theirs. He waited years until He was ready to deliver them from bondage in Egypt to set out for their Promised Land. And even then He warned them not to expect a "fast fix." He reminded them of His faithfulness, but cautioned them to remember His timing as they headed for the enemy-inhabited Promised Land.

> You may say to yourselves, "These nations are stronger than we are. How can we drive them out?" But do not be afraid of them; remember well what the LORD your God did to Pharaoh and to all Egypt. You saw with your own eyes the great trials, the miraculous signs and wonders, the mighty hand and outstretched arm, with which the LORD your God brought you out. The LORD your God will do the same to all the peoples you now fear. . . . The LORD your God will drive out those nations before you *little by little. You will not be allowed to eliminate them all at once.*" (italics ours)[10]

They were ready to take over in one fell swoop, but God knew that for their good, and the long-term effectiveness of His plan, His timing was better than theirs. It's the same in our walk with God and being *on mission* with Him wherever He's placed us. We're ready for radical change tomorrow with us as the catalyst, but He's looking for eternal transformation, and that takes time. We become impatient with coworkers, concluding prematurely that God could never change their lives. We tend to overestimate what we can accomplish in one year, but underestimate what we can accomplish, with God's blessing, in five years. Sometimes it takes years of ministering to someone's needs before they're ready to grasp the love of Christ.

Connect the Dots from Work to Existing Need

Steve Puckett. He leads one of the most innovative medical companies in America, MedCath. Founded in 1988, it's an innovator in advanced cardiac treatments, surgery, and restoration. Its entrepreneurial partnerships between the corporation, hospitals, and physicians have created cost-effective solutions in cardiac patient care. With multiple hospitals and a fleet of mobile cardiac cath labs, MedCath is contributing to the revolution in cardiac care.

Steve serves as the chairman of the boards of MedCath, Hospital Partners of America, and several other companies, including a land development and building corporation as well as a heating and air conditioning business. He and his wife, Beth, have a heart for helping the less fortunate. They live in Charlotte, North Carolina, where they apply their business skills and personal resources to help transform the lives of people through a ministry called Jackson Park Ministries (JPM). It's the place where they found a dire need for their business expertise.[11]

The ministry began eighteen years ago in a Baptist church with a for-sale sign hanging on the front door. It was established to minister to the pressing needs of a depressed inner-city area.

JPM launched a transitional housing program designed to stitch dysfunctional families back together. Four interviews are required for a family to be accepted in the program. They must have a job and, if they don't, Jackson Park Ministries provides them opportunities in the community with supportive partners. They are asked to attend Steele Creek Community Church for the first two months and go through a discipleship program. One aspect of the program is financial management training sponsored by Crown Ministries. This training encourages participants to submit their weekly paycheck to a financial counselor who helps them establish and stick to a budget. They also learn the importance of debt reduction and saving for the future.

Fractured marriages are rebuilt through interactive marriage classes based on the Word of God, practical parenting training, and monthly family days where families spend the entire weekend together just having fun.

The program has two disqualifiers for candidates—lying to the JPM staff about any issue, and not fulfilling the requirements agreed upon. While the program takes a year to fifteen months to complete, the recovery rate is remarkable. Prostitutes, drug dealers, shattered families, and many others without much hope have been restored to productive and fulfilling lifestyles. Steve and Beth connected the dots. They looked for a way to use their business skills and resources to help those shattered by the inner-city jungle. They discovered Jackson Park Ministries and decided to help. Beth serves on the board and volunteers with friends to clean, paint, repair, and decorate existing apartments. Steve's company maintains the ministry's heating and air conditioning equipment.

Have you connected the dots from your skills and talents, plus your daily work and experiences—all God-given—to a need in your workplace or community? If not, what are you waiting for?

So What Is Success Really?

Our culture consistently tells us we deserve bigger, better, pricier, and trendier stuff. And the promise is that when we get it, we'll have fulfillment. Most often we find when we arrive there, it's not nearly what we anticipated. That's because there are only a few things that make an eternal difference— God's Word and mission, and God's people. When you combine them, fleshing out God's Word and reaching out to impact His people for His cause, significance results.

So step back and look at your profession. Have you come to the clear understanding that it is a vocation, a part of your calling from God? Do you realize that God wants you to be *on call* to impact the lives of others, finding creative ways to share His message and see lives changed? Perhaps the governor of Georgia, **Sonny Perdue,** summed it up best in our interview with him when he compared our vocation to a specific set of marching orders:

> If we see where God has placed us *the way God sees it*, we'll recognize our work to be a calling. These things don't happen by chance. God

knows how He made us, and He places us strategically where He needs servants to make a difference. We've been dispatched. Just as our military has orders to a specific location, God orders us in every aspect of our lives—into our location, into our work, into a service where He needs something done.[12]

PRINCIPLE 5

God reveals His mission through His Word, His Spirit, wise counsel, and His work in circumstances around you.

Key scriptures:
- His Word—"All Scripture is God-breathed and is useful for teaching, rebuking, correcting and training in righteousness, so that the man of God may be thoroughly equipped for every good work" (2 Timothy 3:16–17).
- His Spirit—"But when he, the Spirit of truth, comes, he will guide you into all truth. He will not speak on his own; he will speak only what he hears, and he will tell you what is yet to come" (John 16:13).
- Wise counsel—"Plans fail for lack of counsel, but with many advisers they succeed" (Proverbs 15:22).
- His work—"And we know that in all things God works for the good of those who love him, who have been called according to his purpose. For those God foreknew he also predestined to be conformed to the likeness of his Son, that he might be the first-born among many brothers" (Romans 8:28–29).

Key points:
- When God formed you, He hard-wired you for success in your mission. He will not work at cross-purposes with His own creative work.
- The Bible is the owner's manual for our life. God will never call us to do anything inconsistent with His will as revealed in Scripture.
- God does not play guessing games with our lives. If we earnestly seek Him, He will guide us through His Spirit and His work in circumstances around us.
- We should seek the counsel of mature Christians who can help us discover God's will for our lives. But we should remember that God will ultimately reveal His plan for our life to us, not them.
- There are no shortcuts or gimmicks that reveal God's will. Fleeces, our feelings, and "open doors" can sometimes steer us wrong.

Understanding How God Wired You

Have you ever noticed the critical role questions play in life? Court cases are won or lost on the strength of questions asked in cross-examination. "Cross-examination," said the legendary jurist William Blackstone, "is the greatest legal engine ever invented to discern the truth." Strategic planners often say that asking the right questions is about 80 percent of the key to finding the right strategy. Great teachers use the "Socratic method" to ask penetrating questions and help students discover truth on their own. Just sit back for a moment and think of the powerful impact of questions in living. Life changing moments are often characterized by questions like:

- Will you marry me?
- Would you like to invite Jesus Christ into your life?
- Have you decided about the job offer yet?
- Honey, how would you feel about being a father?

Or, how about emergencies:

- Quick, where's the bathroom?
- Dad, how much is the deductible on our car insurance?
- How can the pregnancy test strip be turning blue? We're still in graduate school!

Foundational questions can establish our life's future:

- Does the Bible really speak to my everyday life?

- Are you certain you'll go to heaven when you die?
- What are the principles for having a marriage that will last a lifetime?
- How can I see my job as something sacred when all I do is work in a manufacturing plant making parts that have nothing to do with changing the world?

Or acquiring wise counsel:

- How do I know that the person I'm dating is the one God wants me to marry?
- What do you see as the major strengths in my life? Why don't you go ahead and tell me my weaknesses as well?
- How do I become more useable in God's hands?
- How do I determine what vocation to pursue?

Look at any great teachers, and you'll often find them interweaving questions into their presentations. Their purpose is not to dump a load of cognitive knowledge on the listeners, but to be a catalyst for the listeners to think, evaluate, and get to the core issues. Christ was the greatest teacher of all time, and His teaching was laced with riveting questions that penetrated to the bottom-line issues of life:

- What is the kingdom of God like? (Luke 13:18)
- Who would begin construction of a building without first getting estimates and checking to see if there's enough money to pay the bills? (The implication is, "Don't follow Me without first counting the cost.) (Luke 14:28)
- Who is your neighbor? (Luke 10:29)
- Simon, son of John, do you truly love me? (John 21:15, 16, 17)
- Who do people say the Son of Man is? Who do *you* say I am? (Matthew 16:13, 15, italics ours)
- What do you want me to do for you? (Luke 18:41)

Jesus had a way of putting His finger on things that really matter. In just a few words, He would cut through the superfluous "fluff" of our existence and penetrate down to the intents and motives of the listener's heart.

Following His example, we want to look at some key questions that will help us get a grip on how God uniquely hard-wired us, questions that will get below the surface of life and down to the core realities of who you are, how God made you, and how that fits with what He wants to do with your life. This is a critical step in understanding His mission for you. As we explained in the very first principle, God prepared a unique plan and calling for your life even before you were born. Then He designed you for that destiny, creating you with all the gifts, resolve, personality traits, and desires necessary to get the job done.

God does not work at cross-purposes with His own creation. We need to keep this in mind in the next few chapters as we look at the specific ways that God guides us. But we also need to be aware that, while God created us with certain strengths and abilities necessary for our mission, He also delights in sometimes working through our weaknesses. And we need to remember that God gives us missions we could never complete alone. Relying on His strength, not ours, is the only way to fully realize our calling.

> **God does not work at cross-purposes with His own creation.**

With those thoughts in mind, let's turn to a few helpful questions designed to dig deeper into the way God designed you for your destiny.

- When I have leisure time, how do I like to spend it?
- What ignites the passion of my life and excites me when I think about doing it for a vocation?
- What are three core strengths that God has placed in my life?
- What rewarding experiences has God given me that may have been preparation for my future?
- Do I enjoy being in the lead and responsible, or in the background and supportive?
- What kind of activities make time fly for me?
- What are the activities and work that cause me to sense God's pleasure as I do them?
- When a book, sermon, speech, event, or activity ignites an interest in me, what's the subject matter?

- What are the things that most make me feel alive when I participate in them?
- In what ways do I most enjoy giving myself away to others?
- Do I feel excited or apathetic about the work I'm presently doing?

These questions should get you thinking about the passions and abilities that God has hard-wired into you. Both are critical as you assess God's mission for your life. Many times, we like to focus on our interests and passions, but forget that passion alone is seldom enough. Randy may have a passion to become a professional football player. And since he doesn't mind conflict, maybe his personality would be well suited for that vocation as well. But there's still a major three-part challenge: size, speed, and age. Randy needs to stick to writing.

Writing to the church at Philippi, Paul recognized this critical balance as well. "For it is God who works in you," Paul said, "[both] to will and to act according to his good purpose."[1]

Do you see what Paul is saying here? When God works in our life to guide us according to His good purpose (and by the way, His purpose for us is always good), then He works within us on both the will (our desires) and the actions (our abilities). So when you see this alignment between passions and abilities in your own life, you can usually trace it back to the God "who works in you."

GOD HAS GIVEN YOU A UNIQUE PERSONALITY.

Understanding our interests will help us identify what God created us to do. Likewise, getting a better handle on our abilities will help us learn about those things we are best able to do. But another key factor in this mix of how God created us is personality and temperament. Better understanding our own personality and temperament will teach us *how* we like to do things. This, in turn, will have a significant impact on determining *whether* God is calling us to a particular task and *how* we should best accomplish that task consistent with our own unique personality.

Everyone who goes to the doctor knows the value of diagnostic tools. They help us understand our physical strengths, limitations, and ailments. In the same manner there are tools that can help us better understand ourselves, how we function, and how we are made by our Creator. These tools help us probe the realities of our personality, temperament, or our likely tendencies in handling conflict. What *must* be remembered is that diagnostic tools are simply that—just tools. They cannot be used as a definitive final word about us or anyone else.

But they can help us understand ourselves better. That understanding can make a huge difference in the way we live. Have you ever noticed that when the family is getting ready to take off on a major trip the air crackles with tension? A few family members are impatient, frustrated, and snapping at each other while somebody else is withdrawing into his or her silent shell. Another family member just slips away to avoid the challenge.

Why?

Because everybody is different. Some are addicted to being on time, while others don't even know what time is! Some want everything packed neatly, while others just throw stuff in a bag, whether it's clean or not. And when someone reacts in tension, his or her mode of reaction often sets off someone else in the family. All because each family member is created differently.

For Randy and Rhonda, any trip to the airport is a challenge. Rhonda likes to get there early enough to catch the previous day's flight. Randy likes to get there just in time to stick his foot in the door to the Jetway as the boarding gate closes. You don't stay married twenty-five years without understanding each other's personality enough to make the compromises necessary so you don't kill each other.

Knowing how others are wired is a great help in the workplace too. When a coworker does something you can't figure out, you could say, "That's the dumbest thing I've ever heard of," or you could focus on what you know about your coworker's temperament and strengths. With the right knowledge, you can understand why he reacts the way he does. Bob keeps a file with the personality profiles of the employees with whom he works closely. When he's perplexed about a situation at work, he regularly pulls out that file and says, "That's why John or Mary reacted like that." Bob believes that having that kind of insight into your coworkers and associates can be a real lifesaver throughout your career.

Made to Count!

We want to provide some additional help for you to discover your own unique personality and your own unique giftedness. Our friend Dr. Mels Carbonell of Uniquely You Leadership Center has graciously worked with us to provide an online instrument to help you explore these areas of your life.

If you look under the front flap of the dustcover on this book, under it you will find an individually numbered eight-digit code. Enter your personal eight-digit code on the Uniquely You website (www.uniquelyyou.com), and you will be allowed to complete one personality temperament profile as well as one evaluation of the spiritual gifts profile. (On the spiritual gifts profile we have decided to stay with the spiritual gifts that are the most broadly accepted across the evangelical world and not to focus on those that are controversial in some quarters.) If you would like to have your spouse, family, leadership team, or others use the profiles, you will be able to do so for a very reasonable fee.

We hope these diagnostic instruments will help you affirm and clarify some realities about how you are made and possibly clear up some misperceptions about yourself or others. It's beneficial to sit down with your spouse, your family, or your team at work and talk through how different personalities and giftedness can best relate to each other. Some of the greatest points of conflict and misunderstanding in our life arise from two areas:

1. Unmet expectations
2. Lack of understanding another's perspective

Both of us have found it immensely helpful to walk our leadership team at work through these instruments and then debrief so everyone understands one another better. And we've gone through that same type of process with our spouses.

When you've completed the online profile assessment, please turn to Appendix A for some interpretative information provided by Dr. Carbonell and us to help you understand how to best relate to others based on these personality assessments. After all, the greatest things in life happen not as we try to do something on our own, but as we recognize our need for others who can complement us and whom we can complement! Remember, God calls you to a life-changing mission *that is bigger than you are*.

Understanding our unique interests, personalities, and gifts is a critical step in making our lives count. By honestly answering the questions at the beginning of this chapter, you should get a good idea of the interests and strengths that God has hard-wired into your life. The Uniquely You diagnostic tools will provide a helpful assessment of your personality and your spiritual gifts. When you have completed these instruments, you'll have a much better context for determining what God is saying to you through His Word, His Spirit, wise counsel, and His work in circumstances around you. Remember that God created you for a life-changing mission. And God never works at cross-purposes with His own creation.

How God Reveals
Your Mission

Years ago a French aerialist named Charles Blondin was the first man to walk a tightrope across Niagara Falls. Having seen an aerialist as a small child, Blondin set his mind on becoming the best in the world. By the time he was eight, he was dubbed "The Little Wonder." And year after year he only got better. In 1858 he saw Niagara Falls for the first time. He decided then that he would be the first aerialist to conquer the falls.

On June 30, 1859, before a mesmerized crowd, Blondin stretched a three-inch hemp cord across the raging river, right above the falls. At one end it towered 160 feet high. At the other end it was 270 feet above the ground. He crossed with ease and became an immediate legend.

Blondin returned numerous times to cross the surging waters in a variety of ways. One time he balanced a chair midway across and then stood on the chair. He crossed the river on a bicycle, on stilts, in a sack, and once he crossed blindfolded! One of his most popular feats was to take a small stove, stop part way, cook breakfast and then lower it to cheering passengers on the Maid of the Mist tour boat below.

In September 1860, the Prince of Wales was in the audience. That day Blondin carried his own manager, Harry Colcord, across the falls piggyback. The Prince was amazed but begged Blondin not to do it again. With a mischievous grin, Blondin asked if the Prince believed he could push the Prince himself across the falls in a wheelbarrow.

"Sure," the Prince replied. And before he could say another word, Blondin commanded, "Then get in!"

The last time anyone saw the Prince that day, he was scrambling away as fast as he could!

Do we sometimes respond in the same way to God? He asks, "Do you think I can successfully guide your steps and order your life?" And we say, "Sure!" But when He says, "Then get in," we start backtracking. He asks us to do something outrageous and exciting, and we start walking away from the falls. Could it be we're really saying, "I believe you can guide my steps, *as long as it makes sense to me*, but there are more choices out there, and I want to keep my options open"?

> The bottom line is we either trust God or we don't. We're either willing to be obedient, or we leave our options open.

The bottom line is we either trust God or we don't. We're either willing to be obedient, or we leave our options open. The choice is up to you. In this chapter, we'll be looking at the specific ways God guides your steps. But before we do that, we wanted to give you the same reminder that we did at the beginning of the book. Figuring out what God is saying to you is not always the hard part. God will make His will for your life crystal clear. The hard part is trusting God enough to do it.

In many of the stories we profile in this book, a big breakthrough occurs when someone acts out of obedience to God—an obedience so radical that it can look crazy from a human perspective. God isn't looking for those who want a debate. Rather, He's looking for those who are committed to obedience, even *insane* obedience. Are you willing to show that level of trust?

Before you read any further, why don't you just stop for a few minutes and spend some time in prayer. Promise God that you will do whatever He asks without question or delay. Don't leave your options open on this. It may cost you relationships, finances, or other comforts of life. But it will be well worth it. Get in the wheelbarrow. And keep your eyes heavenward, because it's a long way down.

Commit to the Word as Your "Owner's Manual"

Every vehicle has an owner's manual. According to car manufacturers, the recommendations in the owner's manual are there for a two interrelated reasons:

1. To keep the vehicle operating at maximum effectiveness
2. To avoid major breakdowns

Unfortunately, too many of us wait to read the owner's manual until—you guessed it—our vehicle has broken down!

Isn't it strange that we do the same thing with the Bible? God gave it to us with principles to follow so our lives can operate at maximum effectiveness and we can avoid major breakdowns. Yet, too often, we don't turn to the Bible until we've experienced a significant breakdown.

At the North American Mission Board offices in Atlanta and Fort Worth, we've provided every employee with a copy of the Bible. Engraved on its cover are the words, *The Owner's Manual.* We encourage our employees to keep it handy on their desks for when they face significant challenges. But we don't want them to wait until there's a problem to open *The Owner's Manual.* We want them using it every day for preventive maintenance.

If we are to fulfill God's call in our individual lives, we must get a strong grip on the importance of reading God's Word on a regular basis. God made it very clear that His Word will do a work in us:

> All Scripture is inspired by God and is useful to teach us what is true and to make us realize what is wrong in our lives. It straightens us out and teaches us to do what is right. It is God's way of preparing us in every way, fully equipped for every good thing God wants us to do.[1]

Let's look at these verses in another version that elaborates a little more.

> Every Scripture is God-breathed (given by His inspiration) and profitable for instruction, for reproof and conviction of sin, for correction of error and discipline in obedience, [and] for training in righteousness (in holy living, in conformity to God's will in thought, purpose, and action), so that the man of God may be complete and proficient, well fitted and thoroughly equipped for every good work.[2]

God says that if we're paying attention to His Word and following it in our daily living, it will

1. teach us the right way to walk;
2. give us a stab of conviction when we're not walking that way;
3. show us how to get back on the right path to do the right thing;
4. show us how to stay on that path.

And the ultimate purpose of all these steps is to be thoroughly equipped and ready to fulfill God's call, live out His plan and receive His provision.

God has revealed His will to us from one end of Scripture to the other. The Bible is full of truths and practical ways of living that can be applied to the life of every Christ-follower. By putting those truths into practice, God's call on our life comes alive. Such is the promise God made to His followers in the Old Testament: "Take to heart all the words I have solemnly declared to you this day, so that you may command your children to obey carefully all the words of this law. They are not just idle words for you—*they are your life.*"[3] Jesus says almost the same thing in the New Testament when He declares to His followers, "The words I have spoken to you are spirit and *they are life.*"[4]

God will never ask you to do anything that contradicts His principled will found in Scripture. If we claim to hear God's voice, and claim that God asked us to do something inconsistent with Scripture, then we are really claiming that God is a liar. God does not change. And He does not tell us one thing through His Word, only to give us another set of directions through some other means. God's plan for your life will always be consistent with Scripture. Always. Every time.

LISTEN TO THE HOLY SPIRIT

Jesus gave great counsel early in his ministry when He stood on the mount and declared to His followers:

> Ask and it will be given to you; seek and you will find; knock and the door will be opened to you. For everyone who asks receives; he who seeks finds; and to him who knocks, the door will be opened.[5]

When you read those verses in the original language, you discover that Jesus is talking about *persistent* asking, *continuous* seeking, and *relentless* knocking. In other words, Christ is telling us to be a heavenly pest! We are to be that small child in the backseat of the car with his "Are we there yet?" questions. Or the telephone solicitor who calls . . . and calls . . . and calls in the middle of our meal. You must do everything in your power to know and understand His will. He wants you to persevere, to finish what you begin, especially in asking and searching for the clarity of call and the direction of His plan.

What an amazing promise He gives for those who do just that—ask for the promise He inevitably will answer! In the Old Testament, God guaranteed, "Call to me and I will answer you and tell you great and unsearchable things you do not know."[6] Notice there is no "maybe" or "sometimes" in this Old Testament promise or from Christ's promise in the Sermon on the Mount. God will *always* answer. He doesn't promise that He will always give the answer we *want* to hear, but He does promise to *always* answer with what we *need* to hear.

But many of us pray fervently for God's guidance, just as these verses instruct, then wonder why we are still so confused. One reason may be that we've forgotten prayer is a two-way conversation. It's not just asking, it's also listening. The early Christians understood this and practiced the spiritual discipline of meditating on God and listening for His guidance. But today, with all the noise and chaos of our society, we require God to shout over the competing decibels, or flash his message on a neon billboard, to get our attention. The problem is that God doesn't usually work that way.

You may be familiar with the story of how God spoke to Elijah when Elijah was hiding in the mouth of a cave, afraid of the evil queen Jezebel. Scripture gives us this vivid account:

> There he went into a cave and spent the night.
>
> And the word of the LORD came to him: "What are you doing here, Elijah?"
>
> He replied, "I have been very zealous for the LORD God Almighty. The Israelites have rejected your covenant, broken down

your altars, and put your prophets to death with the sword. I am the only one left, and now they are trying to kill me too."

The LORD said, "Go out and stand on the mountain in the presence of the LORD, for the LORD is about to pass by."

Then a great and powerful wind tore the mountains apart and shattered the rocks before the LORD, but the LORD was not in the wind. After the wind there was an earthquake, but the LORD was not in the earthquake. After the earthquake came a fire, but the LORD was not in the fire. And after the fire came a gentle whisper. When Elijah heard it, he pulled his cloak over his face and went out and stood at the mouth of the cave.

Then a voice said to him, "What are you doing here, Elijah?"[7]

The God who never changes still speaks to us in a gentle whisper. But sometimes He must be wondering: *Is anybody listening?*

Picture a teenager on the Internet. If they're like the teens in our houses, they will have fifteen IM chats going on simultaneously with fifteen different friends. (Sometimes, we've found that we can be working on this book on a computer in a different room from the kids, and we'll get an IM message from one of the kids *in our own house!* Do our families need counseling, or what?) While simultaneously talking to fifteen friends, they'll be surfing the Internet, listening to CDs from the computer on their head phones, and explaining to their parents how they will clean their room or do their homework later. And if the computer happens to be in the same room as the television, they'll have it going too "just for background noise, Dad."

Or take a busy business executive. She might be involved in a phone conference from her office. She wears a headset so her hands are free even as she talks. Maybe she hits the mute button to shout an instruction to her assistant. Then, while still on the phone call, she turns to her computer and bangs out a couple of e-mails, checking the scrolling ticker of her stocks as she does so. Did we mention that she's probably drinking coffee or eating lunch this entire time?

We are a nation of multitaskers addicted to noise. But God's Word says the same thing to us that it did centuries ago to the agrarian nation of Israel. "Be still, and know that I am God."[8]

How long has it been since you've been still and listened to God? Are your devotional and prayer times filled with lots of requests but little time spent listening? Do you need to come apart from your crushing schedule and pray earnestly for God's guidance and then take time to listen for a response?

The pages of this book are filled with Christians who did just that. In chapter 14, you will read the story of Phillip Johnson, a Berkeley law school professor in the academic fast lane, climbing and clawing his way to the top, "writing law review articles that nobody read." He found it necessary to take a semester sabbatical and seek God's will. He left his normal environs and moved to England, praying that God would provide him with an insight to make his life count. And wait until you see the world-changing insight that God provided.

But maybe you can't take time away right now. That's okay. Remember Ruth Okediji? She would get up at three or four in the morning, praying to God for direction. After months of seeking God's direction with all her heart, Ruth received her dramatic answer. She had no doubt it was God. "God speaks!" Ruth exclaimed to her sleepy roommate. "God speaks!"

> **The question is not whether God still speaks. The question is whether we're still listening.**

And still He speaks. Through His Word (and remember, the Holy Spirit will never prompt us to do anything inconsistent with the revealed Word of God). Through that small whisper. Through the counsel of godly friends. And through the circumstances of our life.

The question is not whether God still speaks. The question is whether we're still listening. And whether we will be able to recognize His voice.

If you feel like it's been a long time since you've heard from God, then we urge you to do two things. First, come apart from your normal routine and listen. And second, focus on strengthening your walk with Christ. Don't approach Him as a celestial guide dog, worship Him as God and snuggle close in His love. Let Him become your loving Shepherd, walking with you day by day. Then when He speaks, you will know His voice, and you will follow.

> The watchman opens the gate for [the shepherd], and the sheep listen to his voice. He calls his own sheep by name and leads them out. When he has brought out all his own, he goes on ahead of them, and

his sheep follow him because they know his voice. But they will never follow a stranger; in fact, they will run away from him because they do not recognize a stranger's voice.[9]

Seek Wise Counsel

God loves us enough to send mature, seasoned, and integrity-filled believers into our lives. We watch them model wisdom and godly living. We see first-hand the impact they make. It doesn't take us long to determine that we want to have vertical and horizontal relationships and influence like they do.

We encourage you to seek some wise counsel from those people, but first, a warning. They may be godly, but they are not God. Like all of us, they have a sin nature and they are only one step away from disobedience. If they are truly godly, they would be the first to tell you not to put your faith in them. Put your faith in Christ. Look to others for counsel but not for salvation. Men and women will disappoint, only Christ is perfectly faithful.

Once you find a godly man or woman who represents the kind of Christian you would like to become, set up a private time over lunch, dinner, or coffee. Say you're looking for some counsel and a sounding board as you seek to understand God's call on your life. Be ready with some questions that will help you learn from the person's journey such as:

- How did you discover God's call and plan for your life?
- How did you discover your passion, and how did that tie in with God's call?
- What are some ways God helped you "hear" His call on your life and understand His plan for your future?
- Was it a sudden experience or was it an unfolding journey?
- How did God use your temperament, talent, spiritual giftedness, and experiences to reveal His call and plan?
- What would you do differently if you were going through the journey all over again?

Notice that we are not suggesting you ask them questions about what God's plan is for *your* life. This is a mistake that's made all too often. We determine God's plan for our life like a Gallup poll, asking everyone we know what they think we should do. How many of Noah's friends would have voted for him to build an ark? How many of Joshua's generals would have suggested that he march around Jericho seven times and then shout at the top of his lungs? How many of Gideon's friends would have voted that this farm boy should lead Israel into battle against the Midianites? You get the idea. God's call on your life is personal between you and God. If you're married, you sure need to involve your spouse. If you have older children, involve them. But to others, God's call on your life may not make sense. It doesn't matter.

When the apostle Paul prepared to return to Jerusalem after his third missionary journey, a man named Agabus warned Paul not to go. Agabus grabbed Paul's belt, tied his own hands and feet with it, and prophesied that the owner of the belt would be bound by the Jews in Jerusalem and handed over to the Gentiles. Paul's response? "Why are you weeping and breaking my heart? I am ready not only to be bound, but also to die in Jerusalem for the name of the Lord Jesus."[10]

Then Luke, the writer of the book of Acts, makes an interesting comment. "When he would not be dissuaded, we gave up and said, 'The Lord's will be done.'"[11]

Did you catch that? "The Lord's will be done." Against the advice of his friends, Paul went to Jerusalem. Agabus was right; Paul was bound up and delivered to the Gentiles. He was tried in the Roman legal system, eventually appearing before Caesar himself. Because he went to Jerusalem, Paul was able to present the gospel to the Gentile rulers, including Caesar's household. Because he went to Jerusalem, Paul wrote the book of Romans. Because he went to Jerusalem, Paul was able to faithfully fulfill his mission to take the gospel to "Gentiles, *kings*, and the children of Israel."[12]

Our point is not to discount the advice of friends, but to use it wisely. Seek wise counsel on *how* to discover God's purpose for your life. Ask those you respect how God worked in their life. But remember, God's calling is always *personal*. He calls *you* by name. And He reveals that calling to you personally.

Rely first and foremost on Scripture. But don't be afraid to read other stories that will inspire you and other resources that will help make life count. If you're going to make an impact, you've got to be a reader. Learn from the experiences of others. There are many great books available to you that will help you immensely on this journey. In Appendix B, we've listed a number of books that we've found the most useful.

Made to Count!

FIND GOD AT WORK AROUND YOU

Our friend Henry Blackaby has helped many Christ-followers look at God's will from a very different perspective. In his book *Experiencing God*, Henry urges us to find where God is working and join Him in it. This type of thinking helps keep our focus where it should be—on God. As Henry explains it:

> Once I know God's will, then I can adjust my life to Him. In other words, what is it that God is purposing where I am? Once I know what God is doing, then I know what I need to do. The focus needs to be on God, not *my life!*[13]

But this is not a call to bandwagon Christianity. We are not called to always join the largest and fastest growing church or to go to the most fruitful mission field or to pursue occupations where God is doing a great work. Some of us are called to be pioneers and to labor faithfully in arenas where we'll never personally see much fruit. *God is at work just as much in the sowing as in the reaping.*

God may be calling you to a career or a place that has long been spurned by the church as a "secular" arena where God is not at work. But perhaps the very reason that we see no fruitfulness in that arena is because Christ-followers have abandoned the field. Later in this book, we'll be challenging you to consider some specific "secular" areas that greatly impact our culture. For years, Christ-followers have tended to avoid these areas as barren fields, too secular for God to redeem. But now we see God starting to turn many hearts to these unreached "mission fields" in North America. At the same time, He's beginning to stir the hearts of those already there.

Our point is simply this: When you look for God at work in circumstances around you, don't focus exclusively on where God is bringing in the harvest. God is at work when He breaks our hearts over a need or creates new opportunities to share the good news or helps us establish meaningful relationships or gives us a platform of credibility or success that can be used to increase the effectiveness of our sharing. God works in an infinite number of ways. In chapter 4, we threw away the box that we sometimes try to put God in. Let's not drag that box out now.

The funeral of the great Egyptian leader Anwar Sadat was attended by nearly every dignitary from around the globe. A Nobel Peace Prize winner, Sadat had been a key player in negotiating a Middle East peace compromise for his time, a feat that lesser politicians before and after have failed to duplicate. At the funeral, a network correspondent asked Sadat's chief of staff a penetrating question about the key to Sadat's effectiveness. "What made this man so highly respected by friend and foe alike?" asked the correspondent. "Why do all these world leaders speak so highly of this man and his legacy?" The chief of staff answered without hesitation: "Because Prime Minister Sadat was willing to plant shade trees under which he would never sit."

As you evaluate God's work in the circumstances around you, and determine to join Him in what He's doing, keep in mind that He may not be calling you to be part of a great movement that's already bearing visible results. Instead, He may be calling you to the quiet and thankless job of planting shade trees under which you will never sit.

13

A Fleece, a Closed Door, a Sense of Peace—Does God Guide Like That?

Sometimes God watches out for angels and fools.

The Singer family was on their way to the airport. Rhonda was driving so she could drop Randy off at the terminal. Little Joshua was not yet school age so he was along for the ride, strapped into his car seat in the back of the mini-van, sucking his thumb and holding his blankie.

"I'm going to get him out for a few minutes and give him a hug," said the fool in the passenger seat.

"I don't think that's a good idea," said the angel driving. "We're almost there. Why don't you just wait?"

Deciding that it wasn't worth fighting over, Randy hunkered down in his seat to begin a quiet pout. It would turn out to be a short one.

Less than three minutes later, it happened. A little old gentleman driving a four-door sedan approached the highway from a side street, didn't even slow down, and pulled out right in front of Rhonda.

Brakes squealed, metal crunched, and glass shattered. When the cars stopped spinning, both were nearly totaled but, miraculously, the passengers and drivers were pretty much okay. (You can bet Randy heard "Aren't you glad you listened to me?" a few times after that one.)

When a police officer showed up to investigate, an interesting thing happened. He interviewed the poor little man who had pulled directly in front of the Singer minivan, and here's how that conversation went:

Officer: "Why did you pull out in front of the van?"

Driver: (After a fairly long pause). "I thought the yellow blinking light gave me the right of way."

Officer: (After an equally long pause). "I think I'm starting to understand exactly how this accident happened."

The problem was simply this: Not only doesn't a yellow blinking light give someone the right of way, *but there was no yellow blinking light at this intersection!* None at all. Nowhere.

This man had somehow imagined a traffic signal that didn't exist, then proceeded on the blind faith that this "signal" gave him the right-of-way.

Sometimes, our spiritual journey can be that way. In this chapter, we will briefly address a few false traffic signals we might construct at a crossroads in our life. Keep in mind that we're not saying these methods are *always* bad— far from it. But they have the *potential* to lead us astray if they're not handled properly.

A FLEECE

The idea of a *fleece* has often been promoted as a great way to determine God's will. It was first used by Gideon, as recorded in Judges chapter 6, to confirm God's promise that He would deliver Israel from the Midianite enemy. For hundreds of years, Christians have used this example to justify putting out their own "fleece," trying to divine the will of God by whether or not He brings about a certain event. We lose sight of the fact that Gideon's act was not an act of faith, but an act of doubt and disbelief. He didn't use a fleece to determine God's will. God had already made that part real plain. God sent an angel of the Lord with clear instructions while Gideon was threshing wheat in the winepress. The following exchange took place:

> The LORD turned to [Gideon] and said, "Go in the strength you have and save Israel out of Midian's hand. Am I not sending you?"
>
> "But Lord," Gideon asked, "how can I save Israel? My clan is the weakest in Manasseh, and I am the least in my family."

The LORD answered, "I will be with you, and you will strike down all the Midianites together."[1]

Gideon was shocked that God chose him, a farmer, to lead the nation of Israel into battle. So he sought confirmation. Twice. By putting out the fleeces, Gideon was basically saying, "Are you sure about this, God?" or, "There must be some mistake." Gideon wasn't really *seeking* the will of God; he was *questioning* the will of God.

That's why we don't recommend using a fleece to determine God's will for your life. God speaks to us in a variety of ways. God reveals His will through His Word, through His Spirit, through the counsel of others and through circumstances. But God doesn't normally *reveal* His will through a fleece. And there is no scriptural precedent for this approach, certainly not in the story of Gideon.

The problem with Gideon is that he was being driven by his feelings— feelings of intimidation, fear, and uncertainty. If he had quickly and simply put his faith in God's promise, he would have been a stronger follower.

You may have heard the catchy phrase: God said it, I believe it, that settles it.

It may roll nicely off our tongue, but it's also biblically misleading. When it comes to God's declared will, we should say, "God said it, that settles it."

We don't have to grasp or personalize God's declared will for it to happen. If we don't "buy into" God's will, it will still come to pass. It just means that we'll be out of sync with God and miss out on the blessings of what He's doing.

Years ago, Bill Bright, founder of Campus Crusade for Christ, wrote a booklet that gained worldwide popularity named *The Four Spiritual Laws*. It includes a simple yet profound diagram of a train, shared here with the permission of Campus Crusade for Christ.

Notice that the steam engine is labeled *Fact* (as in God's declared Word), the coal car is labeled *Faith*, and the caboose is labeled *Feeling*. In a train like this, it doesn't matter whether the caboose stays hooked on or becomes disconnected. If there's coal in the steam engine, the train will run. In the same way, when we put our faith in God's declared Word, regardless of our feelings, the train runs. And the amazing thing is this: when we do so, our feelings begin to follow our faith.

If you're tempted to make a decision to clarify or authenticate God's call and plan for your life based on the story of Gideon, realize that you're using a story of struggle and doubt as your guide. And remember that buildings constructed on faulty foundations often tumble.

A Sense of Peace

Some would never use a fleece, but instead insist that an "internal sense of peace" is the key to knowing and affirming God's plan. They look at Scriptures such as Colossians 3:15 ("And let the peace of Christ rule in your hearts, since as members of one body you are called to peace.") and Philippians 4:6–7 ("Don't worry about anything; instead, pray about everything. Tell God what you need, and thank him for all he has done. If you do this, you will experience God's peace, which is far more wonderful than the human mind can understand. His peace will guard your hearts and minds as you live in Christ Jesus." NLT).

But neither of these passages is found in the context of determining God's will for our lives. The passage in Colossians is focused on peace between individuals relationally while the passage in Philippians is in the greater context of experiencing God's joy even when times are difficult.

Scripture is clear that God will give us an assurance of His will for our lives, but we must be careful not to substitute a *feeling* of peace for the fact of God's guidance. (Remember the train!) While it is true that God will often stir our hearts just before He causes a major change in our lives, or give us a calm assurance when we follow Him, we cannot rely on feelings alone. This is especially true if our relationship with God is fractured as a result of disobedience. We can have a false sense of peace, because we've stayed in our comfort zone instead of following God's lead into an area of risk and adventure.

An excellent example is the Old Testament prophet Jonah. When God called him to go to Nineveh and bring a great revival to the city, Jonah ran in the opposite direction. Jonah attempted to escape God's call and boarded a ship headed away from Nineveh, but God sent a storm that put the entire ship and its crew in grave jeopardy. Jonah was as far outside of the will of God as anyone can get. But during the storm, where was he? Take careful note here. The Bible says that he was peacefully asleep down below the deck!

It's possible to so deceive yourself that you can "feel at peace" when you're outside God's call and plan for your life. This is another clarion warning that feelings *alone* cannot be trusted as the primary authentication of God's plan.

> Be careful not to substitute a feeling of peace for the fact of God's guidance.

A Door of Opportunity.

As we discussed in the previous chapter, God frequently works through circumstances. And we've both seen Him open and close doors so that we can't possibly make mistakes about following His will. The stories in this book are replete with Christ-followers who recognized when God was opening a door just for them and with Christ-followers who saw God do some pretty incredible things with closed doors as well.

But again, this is not a sure-fire way to determine God's will. In chapter 17, you will be reading the story of Hugh Hewitt, an attorney who God has used in a variety of powerful ways. The first time Hugh applied to law school, he ran smack into a closed door. But that didn't stop him from applying to the very same school a few years later, confident that God had called him to do so. Hugh learned that if you let every rejection tell you that you're not supposed to do something, you're substituting the roadblocks of men for the will of God.

On the flip side, we also need to realize that *every open door does not constitute a call.*

We would do well to learn from Paul's missionary journey recorded in Acts 16. He and Silas on two occasions were headed to regions on their journey—first to Phrygia and Galatia and then to the borders of Mysia and Bithynia—yet they didn't enter either region. At neither juncture does Acts record any situation that would have hindered them from entering physically or circumstantially. In essence, they had "open doors" before them. But, Scripture does make clear that God's Holy Spirit convicted them internally not to enter those regions but to go to Troas instead. Why? If you read the rest of the story, you'll find that it was at Troas that God had planned a divine encounter for them. From there all of Europe would be exposed to the gospel. What if they had gone through one of the other "open doors" and missed the critical encounter God planned at Troas? What does that say to us?

Notice that this time it was an internal conviction that prevented Paul and Silas from walking through an open door. But this internal conviction is different from following our feelings. Feelings come and go, they wax hot and cold. We must learn to recognize the critical difference between our temporal feelings and that still, small voice that represents the guidance and conviction of the Holy Spirit in our lives.

And finally, remember that even "doors" opened by God in the journey of our lives are not a guarantee of easy circumstances. Paul, writing to the church at Corinth about his time at Ephesus declared, "A great door for effective work has opened to me, *and there are many who oppose me.*"[2]

At the same time, to the church in Colossae he requested,

> Pray for us . . . that God may open a door for our message, so that we may proclaim the mystery of Christ, for which I am in chains.[3]

Should you pray for an open door? Yes. But also ask for God's discernment as to whether He is the one who opened the door *and* realize that God's purpose for open doors is to further His message and kingdom impact, not merely as a way to guide our career.

So, when you're tempted to rely on fleeces, feelings, or open doors of opportunity, it might be helpful to imagine your own yellow blinking light. Caution! Proceed prayerfully. Don't let these things dictate your actions. Look for God's guidance through His Word, His Spirit, wise counsel, and circumstances.

And if a police officer shows up, you might want to think about taking the Fifth.

PRINCIPLE 6

God will repeatedly bring you to crossroads of choice as He forges you for His mission.

Key scripture:

- "But Daniel resolved not to defile himself with the royal food and wine, and he asked the chief official for permission not to defile himself this way" (Daniel 1:8).

Key points:

- God will bring us to critical junctures in our life and give us the choice of whether to follow Him.
- When we choose God at the crossroads for seemingly minor things, He will send us down a path toward greater responsibility and impact.

14

God at the Crossroads

There ought to be a Sunday school hall of fame. You know what we mean—the kinds of stories that mesmerize little kids. Lots of action. Unpredictable results. A nasty bad guy. Heroes so famous you've heard about them even if you never set foot in Sunday school.

David and Goliath. Now there's a hall of fame pair. Everybody loves an underdog. Especially we smaller or skinnier kids who had to be on the constant lookout for bullies. It was the revenge of the nobody, the kid who gets chosen last for dodgeball. No doubt about it, David makes our hall of fame.

Jonah and the whale. That's a cool story, too. Our little imaginations would run wild wondering what it must have been like inside the belly of that big fish. And if you had a really good Sunday school teacher, one who specialized in sound effects and role playing, the whole thing could get pretty interesting. "And after three days," our teacher would say in nearly a whisper, "with Jonah in the belly of the whale . . ." We would all slide forward on the edge of our seat, wide-eyed. Then suddenly . . . "bluuughgghg!" and the teacher would practically spit all over us. You could just about smell the seaweed. Yep, Jonah and the whale. Rated PG-13. Another hall of famer.

And there would be two moments right out of the book of Daniel. The most famous, of course, would be Daniel in the lions' den. You especially had to love the way the artists pictured that story. Daniel just kind of lounging around, not a care in the world, maybe petting a lion or two, all dressed up in a nice white robe. It was the greatest circus act of all time. A few chapters before that there was Shadrack, Meshach, and Abednego, smiling in the middle of that fiery furnace, refusing to bow down to the king's idol. They're probably not as famous as Daniel, but maybe we could vote them in on the second ballot.

Somehow our Sunday school teacher would always slip a fourth person in that fiery furnace, taxing our little mathematically-challenged brains. But pretty soon we'd figure it out and she would explain that it was actually Jesus, who never leaves us. It's a great story with an awesome twist at the end, but we suspect that it probably owed a lot of its popularity to those great-sounding names. The fiery furnace just wouldn't have been the same with Harry, Fred, and Billy Bob.

But the interesting thing about these stories, and dozens more like them from the pages of Scripture, are the things that happened just a few chapters earlier. Before these heroes were ready for their high-profile stands, God forged and equipped them at a crossroads of choice. Most of the time, the crossroads occurred on an issue of lesser importance in the eyes of the world, but from God's eternal perspective, it was a moment that determined a destiny. "You have been faithful with a few things." God says, "I will put you in charge of many things."[1]

FORGED AT THE CROSSROADS

For David, a critical crossroads came years before he encountered Goliath, when he was tending the family sheep on the deserted hillsides of Galilee. It was in that setting, with nobody else around, that David had to decide if he was a runner or a fighter. When a bear or a lion would come and carry one of David's sheep away, he was faced with a crossroads of choice. Let the beast go—what's one lousy sheep, anyway?—or risk everything to rescue that one sheep in danger. David chose danger. "I go after [the lion or bear] with a club and take the lamb from its mouth. If the animal turns on me, I catch it by the jaw and club it to death."[2]

And God took note. Later, God would orchestrate the circumstances to bring this shepherd boy to the front lines of the battle between the Israelites and Philistines. There, David would hear the trash talking of the nine-foot-tall Goliath, and would watch the Israelite soldiers run in fear. It was more than David could take. He talked Saul into letting him go to battle against Goliath, telling Saul about his exploits with the lions and bears. David felled the giant with one shot from his trusty slingshot, and David became a Sunday school icon.

It worked just the opposite with Jonah. He chose wrong at the crossroads, but his story is still an encouragement. Jonah is an example of how God can redeem even a bad crossroads choice, though we will certainly have to suffer the consequences.

God told Jonah to go to Nineveh and preach, and Jonah took off in the opposite direction. Jonah's mistake was not one of the head but of the heart. He knew the right path, but he still chose the wrong one. You probably know the story. While Jonah was sailing away from Nineveh as fast as possible, the Lord caused a storm to nearly capsize the boat. The sailors figured out that the disobedient Jonah was the cause of their problems. They threw him overboard, where he was swallowed by a large fish. By the time the fish regurgitated Jonah three days later, he was definitely ready to go to Nineveh. This may sound crazy, but Jonah was fortunate. He was given a second chance and another crossroads. Many times, disobedience at the crossroads will cost us more dearly, making us completely miss the joy of fulfilling God's mission for our lives.

And then there is the gang from Daniel. Two chapters before Shadrach, Meshach, and Abednego took their stand in the fiery furnace, and five chapters before Daniel faced down the hungry lions, we see these young captives from Israel take a seemingly insignificant stand in the Babylon cafeteria. These young men from Israel were part of a select contingent of captives being trained in the king's court to eventually serve the king. They were given the finest education and the best provisions, being assigned a "daily amount of food and wine from the king's table."[3] And for Daniel and his compatriots, the food and wine became a crossroads of choice. They could either follow the dietary laws that God had given to the Jews, or they could rationalize a way to eat these choice provisions. After all, wasn't God providing for them even in their captivity?

Think of the enormous pressure for Daniel and his cohorts to just go along with the crowd. Everybody else was eating the king's meat and drinking the king's wine. And it's not like this was a really big deal. They weren't asking Daniel to worship an idol or deny his faith. He could have saved his stand for the big issues—we've all got to be willing to make a few little compromises just to get along.

But for Daniel, the choice was clear. There was no such thing as a little compromise. "Daniel purposed in his heart that he would not defile himself with the portion of the king's delicacies, nor with the wine which he drank; therefore he requested of the chief of the eunuchs that he might not defile himself."[4] He asked for a ten-day test period—give my buddies and me just vegetables and water for ten days, and see if we don't look as good as all the other young men.

Daniel's test was a success. At the end of ten days, Daniel, Shadrach, Meshach, and Abednego looked healthier and better nourished than all the young men eating the king's meat. And God rewarded this crossroads choice by giving these four young men superior knowledge and understanding, and by giving Daniel the ability to understand dreams and visions of all kinds.

When the big tests came a few years later, there was never any doubt about how these men would respond. If they didn't eat the king's meat, you could rest assured that they weren't going to bow down to a ninety-foot-tall idol erected by the king. And if they didn't drink the king's wine, then they weren't about to stop praying to God just because the king issued a cease and desist order. These were young men who couldn't be bought or intimidated— hall of famers because they chose God at a seemingly insignificant crossroads in a Babylon cafeteria.

CROSSROADS CHARACTERISTICS

When you review the stories of these four biblical heroes, and dozens of others like them, you discover that each crossroads, though unique to the life of the individual believer, also has certain characteristics that remain fairly common. Recognizing them will help you understand when you have hit one of your own crossroads, a life-altering choice between God's way and the world's.

The Crossroads Choice Is a Tough Choice

There is nothing glamorous or easy about choosing God's way at the crossroads. Even the very first crossroads we encounter in our spiritual lives is a tough one. Remember the second principle that we discussed toward the very beginning of this book? God calls you to a life-changing relationship with Him through Jesus Christ. This critical decision, whether to accept Christ or reject Him, is the first and most important spiritual crossroads we will ever encounter. Listen to the way that Christ describes it:

> Enter through the narrow gate. For wide is the gate and broad is the road that leads to destruction, and many enter through it. But small is the gate and narrow the road that leads to life, and only a few find it.[5]

And this first crossroads is by no means the only tough choice we will encounter. David had to face down the lion and the bear. Jonah had to preach to a people he despised. Daniel, Shadrach, Meshach, and Abednego had to risk the wrath of the king and the ridicule of their peers.

Crossroads choices are tough choices. The road less traveled is seldom smooth and broad, with lots of amenities and fellow-travelers. Instead, it is a rocky and foreboding road, with few companions, that we can travel only through the power of the Holy Spirit.

The Crossroads Choice Is a Crisis Choice

While this is not always true, as a general rule a crossroads choice will come without warning, requiring you to make an instinctive decision without a lot of time for planning or counsel. Crossroads choices are choices made from the heart, reflecting the depth of our character. David had precious little time to decide whether to pursue the bear. Daniel and his friends had to decide whether to eat the king's meat or not as it was placed in front of them. Jonah is the exception, as he had a little more time to decide whether to go to Nineveh. And Jonah is the one who got it wrong!

The key to Daniel's choice is that he had resolved *ahead of time* not to defile himself while in Babylon. He had "purposed in his heart" to remain pure.[6] He didn't have to make a split-second choice under the pressures of the moment; he had already determined the path he would choose. He didn't panic when the king's meat and wine were placed in front of him. Even for a strong believer like Daniel, the pressures could have been overwhelming, distorting his judgment. Instead, he simply recalled his commitment not to defile himself and acted on it. The choice had already been made in the quiet moments between Daniel and his God. Then God gave him the courage to follow through.

From David, we can learn another key principle of what will help us make the right call when the pressure is on. In Psalm 119, David writes "I have hidden your word in my heart that I might not sin against you."[7] It wasn't enough for David to be familiar with God's Word, or to know it in a vague or general sense, he wanted to "hide it in [his] heart." David understood the importance of memorizing God's Word, of allowing it to become a part of his fiber and being. Over and over again, David would meditate on God's law, and memorize God's Word, until it became as natural to him as breathing. David not only got into God's Word, he made sure that God's Word got into him. When a crossroads came, and there was no time to conduct an eight-week Bible study or make an appointment with a spiritual counselor, David would know the right path *instinctively*, because God's Word had become a part of who he was. (Of course, like all of us, David did not always *follow* the right path. But that's another story.)

> A crossroads choice is usually an unexpected choice. But it doesn't have to be an *unplanned* one.

How about you? Are you hiding God's Word in your heart, preparing for the next crossroads of choice? Here's a quick test. Count up the number of years that you've been a Christ-follower. Now, multiply it by four. Whatever that number turns out to be, ask yourself this question: Do I know that many verses of Scripture along with the reference? We're only talking about learning one verse every three months, something that anybody can do. How can we claim that we are serious about choosing God's way at the crossroads if we're not willing to commit some of His great roadmap to memory?

A crossroads choice is usually an unexpected choice. But it doesn't have to be an *unplanned* one. When you go around a turn and a crossroads suddenly appears, God will help you recall the precise verses of Scripture that will illuminate His choice, so long as you've done your part and hidden His Word in your heart ahead of time.

The Crossroads Choice Is a Life-Changing Choice

Following God's will is a daily decision. As we will discuss in the seventh principle, God guides you and provides for you to carry out your mission one step at a time. Often, we want to see way down the road, but God promises to show us the next step and no more.

> In your ears you will hear a word behind you, saying, "This is the way; walk in it," when you turn to the right hand and when you turn to the left.[8]

> The steps of a [good] man are directed and established by the Lord when He delights in his way [and He busies Himself with his every step].[9]

But here's an important corollary: While following God's will is a step-by-step process, there are certain crossroads in life that will determine our destiny and change every step we take thereafter. These choices will make a permanent mark on us, defining who we are and where we're going. And most of the time, we're not given a second chance at that crossroads—ignoring God's path can have devastating consequences.

Even secular writers appreciate this principle. Shakespeare captured the very essence of it in his play *Julius Caesar*, as Brutus rallied his co-conspirators against Caesar. Though he chose the wrong path, Brutus eloquently articulated the fleeting opportunities these crossroads present:

> There is a tide in the affairs of men which, taken at the flood, leads on to fortune; omitted, all the voyage of their life is bound in shallows and in miseries. On such a full sea we are now afloat, and we must take the current when it serves, or lose our ventures.[10]

Such is the nature of the crossroads. History is made there. Martin Luther and his Ninety-Five Theses. George Washington and his crossing of the Delaware. Jesus Christ and the road to Golgatha.

Your own personal history will be impacted in unchangeable ways from your choice at each crossroads. Do not lightly shrug off the path that God is directing you to follow. We have no way of knowing where it will lead, or how many lives it will change. We only know this: If it wasn't the best path for us, He wouldn't call us to walk down it.

The Crossroads Choice Is Not Usually a High-profile Choice

The choices that determine our destinies are not always the choices that make the headlines. In fact, this is one of the ways that Satan entices us to walk down the wrong road. "It's not that big of a deal," he says. "The other road is tough and dangerous. Don't you think you're entitled, just this once, on such a small matter, to take a road that's smooth and comfortable?"

But to God, there are no insignificant crossroad choices. Each choice shows our character and tests our obedience. Each time we must either chose God's way or chose our own. And though the issue might seem insignificant to us at the time, it may be God's way of forging our lives for a point of much greater impact farther down the road.

Do you think God was any more pleased with David when he took on Goliath than He was when David went after the bear? And what about Daniel? Was God more concerned about Daniel continuing to pray after the king said he couldn't or about Daniel's refusing to defile himself with the king's meat?

For God, the issue is never one of "show," taking a high-profile stand that gets a lot of attention but one of obedience, being faithful in the small things even when nobody else notices. This was the painful lesson learned by Saul, king of Israel, when he returned from doing battle with the Amalekites.

Saul was proud of himself. He had destroyed the enemies of Israel and returned with the Amalekite king in tow as well as the best of the Amalekite sheep and cattle. Saul planned to make a big sacrifice to the Lord with the sheep and cattle, and make a big spectacle out of King Agag. It would be quite a victory party, celebrating a major victory over a vanquished foe.

There was only one problem. The guest of honor at the party was not pleased. Instead of congratulating Saul, God chastised him. Speaking through Samuel, His prophet, God reminded Saul that He had instructed the Israelites to completely destroy the Amalekites and all their animals. And then Samuel asked a piercing question and spelled out the consequences for Saul's disobedience at the crossroads:

Does the LORD delight in burnt offerings and sacrifices
  as much as in obeying the voice of the LORD?
To obey is better than sacrifice,
  and to heed is better than the fat of rams.
For rebellion is like the sin of divination,
  and arrogance like the evil of idolatry.
Because you have rejected the word of the LORD,
  he has rejected you as king.[11]

It would be well for us to remember Samuel's point when we come to a crossroads today. God wants complete obedience, even in the little things, even
when nobody else is watching. Saul chose pomp and circumstance at the
crossroads rather than obedience. As a result, God rejected him as king,
preparing instead a young shepherd boy who was that moment being faithful
at his own crossroads, somewhere on the Galilean hillside, tending his sheep
with nobody watching, chasing after lions and bears.

"I Felt Like I Had Wasted A Talent"

Phillip Johnson knows a thing or two about crossroads choices. And he has also
come to appreciate the ironies that God sometimes weaves into the crossroads of
our lives. He still remembers sitting in the Harvard Square theatre as a died-in-
the-wool liberal undergrad, with a gnawing sense that something just wasn't right.
He was watching *Inherit the Wind,* a film loosely based on the Scope's Monkey
Trial from decades earlier that had established the right to teach evolution in our
public schools, and the reaction of the raucous crowd bothered him.

> The Harvard Square audiences were always demonstrative. They
> would cheer and boo and holler throughout the movie. When the
> William Jennings Bryan character [the lawyer defending creationism
> in schools] came on he would be booed. And the Clarence Darrow
> character [ACLU lawyer attacking creationism] would be cheered. I
> just got this sense that the Harvard student audience was acting like
> the people in that Tennessee town—the mindless Bible thumpers.
> But the students were being the mindless Bible bashers.[12]

In the film, Darrow ultimately makes a monkey of Bryan, as the enlightened intellectual puts Bryan himself on the witness stand, ridiculing him with a withering cross-examination. The crowd cheered. But Johnson did not join them.

> I've probably always had this tendency to look for the dissenter, the maverick. And I thought the real maverick and the real dissenter was now the Bible believers, and maybe they weren't getting a fair shake.

Little did Johnson know that he would one day be that maverick. Nor that his life's purpose—his one consuming passion—would be to lead the challenge against evolution and usher in the modern day intelligent design movement. But first, Phillip Johnson had a few choices to make at the crossroads. And God had a little molding and trimming to do. It would take Him nearly twenty years to get it done.

He started by molding a sharp and critical mind. Like He did with the apostle Paul, God used some institutions that opposed the Christian worldview to get it done. Harvard undergrad. Then law school at the University of Chicago, where Johnson graduated first in his class. This was followed by a clerkship with the most prestigious state supreme court judge in the United States, Roger Traynor of California. Next, Johnson stepped up to the U.S. Supreme Court, clerking for Chief Justice Earl Warren, the architect of the liberal social agenda that decades later still haunts America.

From there, Johnson went to a prestigious job teaching at ultra-liberal Boalt Hall Law School (at the University of California at Berkeley), building a national reputation in criminal law and procedure. He was following the world's prescribed path for success for someone with such an intimidating intellect. But he couldn't shake this gnawing feeling that something was wrong, the same type of feeling that had haunted him in the Harvard Square Theatre so many years ago.

> I had assumed that the purpose of life was to rise higher in the hierarchy of the values of the world. One way to do this was to become a high-prestige law school professor, to get the most merit badges. I had made a very good start on that measure of success. But I was now

wondering what the meaning of it was. Just writing law review articles and teaching classes did not seem to be an adequate foundation to build one's life on.

At the same time that he started experiencing these misgivings about the world's definition of success, his marriage and family life started crashing around him. When his wife said she was leaving him, Johnson knew it would be useless to argue. In reality, the marriage had been over for quite some time. That night, with a heavy heart, he approached the most critical spiritual crossroads he would ever encounter. He accompanied his eleven-year-old daughter to a Vacation Bible School dinner. The plain-spoken pastor shared the basics of the gospel message in a way that, for the first time, made this intellectual law school professor think that it might just be for him. "At that time, I asked myself: *Why do I think that what I have as an intellectual is so much superior to the gospel that so many simple people have come to accept?*"

For two years, Johnson began exploring the claims of Christ. And at the age of thirty-eight, this intellectual giant embraced the gospel of the "simple people," giving his life to Jesus Christ. He began attending First Presbyterian Church in Berkeley, and there met his second wife, another adult convert to Christ. But at work, he continued to sense an emptiness and frustration while working his way up the intellectual food chain.

There was, as Johnson describes it, "this feeling that I had wasted a talent. I felt like I had been given a gift and might have done something really important in my life, but wasn't doing it. That feeling continued until the great pivotal year in my life, 1987, when my wife, Kathie, and I went to England on a sabbatical."

On a hike in the Welsh border country, Johnson prayed desperately for an insight. He was looking for something that would make his life count— something he could pour his intellectual energies into. He had no idea what it might be. "I now tell people to be careful about what you pray for," Johnson quips, "because you just might get it."

God gave him the insight in a most unusual way. In London, Johnson would take the bus to work, walking from the bus stop to his university office each day. On the way was an old bookstore, and Johnson had never been able to walk by a bookstore without stepping inside and "fondling a few books."

His first time by, a book by an esteemed Oxford scientist named Richard Dawkins caught his attention. That book, *The Blind Watchmaker*, was the preeminent defense of the theory of macroevolution then in existence. Johnson quickly devoured the book, then another, then another. After a few weeks of reading the best arguments that evolutionists had to offer, God gave Johnson more of an insight than even Johnson bargained for: "I had this insight into the basic logical flaw at the heart of Darwinism. And Darwinism was the pillar at the heart of the whole intellectual establishment."

It was an unexpected crossroads. Sure, he had been praying for an insight, but Johnson was expecting something a little more conventional, something that might make sense for a law school professor. Was this man who had been trained in the law really ready to take on the *scientific* geniuses behind the theory of macroevolution? Was this former intellectual liberal, trained in the chambers of the great Chief Justice Warren, ready to declare war on the entire liberal intellectual establishment?

A few weeks after picking up Dawkins's book, Johnson had a heart-to-heart talk with his wife. "I think I understand this stuff," said Johnson. "I know what the problem is. But fortunately, I'm too smart to take it up professionally. I'd be ridiculed. Nobody would believe me. They would say, 'You're not a scientist, you're a law school professor.' It would be something, once you got started with it, you'd be involved in a lifelong, never-ending battle." And with one foot now heading down the wrong path, Johnson heard his own words echoing in his ears. *A never-ending battle.* As a dissenter, no less! "And that," says Johnson, the maverick, "was of course irresistible. I started work the next day."

Johnson's first book on the subject, *Darwin on Trial*, was published in 1991 and sent shockwaves through the scientific community. In it, Johnson exposed the logical inconsistencies and the flawed presuppositions inherent in Darwinism. Criticism was swift and strident. Stephen Gould, for example, predictably condemned Johnson for even addressing the subject as a law school professor. Gould argued that a lawyer "cannot simply trot out some applicable criteria from his own world and falsely condemn us from a mixture of ignorance and inappropriateness."[13]

Johnson shrugs at the criticism. "If I'm right in what I'm saying, I should expect to be treated about the way I'm being treated." The charge that a lawyer should stay out of this "scientific" arena concerns Johnson least of all.

The problem of Darwinism is a problem that is just right for a law school professor. It is really about God and the logic of arguments and the way assumptions are hidden in order to smuggle a conclusion across. I often joke that who would know more about dishonest methods of reasoning than a professor of law.

And so Johnson soldiers on, laying bare the assumptions of Darwinism in a bevy of books and an endless series of lectures and debates. Though he doesn't consider himself a particularly strong debater, he frequently wins over audiences with his friendly and self-effacing style. And often, he will come away from the debate with a new friend, the same person who served as Johnson's opponent on the debate platform.

When asked about the strongest argument of Darwinism, Johnson pulls no punches. "Their strongest argument isn't really an argument at all in the strictest sense. It's authority. These are the people our culture regards as wise. They're the scientists and engineers we rely upon to make sure our airplanes don't crash and to see that our diseases are cured. So how could they be wrong about something so fundamental?"

When reminded of the scriptural admonition that "God chose the foolish things of the world to shame the wise" (1 Corinthians 1:27), Johnson laughs and says, "Maybe that's what I am, one of the world's foolish things."

Others would not rate him so harshly. He has managed to put a crack in the solid fortress of Darwinian belief, and others have joined the cause. Biochemist Michael Behe, for example, recently wrote *Darwin's Black Box*, showing how evolution could not possibly have worked at the level of molecular cell biology. Johnson compares himself to an offensive lineman in football: "The idea is to clear a space by legitimizing the issue, by exhausting the other side, by using up all their ridicule."[14]

It sounds like thankless work, taking the heat so others can advance the intelligent design arguments, but Johnson seems to relish it. "I'm like a kid in a candy store. I can't think of anything I would rather be doing."[15]

Don't be surprised to find Phillip Johnson debating the creation of the world against some brilliant scientist at a secular university near you. If the crowd cheers his opponent, and boos for Johnson, don't waste time feeling sorry for him. You'll probably notice a slight smile curling at the corner of his lips. After all, he's always been a bit of a maverick. And he will never regret the choice he made at the crossroads.

There are many lessons we can learn from this brilliant professor. Be patient as God prepares you for your calling. Don't worry if you're struggling with trying to figure out what to do. Pray for insight. Then be ready to show insane obedience at the crossroads, even if it means that a lifelong battle looms ahead.

And one more thing. Don't be afraid to wander into a few old bookstores. God's answer may come in a very unexpected way.

PRINCIPLE 7

God guides you and provides for your mission one step at a time.

Key scriptures:
- "I will instruct you and teach you in the way you should go; I will counsel you and watch over you" (Psalm 32:8).
- "The steps of a [good] man are directed and established by the Lord when He delights in his way [and He busies Himself with his every step]" (Psalm 37:23–24, Amp.).

Key points:
- Though God reveals His mission for us in advance, He reveals His plan only one step at a time.
- Sometimes God is calling us to take a step that just doesn't make sense. Take it anyway.
- God is not just guiding the steps of your vocational mission, He is also guiding your steps as you seek to bring others into a personal relationship with Christ.

15

In Step with God

Austin slammed the steering wheel in utter frustration. Traffic on Route 400 had slowed to a crawl—nope, a standstill! He was running late, *real* late, and his blood was in a boil. He inched closer to the pickup in front of him, so close he could just about scratch the driver's back. Though he sat high in his own SUV he felt powerless against the crush of Atlanta traffic. In front of him was some Georgia boy in his Dodge Ram, with a bumper sticker informing Austin that if he wanted Bubba's gun, he'd have to pry it out of the man's cold, dead hands. To his right—Hey! Why did that lane start moving? He started inching over. The drivers in the right lane closed the gap between cars, but Austin knew they'd make room for his Suburban. He cut in front of a woman applying makeup.

What a mess. He had a critical meeting in half an hour, and it was fifteen miles away. He started praying that God would part traffic like He did the Red Sea. As if to mock Austin, the traffic in his lane stopped, while the cars to the left of him inched forward. He looked in his rear view mirror. Now she was applying eye shadow!

"This stinks!" he yelled. "I hate this stuff!" He glanced left—they were picking up speed. The guy floating by in the next lane was bouncing around to his music, the radio blaring so loud that Austin felt the pulse of the bass.

Made to Count!

He turned on his own radio to drown it out. Just his luck—he caught the tail end of the traffic report. "So motorists can expect big delays on that route," the traffic guy reported. Austin could hear the whir of the helicopter blades in the background. "This is Captain Crash Peterson, with your eye-in-the-sky traffic report signing off. Safe motoring."

Austin leaned forward and peered out his front window, checking for any helicopters in the vicinity. He was coming to a critical juncture where Route 400 intersected Interstate 285. Taking the 285 Loop would be a little longer, but if the traffic was better . . . His lane started moving. He hit the scan button on the radio, searching for another traffic report.

The intersection was approaching fast and Austin needed some help. Should he go 400 South to Route 85 or take 285 West? Which lane would be fastest? Where was Mr. Eye-in-the-sky when you needed him? He only had a few more minutes to decide. He slowed down a little to give himself more time. The makeup woman behind him put down her lipstick and laid on the horn. *Some nerve.*

Austin found himself wishing he were flying that helicopter. That way, he could see the entire Atlanta traffic grid at one time. None of this guessing which way to go based on the traffic in front of you. If he only knew which route to take at this next intersection, he still had a chance of making it on time. His cell phone rang.

"What!"

"You okay?" asked Carli. Hearing his wife's voice calmed him a little.

"Traffic's a mess. And I'm running late."

"That's why I'm calling," said Carli. "The television news is reporting a big pile-up on 400 just north of the city. Maybe you ought to think about going 285."

Austin smiled to himself and pulled into the exit lane. What timing! "Thanks," he said. "I'll do that." Already traffic had started moving faster. "Did they say what happened?"

Carli laughed. "They said some lady was applying makeup. She rear-ended the guy in front of her and caused a chain collision."

"Oh," said Austin, as he glanced suspiciously in his own rear-view mirror. He flicked on his turn signal to merge left.

YOU REALLY WANNA FLY THIS THING?

Like our hypothetical driver (but trust us, the traffic in Atlanta is *not* hypothetical), many of us get impatient with God's guidance in our lives. We'd rather be up there flying that helicopter ourselves, enjoying the bird's-eye view of the entire city traffic system. That way we could plan not just our next move, but our entire trip, confident that we possess all the knowledge necessary to make the right turns.

If we could just be that helicopter pilot, our problems would be over. Really?

Think about throwing our friend Austin behind the controls of the traffic helicopter. If he's like most of us, he'd be overwhelmed and have an immediate panic attack while staring at the maze of controls and gauges that need constant attention. Helicopters are notoriously hard to fly. And within minutes, Austin would be in freefall. When he was with ABC News, commentator Harry Reasoner summed it up this way:

> An airplane by its nature wants to fly, and if not interfered with too strongly by unusual events or by a deliberately incompetent pilot, it will fly. A helicopter does not want to fly. It is maintained in the air by a variety of forces and controls working in opposition to each other, and if there is any disturbance in this delicate balance the helicopter stops flying, immediately and disastrously. There is no such thing as a gliding helicopter. . . . [Helicopter pilots] know, if something bad has not happened, it is about to![1]

So if Austin were put at the controls of that helicopter, he would soon have a lot more problems than just the traffic.

It's every bit as ludicrous for us to beg God for a longer-range view, instead of being guided step by step. Do you really want to be guided more than one step at a time? How many times in your life have you been through something so tough that you would never have been able to face it if you knew it was coming? How much time do we spend worrying about the few things we do know about the future? And how much more would our lives be absolutely consumed by worry if God showed us what was coming in the next five or ten years?

Made to Count!

Plus, we really aren't qualified to fly that helicopter. God doesn't just know the future, He also knows the intents and purposes of the heart. He alone is all-powerful. He doesn't just see the future coming like some train wreck that He's powerless to prevent. The future is in His hands.

It's the same point that God made to Job when Job got done complaining about his difficulties. God is God and we are not! He doesn't owe us an explanation. Listen, as God performs one of the most powerful cross-examinations of all-time:

> Who is this that darkens my counsel
>   with words without knowledge?
> Brace yourself like a man;
>   I will question you, and you shall answer me.
>
> Where were you when I laid the earth's foundation?
>   Tell me, if you understand.
> Who marked off its dimensions? Surely you know!
>   Who stretched a measuring line across it?
> On what were its footings set,
>   or who laid its cornerstone—
> while the morning stars sang together
>   and all the angels shouted for joy?
>
> Who shut up the sea behind doors
>   when it burst forth from the womb,
> when I made the clouds its garment
>   and wrapped it in thick darkness,
> when I fixed limits for it
>   and set its doors and bars in place,
> when I said, "This far you may come and no farther;
>   here is where your proud waves halt"?
>
> ---
>
> Have the gates of death been shown to you?
>   Have you seen the gates of the shadow of death?

Have you comprehended the vast expanses of the earth?
  Tell me, if you know all this.

What is the way to the abode of light?
  And where does darkness reside?
Can you take them to their places?
  Do you know the paths to their dwellings?
Surely you know, for you were already born!
  You have lived so many years![1]

Did you catch that last tinge of sarcasm? Can you imagine having to answer those questions and dozens more like them? Probably we would all do the same thing that Job did—repent in dust and ashes.

BLIND OBEDIENCE

God promises to guide our steps. There can be no doubt about that.

Your ears will hear a word behind you, saying, "This is the way; walk in it," when you turn to the right hand and when you turn to the left.[3]

The steps of a [good] man are directed and established by the Lord when He delights in his way [and He busies Himself with his every step].[4]

I will instruct you and teach you in the way you should go;
I will counsel you and watch over you.[5]

But God doesn't promise that it will always make sense to us:

As the heavens are higher than the earth,
  so are my ways higher than your ways
  and my thoughts than your thoughts."[6]

Nor does God promise that the steps He orders will be exactly where we would have gone:

Made to Count!

In his heart a man plans his course,
  but the LORD determines his steps.[7]

Sometimes, God directs our steps for reasons that we will never understand until we meet Him after we die. But often, God's plan unfolds in a way that seems crazy at the time but in hindsight is obvious to everyone, and we marvel. We need to celebrate those moments, and allow them to further buttress our trust and confidence in God's amazingly intricate plan, even when He asks us to take steps we don't understand.

Randy had a chance to see just such a moment this past summer. He was on a mission trip in Norfolk, Virginia, with about four hundred World Changers—high school students who spend a week rehabilitating inner-city homes and sharing the gospel. These students were part of the nearly 25,000 World Changers who fixed up thousands of homes in cities across the continent and around the world last year.

One particular crew of twelve had painted, cleaned, set in new windows, and installed new gutters on their designated house. They had also built a strong relationship with the owner of the house and shared the gospel in the surrounding neighborhood. Things were proceeding right on plan, and it even looked like the crew might finish by noon on Friday. They could eat lunch and then head back to the school where they were staying and take the rest of the day off.

Their last job was to cut down a rotten limb that was hanging over the roof of the house. To be extra careful, they sent one of the students up on the roof to make sure that when the branch fell it would not puncture the roof. As he was bracing and waiting for the branch, he stepped back, and his own foot went right through a rotten section of the roof!

Needless to say, the students were dismayed. They had no roofing materials so they had to order some and wait. Now, they would have to find out how much of the roof was rotten and try to get it repaired before the end of this, their very last day. There would be no afternoon off.

Later that day, the therapist for the disabled homeowner stopped by the house. This particular therapist hadn't been there all week. He asked the kids what they were doing. They had a chance to share with him about Christ.

The therapist had been searching spiritually for something real, and before he left that afternoon, he gave his life to Christ.

Think about that. At noon, that one step back seemed to create a tragedy. But by early evening, God's plan was apparent. Not only did He reveal some weak spots on the roof badly needing repair, but He also gave the students a chance to lead the therapist to Christ. One small step back, and two giant leaps forward. And God orchestrated every one of them.

God's Mission and God's Plan

Throughout this book, we've been careful to talk about both God's mission for your life and God's step-by-step plan for your life. Notice the interaction between them in this seventh principle: God guides you and provides for you to carry out your mission one step at a time. This principle implies that God will reveal the mission for your life, and you will have to seek daily guidance for each step to help you fulfill it.

Some people have a tendency to take this principle too far, believing that God never even reveals to us the mission for our lives. This philosophy makes life easy. You take it one step at a time and wherever you end up must have been God's mission all along. It's like shooting the arrow and then running to draw a target around where it landed. It may be easy, but it virtually guarantees that your life will have no real impact. And it makes you wonder what Bible those people have been reading.

From Genesis to Revelation, God is in the business of calling His followers by name, giving them a mission, and then directing them to fulfill it. We've already mentioned many of them in this book: Abraham, the father of many nations; Moses, God's spokesman to Pharaoh; Gideon, Israel's deliverer from the Midianites; Esther, a queen called to stop annihilation of the Jews; David, a king whose lineage would rule forever; Mary, the mother of the Christ-child; Paul, God's vessel to take the gospel to the Gentiles. Each was called by God, and each perfectly understood their precise mission. Each relied on the power of God—one step at a time—to help them accomplish something they could never do alone. And it still works that way today.

"This Book Is My Story"

Janet Parshall. An unusual thing happened when we interviewed Janet Parshall for this book. We started off the way we always do, explaining a little about the book and the reason we wanted to ask so many questions. We knew Janet was the busy host of a radio talk show, and we wanted to be good stewards of her time. But when we finished explaining our purpose, an uncomfortable silence filled the phone line.

"Are you still there?" we asked.

"Yes," Janet replied. "But I've got to tell you that as you explained the thesis of this book, I had tears in my eyes. The theme of this book is my life's story. I've been waiting for years for somebody to write this book."[8]

As we listened to Janet over the next hour, we found ourselves asking, "How could we possibly improve on the way she tells this story?" We realized that we couldn't. Instead, we want you to hear Janet's story in her own words, because it so powerfully illustrates the way that God gives us a mission, then provides for us to carry it out one step at a time.

> I came to know the Lord as my personal Savior when I was six years old. At fourteen, I dedicated my life to Him. I went to church camp where we had visiting missionaries for the week who challenged us to fully dedicate our lives to Christ. At the end of the week we participated in a bonfire service. We took a small stick and threw it on the fire as a way to exemplify a life consumed in service to Christ. I just felt the Lord saying, "Janet, will you serve me with all your heart?" And, boy, I said, "Yes, Lord." And I was absolutely convinced that God was calling me to foreign missions.
>
> And He did! He sent me to Washington, D.C. That's my people group. It doesn't get any more foreign than that!
>
> But the way He sent me was amazing. He sent me through the portal of my family home. I had always assumed that He would send me to Bible college and then to medical school and then to the mission field. Instead, he sent me to college and then to the classroom of family. I married Craig and then had these four little babies, boom, boom, boom, boom—four little steppingstones right in a row. And

God designed a custom classroom for me to know what it meant to be profamily.

First, I had to fill their hearts with the precepts of God's Word. I had to learn what it meant for God to parent me by being a parent to them. *What is unconditional love, Janet? Can you practice it the way I gave it to you? Can you give them tender mercies? Can you forgive seventy times seven?* That was a powerful, powerful classroom.

The next step in my tutorial I'll never forget. One night, my oldest came home from her elementary school classroom and, as I always did, I asked, "Honey, what did you do in school today?"

And she said, "Momma, we sat in a magic circle. . ."

Whoop! My antennae went up! I said, "What do you mean by a magic circle, honey?"

And she said, "Momma, they passed around the red scarf and had us answer three questions: 'Do you bite your nails? Do you wet the bed? If there was a divorce which of your parents would you live with?'"

Now I am telling you my stomach flipped, and I thought the floor had swallowed me up. But when I regained my composure, I remembered that I was president of the PTA, so I just decided that I would march into the administration's office and clean this mess up.

Well, Craig and I went to meet with the head of pupil instruction. Now mind you, I'm a stay-at-home mom, and my knees were knocking. We went in thinking it was just going to be a conversation with the head of pupil services, but when we opened the door there was a long table with fifteen chairs around it and two chairs for Craig and me to face the others.

I walked in the door and said, "Oh, my word, we're on trial!"

After we had objectively shared our concerns, praying silently the entire time, the head of pupil services, who sat like a chief justice in the middle of the table, sort of adjusted his position and asked me just one question. "Are you opposed to secular humanism?"

I looked at him and the Holy Spirit was saying, *Be careful, be careful,* so I just asked, "Well, sir, what is secular humanism?"

He looked at me for the longest time, and then he said, "I don't know."

So I just looked back at him and said, "Well, sir, if you don't know what it is, then what difference does it make if I'm for it or against it?" The moment I said that I knew I had just gone from being the head of the PTA to being an agitator in their eyes.

Craig and I decided we needed to talk this over with other parents, because we had learned that our humble little school had become a pilot for this experimental program by the State Department of Public Education to pry into the family lives of the students in order to identify "at risk" kids. So Craig and I started going to Tupperware parties, library clubs, and the local Christian radio show—a little 500-watt mom-and-pop station—to share our concerns.

After I shared my heart on the radio show, the manager of the station came up to me and said, "Janet, how would you like your own talk show?"

I looked at the man and said, "When would you like this to happen?"

He said, "How about noon?" And for two years God taught me how to do talk radio on this tiny little station, listening not only with the ears on my head, but the ears on my heart.

Through that show in the next few years I became friends with the local and national chapters of Concerned Women of America. Eventually, I started representing Beverly LaHaye, president of CWA, in the major press. Then one day she asked me to come to Washington so they could groom me to eventually take over as president of the organization. Well, we were living in the home that my husband grew up in, in this small town in Wisconsin. My roots were so deep they came out the other side of the globe. All of a sudden here comes this call. My precious husband opened up his Bible to the book of Genesis and pointed to a note he had written in the margin ten years earlier where the Scripture said that Abraham would be called out of his father's house. And Craig told me he was ready to leave his father's house.

This little Wisconsin kid packed up and went to my Babylon [We know it as Washington, D.C.] where the Lord eventually led me right back into talk radio. Now my show is nationally syndicated, and it's only God who could have done this. I couldn't make up these details. I am just a wife and mother from Wisconsin!

But my story is just a picture of what it means to be called. If you stand before Him and say, "Here I am. What would you have me to do?" If your heart is His, you're willing to say, "God, anywhere, anything, anytime." What I've learned is this: I'm saving my ticket from God, 'cause this ride is far from over.

And it's Him. It's only Him. I don't know what the future holds. What He has done so far is absolutely amazing. I mean, if He called me home today I would say, "Wow, what a life I've had."

To be able to share the gospel of Jesus Christ with Larry King at a commercial break, to be love in action to the former president of the National Organization of Women—these people need Jesus. This is my transcultural missionary experience. This is my lost tribe. They have three-piece business suits and more initials after their names than I could possibly count, but they still have a hole in their heart that only Jesus can fill. As Oswald Chambers said, "We're not here to make men converts of our opinions, we're called to make them converts of Jesus Christ."

Don't Forget This Step

Before we leave this principle, it's important to remember that God's step-by-step guidance is not limited to our occupational mission. It's easy to focus on that to the exclusion of our daily relationships. But remember that third principle: God calls you to partner with him in a life-changing mission that is bigger than you are. We discovered that part of every believer's mission is to be a part of the Great Commission, to build relationships with others so we can talk to them about Christ.

What really makes this hard is when we realize that God didn't just call us to the fun people, or to the people who see life the same way we do, or to the people we like to hang around. We are part of a mission to redeem *all* of mankind—every dirty corner of this place called earth. That mission will sometimes require us to meet hatred with love, bitterness with forgiveness, and stubbornness with understanding.

Which brings us right back to Janet:

> I once debated a nationally syndicated columnist, and I had been warned ahead of time that she would throw rage and anger at me. So I'm all prepared for this big show and sure enough—Boom!—she throws out the anger. And I took the bait. Returned fire, blow for blow.
>
> But when the debate was over, I got in my car and cried all the way home. I said, "Lord, I broke every rule in the book. You said a soft answer turns away wrath. Father, today wasn't about winning that debate. As far as I know, that women might be spending all of eternity separated from you. The goal is to win her to You! So, Father, please give me just one more chance."
>
> The next time I debated with her I had been praying for days ahead of time. This time I didn't take the bait. After we finished the debate, everybody started clearing out of the green room, and I got the sense that she was just lingering. After everyone else left, she looked at me and she said, "Janet, will you do me a favor?" I said "Sure." She said, "Will you pray for me? My life is falling apart." And I said, "I've already been doing that." A few months later, that woman came to the Lord.
>
> That's when I realized it doesn't matter how many facts and figures you know. The only issue is whether others can see Jesus Christ in you.

How about you? Are you so busy trying to accomplish the next step in your vocational mission that you've forgotten God's mission in those around you? Are you praying that God might give you an opportunity to share with them? And are you ready to share with those people who just about drive you nuts?

Did you ever think about why God's plan has you interacting with certain people on a regular basis? Could it be because they need Christ, and God knew that they would be able to relate particularly well to you?

TAKE FIVE

Before you read any further, we suggest you take a few minutes and fill in the next page in this book. Start with the mission that God has given you. Remember, it's a unique mission that God has been preparing for you even before you were born. It's bigger than you are. And it's life-changing.

> **The only issue is whether others can see Jesus Christ in you.**

Next, write down two crossroads decisions where you've made the tough choice and honored God. What results did you see from honoring God at the crossroads? You may be facing another crossroads decision right now. If so, think about how God used your previous decisions to forge you and equip you for your mission. How does He want to do that in the decision you are facing now?

Then finally, write down several steps along the way where you have seen God guide and provide for you as you carry out your mission. Do you see it coming together? Thank God for each of those steps.

If you don't see it coming together yet, don't worry. God has an awesome plan for your life. Do you remember that trustee of the North American Mission Board whom we told you about in the first chapter? When they were considering Bob to be the board's first president, the trustee just shook his head and said, "In looking at your resume, Bob, either you've made some of the dumbest career moves I've ever seen, or God has been preparing you for this role at every step of your journey."

What may look like a dumb career move now will turn into a beautiful thread in God's tapestry later. You may be at a point in your life like that World Changer crew was at noon on Friday. One step by a student had ruined so much. But hang in there! Before long, you'll be thanking God for what now appears to be a giant setback, and you'll be marveling at how He brings the good out of the bad.

Thank God for the steps you do understand. Trust God for the ones you don't. And, as Janet Parshall said, save that ticket from God, 'cause this ride is far from over.

Made to Count!

MY MISSION:_____

Crossroads decisions:

1. _____

2. _____

Steps toward my mission where God has provided and guided:

1. _____

2. _____

3. _____

4. _____

5. _____

PRINCIPLE 8

When you answer God's call, you will experience His pleasure and change your world.

Key scriptures:

- "So we make it our goal to please him, whether we are at home in the body or away from it" (2 Corinthians 5:9).
- "On the contrary, we speak as men approved by God to be entrusted with the gospel. We are not trying to please men but God, who tests our hearts" (1 Thessalonians 2:4).
- "But when they did not find them, they dragged Jason and some brethren to the rulers of the city, crying out, 'These who have turned the world upside down have come here too'" (Acts 17:6 NKJV).

Key points:

- When we find ourselves doing what God created us to do, we will experience His pleasure.
- God calls us to turn the world "upside down," radically changing those we come in contact with and the professions we pursue.

Follow God's Plan and Experience His Pleasure

Scottish runner Eric Liddle was one of the best athletes to ever represent Great Britain in the Olympic games. A trained sprinter, Eric faced a crossroads of choice when he discovered that the finals for the 100-meter dash in the 1924 Games in Paris would be held on Sunday. He made history when he refused to run in his main Olympic event for religious reasons, and then shocked everyone by winning gold in the much longer 400-meter dash, an event that was held on a different day.

His story, along with that of his friend, Harold Abrahams, another gold medallist from Britain, is chronicled in the Academy Award–winning film *Chariots of Fire*. A poignant scene in the movie occurs when Eric decides that he will join his parents on the mission field in China, but that he first wants to train for and run in the Olympics. He knows this decision will be difficult for his sister to swallow, since she believes that Eric should head to the mission field immediately.

As the two walk along the Scotland hillside, with a panoramic view of their town below them, Eric stops and turns to face his sister Jenny. "I've decided," he says. "I'm going back to China. The missionary cells have accepted me."

Jenny's face lights up, and she lets out a squeal of delight. She gives her brother an enthusiastic hug. "Oh, I'm so pleased."

But then Eric steps back and continues. "But I've got a lot of running to do first," he says. The joy quickly leaves Jennie's face and she stares downward, her disappointment obvious to her brother. Eric takes her two hands and looks directly at her, though she will not return his gaze.

> Jenny, you've got to understand. I believe that God made me for a purpose—for China. But He also made me fast, and when I run, I feel His pleasure. To give it up would be to hold Him in contempt. You were right, it's not just fun. To win is to honor Him.

When they finish talking, Jenny silently walks away, displaying her tacit disapproval of her brother's decision. But Eric Liddle would not be deterred, even by those he loved the most, because he was running to please God and not men.

DOING WHAT GOD CREATED US TO DO

As this scene so vividly demonstrates, when we answer God's call we experience His pleasure. Others may not understand it, but that should never keep us from pursuing that call. "So we make it our goal to please Him,"[1] Paul wrote to the church at Corinth. And to the church at Thessalonica, he made the same point: "We are not trying to please men but God, who tests our hearts."[2]

Nothing pleases God more than watching you obediently pursue His mission for your life. We sense God's pleasure when we do this. Our heart just about leaps out of our chest on the best days. (We'll talk about those other days in a moment.) "Yes! This is it!" Our feet hit the ground every morning knowing that we are doing exactly what God created us to do. We see God work. And we turn our corner of the world a little upside down.

There is a deep contentment that comes from answering God's call in this way, and it absolutely transcends our circumstances. This doesn't mean that you will never have a bad day—far from it—but even in the worst of days you will know that you are doing what God created you to do, and you will *still* experience His pleasure. You will also know, as Eric Liddle did, that to walk away from this calling, the very one that God created you to fulfill, would be to hold God in contempt.

There are people who say that there should never be bad days if you're truly following God's plan for your life. Jesus just wants you happy, healthy, and wealthy. Don't believe them! Others will not so much say it as imply it: God gave us common sense; He wouldn't ever want us to put ourselves in danger or in a hostile work environment, etc.

All these folks have some explaining to do to the apostle Paul.

"Paul, called to be an apostle of Jesus Christ through the will of God"[3] is the same man who was:

> Beaten with rods [three times], once I was stoned, three times I was shipwrecked, I spent a night and a day in the open sea, I have been constantly on the move. I have been in danger from rivers, in danger from bandits, in danger from my own countrymen, in danger from Gentiles; in danger in the city, in danger in the country, in danger at sea; and in danger from false brothers. I have labored and toiled and have often gone without sleep; I have known hunger and thirst and have often gone without food; I have been cold and naked. Besides everything else, I face daily the pressure of my concern for all the churches.[4]

Either Paul had it wrong (as well as the disciples, the martyrs, and the persecuted church through the ages) or some of our health, wealth, and prosperity preachers and believers have it wrong today. We're sticking with Paul.

Our tendency when the tough days come is to look for a way out. The grass starts looking greener somewhere else. We start to question whether this is really what God had in mind for us. We stop trying to please God and start focusing on ourselves. But tough times should never shake your confidence in your calling or dent that quiet satisfaction that comes from knowing you are doing what He created you to do.

What if Eric Liddle had not won a gold medal at the Olympics? What if he had felt crummy on race day, had given it everything he had, and still finished fourth? Wouldn't God have been just as honored in defeat as He was in victory? Of course He would have. (Maybe we wouldn't have the movie *Chariots of Fire*, but that's Hollywood's issue, not God's.) Eric Liddle was doing what God called him to do. He honored God by refusing to race on Sunday. He honored God by training hard and using his athletic gifts to lift up the name of Christ. On a summer day in Paris, he happened to honor God by winning the Olympic 400-meter race. But even if he had lost, God would still have been honored. And Eric Liddle would still have sensed God's pleasure.

The plain truth is that our witness and ministry is often most powerful in the "bad days." Paul was not caught off guard by his challenges. They had been promised to him as part of his ministry. "He is a chosen vessel of Mine," the Lord told Ananias, "to bear My name before Gentiles, kings, and the children of Israel. For I will show him how many things he must suffer for My name's sake."[5]

> The plain truth is that our witness and ministry is often most powerful in the "bad days."

Today, we often focus on the things we must *succeed in* to make a difference, rather than the things we must *suffer through*. While we have a desire to see amazing things happen in our lives, we'll work overtime to avoid the very circumstances where the amazing most often occurs. We call those circumstances "defining moments," and they are most often found in the toughest of times. Think about most of the miracles in the Bible. What were the circumstances? Crisis. Trouble. Trials. Jail. That's why Scripture tells us that we should "consider it pure joy . . . whenever [we] face trials of many kinds."[6]

Paul realized that the legitimacy of his calling did not depend on whether the "good" days exceeded the "bad" days. A calling transcends bad days, trials and disappointments. If you are truly doing the things that God created you to do, you will know it even on your worst days. Paul understood this.

And so does Todd Afshar.

Mr. Afshar Goes to Azusa

Todd Afshar found his calling in junior high, when a history teacher made current events spring to life. Todd started writing to congressmen and senators and subscribed to *Newsweek*. He started watching C-Span and CNN. In *junior high*. At a time when most kids were worrying about their complexion, Todd was concerned about the national debt.

He attended college at Azusa Pacific University in Azusa, California. Todd decided to major in—what else?—political science. And like a lot of other college students, his junior year he decided to get involved in politics.

The difference is that Todd decided to skip the campus politics. Student senate could wait. Others would have to divvy up the student activity fees. Todd set his sights on higher stakes. And since the Democrats and Republicans had already chosen their presidential candidates, Todd decided to run for mayor of Azusa, California—at the tender age of twenty.

The thought had first entered his mind two years earlier when Todd was just a freshman. "Everybody complained about the mayor," Todd explained recently, "antibusiness, against the university . . . all that. But when the elections rolled around, she ran unopposed! I decided that if she was running unopposed the next time [two years later], I would do something about it."

Sure enough, after two more years of hearing complaints about the mayor, Todd heard that she was running unopposed again. "It started with my friends joking about it: You should run. You could win."

"What did you do?" we asked.

"First I called the clerk's office to see what the requirements were. You had to be eighteen years old, a registered voter, and a resident of the city. I qualified."

He more than qualified. He'd been a resident of the city for nearly three years. The humble "Afshar for mayor" campaign was born.

His first challenge, like every politician, was fund raising. He set a modest campaign goal of $7,000. But first, a more immediate problem. He needed $250 for a filing fee.

> I just laid it all before God: "If you want this to happen, I need the resources." I've learned that if God calls me to something impossible, I just pray for His blessing. A little while later I was standing in line at a Starbucks. A friend's father came up behind me in the line and said, "I heard you're running for mayor. I hope this helps." When he left I reached in and opened up the check he had stuffed in my pocket. It was the exact amount I needed to enter the race.

Made to Count!

At first, of course, nobody took him seriously.

> Nobody knew me, and I was running against a political machine.
> The mayor was in her fourth year as mayor, she had been on the
> council for eleven years. And I was a total rookie. I was Mr. Smith in
> the movie *Mr. Smith Goes to Washington*, except this was Mr. Afshar
> goes to Azusa.

But Todd studied the issues and made his rounds. Soon, the businessmen and
businesswomen started backing this fresh face. The critics raised the level of
stridency, even attacking his ethnicity. Todd took it as a sign that he was no
longer somebody to be laughed off.

Todd and his volunteer team from Azusa put up a Web site, held fundraisers, registered college students, and went door to door. When the votes
were tallied on election day, the results were amazing.

Todd finished a respectable second in a three-person race, losing the election by just 700 votes.

Knowing that it must have been tough for young Todd to pour his life
into the election and then lose, we couldn't resist asking how it made him
feel. "What kind of emotions were you experiencing that night?" we asked.
"What thoughts were running through your mind?"

"That I wanted to run again in 2005," said Todd.

Huh?

> A businessman said to me that night: "You don't realize how many
> walls for change you've broken down in this city." This is what I'm
> passionate about. And these passions aren't just something I woke up
> with one day. Passion is different than emotion. If you watch a really
> good episode of *Law and Order*, and say, "I want to be a lawyer," that's
> emotion.
>
> But passion is something that doesn't go away. I had a bad day, a
> tough election, but I still wanted to go into politics. If I get dumped
> by my girlfriend, I still want to go into politics. That's my idea of a
> calling.

This *is* my full-time ministry. I'm not called to lead a church. I'm called to lead a city. Or maybe a nation.

Who knows what the future holds for young Todd Afshar? He wouldn't be the first politician to lose a race but later lead a nation. Abraham Lincoln lost his first race for elected office. Four years later, he suffered a nervous breakdown. He was then defeated for Congress (once), the U.S. Senate (twice) and lost a nomination for vice president. Yet he turned out to be one of the greatest presidents our country ever knew, and he never lost his sense of calling. He realized that his calling did not change with the political winds.

Calling. The sure knowledge that God created you to do exactly what you are doing. The certain knowledge that you will experience His pleasure even in the worst of days.

"*Called* to be an apostle," said Paul. "*Called* to be a politician," said Todd. "*Called* to be a runner," said Eric Liddle.

Called to share the gospel, each one of us. In the good days and bad, experiencing God's pleasure because we are doing exactly what He created us to do.

17

Follow God's Plan and Change Your World

God's call is high-impact. It will rock your world and the world of those around you. This is not just rhetoric. God gives us the most potent spiritual weapons available to accomplish His work in our lives. And He expects us to use them for transformation.

God's plan for our lives will put us at spiritual war with the world. The kingdom of Christ is mutually incompatible with the kingdom of this world. Satan has been given temporary dominion as the "prince of this world."[1] But his days are numbered, and he already stands condemned.[2] As followers of Christ we are new creatures, and Satan has no hold on us.[3]

It should not surprise us then, that Christ-followers change the world around them. And people notice. From the world's perspective, we are turning things upside down. It's been that way since the very first followers of Christ. In Acts chapter 17, we read the story of the apostle Paul and his friend Silas as they came to the city of Thessalonica. To say Paul acted as a change agent would be a monumental understatement. He was a riot waiting to happen, guaranteed overtime for the crowd control police. In Thessalonica, as usual, he proclaimed the resurrection of Christ, and lives were changed. "Some of the Jews were persuaded and joined Paul and Silas, as did a large number of God-fearing Greeks and not a few prominent women."[4] But trouble was not far behind. Some jealous Jews "rounded up some bad characters from the marketplace," started a riot, and then went searching for the apostle Paul.[5]

Though they couldn't find Paul, they dragged the owner of the house where Paul had been staying, a man called Jason, before the city officials. Listen to the indictment against Jason:

> These who have turned the world upside down have come here too. Jason has harbored them, and these are all acting contrary to the decrees of Caesar, saying there is another king—Jesus.[6]

Then they lectured Jason and released him after he had posted bond.

Did you catch the indictment? They "turned the world upside down." Theirs was a topsy-turvy, black-is-white and white-is-black type of mind-blowing impact. And Christ-followers have been having that same impact ever since.

You've already read about many who are doing it today. In this chapter, we will introduce you to four more who are turning the world on its head. Like the people already profiled, they are doing it in some of the most challenging places imaginable—major universities, law, media, politics, big business. They are the embodiment of the eight principles we have been discussing throughout this book, culminating in the promise that when you answer God's call you will experience His pleasure and change your world. You may not start riots, but you will start people thinking about a new way of life, about a radically different worldview.

God does not do things the way the world thinks He should. He often uses those who are untrained and unqualified from the world's perspective to handle the most intimidating assignments. We've already seen that. Need a national voice on radio? Look for a Midwestern homemaker. How about someone to challenge accepted scientific theory? Try a professor at a liberal law school. You want a spokesperson for compassionate conservatism? Find a dedicated communist and convert him. And if you need a defender of our constitutional right to share the gospel in airports, look for a Jewish guy from Brooklyn. Of course. "For my thoughts are not your thoughts, neither are your ways my ways," declares the LORD."[7]

We see it not just in the people He calls, but in the methods He uses.

Leadership to the world means decisiveness and power. For Christ-followers, leaders are first and foremost servants. The world focuses on our strengths; but Christ's power is made perfect in our weaknesses. The world values our individual rights; Christ calls us to surrender those rights to the sovereign will of the Father. These are not incremental differences. The two world systems cannot peacefully coexist. They are black and white. Right and wrong. Rightside up and upside down.

So God works in unexpected people. And He works in unexpected ways. But we've found one other truth that many in the church seem to have forgotten: He also works in unexpected *places*.

That's why we've focused many stories in this book on five major areas of our culture: higher education, media and the arts, law, politics, and big business. We have found that these professions are the disfavored stepchildren for Christians pursuing a calling. As we've mentioned numerous times, some in the church have been building an artificial wall in the last few centuries between the secular and the sacred. Some even take it a step further and define the types of "secular" professions that would be acceptable for Christians. And the church has been building some pretty stout walls around these particular professions.

Frankly, we need an explosion of Christ-followers who will follow God's call to our institutions of higher education, to the practice of law, to Hollywood, Broadway, or Madison Avenue, to politics, or to Wall Street. As Janet Parshall noted in her comments about Washington, D.C., *these places are mission fields*, and a calling to these fields is every bit as God-honoring as a calling to China.

These professions also have enormous impact on our culture. This does not mean that a calling into any of these professions is somehow *more* valuable in God's eyes, but it does mean that a Christ-follower in one of these professions will have a chance to change some of the cultural dynamics that are leading our nation dramatically away from Christ. It is amazing that the very professions that impact our culture the most are influenced by Christ-followers the least.

When Paul went into the sophisticated culture of Athens, he employed a three-fold strategy. First, he preached in the synagogues. Then, he reasoned in the marketplace daily with those who happened to be there. And third, he was given an opportunity to speak on Mars Hill to the cultural influencers, a group of philosophers who spent their time debating new philosophies and religions. Among other functions, they were the gatekeepers in Athens. They alone would decide which speakers would be given permission to speak at cultural events and at other public gatherings. Paul shared the gospel with them, and Scripture records that "some mocked," while others wanted to hear him again, while still others "joined him and believed."[8]

In the next few pages, you will read about a few in today's Mars Hill professions who have "joined him and believed." Whether or not God is calling you into any of these arenas, you will be blessed by their stories and will learn from the way God worked in their lives. And who knows, if you are still wrestling with the issue of where God is calling you, you might just find yourself on Mars Hill, joining them in turning things upside down, experiencing God's pleasure and changing your world.

EXPECT THE UNEXPECTED

Hugh Hewitt. Hugh's life reads like a verse straight out of Proverbs: "In his heart a man plans his course, but the LORD determines his steps."[9] It is a story of unexpected twists and turns, of God's working in surprising ways to impact unlikely arenas. And Hugh Hewitt wouldn't have it any other way.

Nurtured in a strong family environment, Hugh gave his life to Christ at a young age and never doubted his faith. As he studied the teachings of Scripture and some great philosophers, Hugh knew he had a unique calling early in life. The hostile environment of Harvard University couldn't dent it. Nor could the ups and downs of an unpredictable career. He had confidence, not in his own abilities, but in God's plan. And in the role that he would be asked to play.

> I had a public calling from my high school days. When I read Aleksandr Solzhenitsyn, I was convinced that people had to act against communism. Solzhenitsyn made me an anticommunist. He was one of the greatest intellectual influences on my life. I arrived at Harvard certain that we were in the middle of a titanic struggle with the Soviet Union that was a struggle between God's freely created

people and a dictatorial system that destroyed both men and the idea of God.

What a blessing to have Aleksandr Solzhenitsyn as my commencement speaker in 1978. I listened to *The World Split Apart* while sitting in the rain at Harvard. I had a worldview from the beginning that you had America, which is the freest, most religiously inspired country in history arrayed against a maniacal form of Soviet totalitarianism. Nothing dented me. If you read Solzhenitsyn, and understand this spiritual struggle between world systems, you can't be dented.[10]

Hugh's solid confidence would be tested in his final year at Harvard. He applied to law school at Michigan and Harvard, his dream schools, but didn't get in. Many of us would have taken this as a "sign" that God had other plans. A lesser institution, maybe. Or perhaps no law degree at all. But there is a difference between people saying no, and God saying no.

If you let people's initial rejection tell you, "Okay, you're not supposed to do that," then you're clearly not testing God's design on your life. I wouldn't have gone to law school, I wouldn't have had any books published, I wouldn't be a lawyer.

So he took the rejections in stride and furthered his education in a more "nontraditional" way. He went to work for former president Richard Nixon in California. Surprisingly, Hugh says that Nixon was the "best boss I ever worked for." And what an education on global politics and the hubris of man!

After a two-year stint with Nixon, Hugh reapplied to Michigan Law School. This time, he was accepted. During his three years on campus, he proved that he more than belonged. On the strength of his law school performance, he landed a coveted job clerking with the judges of the D.C. Circuit Court of Appeals. He had no way of knowing it at the time, but he would be rubbing elbows with the judges who would become giant figures of the American legal struggles in the '90s and the new century: Robert Bork, Kenneth Starr, Ruth Bader Ginsburg, Antonin Scalia. Huge intellects. Supreme Court justices. A special counsel who triggered an impeachment charge against a sitting president. When God decides to tutor a young man for a career in public service, He pulls out all the stops.

From there, Hugh went to work for six years in the Reagan administration. He joined other ideologues who saw the world through the same lens of good versus evil. They believed in a president who called the Soviets an "evil empire" and challenged Mikhail Gorbachev to "tear down this [Berlin] wall." And they believed it could happen. Not just during their lifetime, but in the next few years, during their term in office. They believed that God was sovereign among the nations of the earth and that He was preparing to turn the communist system on its head. Upside down. Soon.

To the great surprise of all the political prognosticators, He did. An amazing ride for a young man who had believed the words of Solzhenitsyn, and sensed the hand of God, from early in his life.

But God was just getting started with Hugh Hewitt. God wanted Hugh to make a difference through media, to become a strong voice for evangelical Christians on the airwaves. It would take Hugh down a road he had never dreamed about and into jobs for which he never interviewed. The first step was to remove Hugh from the city he had grown to love.

> After six years in the Reagan administration, the phone rang and Richard Nixon wanted me to come back to California and oversee the construction of his presidential library. That wasn't what I had in mind for my life. But at the same time my wife's parents, both of whom were very sick, lived in California and it was time for us to come home and take care of them. So we came back to California and haven't left since.

Which begs the question: How did Hugh Hewitt the lawyer go from overseeing the construction of a presidential library into the world of media, particularly in a competitive Southern California culture where everyone wants to be a star? "Easy," says Hugh. "You do your job."

> I was doing weekly press conferences on the library. A radio programmer from KFI, one of the most influential stations in this area, heard me in these press conferences, and he called me up cold one

day and asked, "Would you like to do a radio show?" I thought, *Why not? That's an idea.* So then it was on to KFI, and the folks at PBS heard me doing KFI and asked me to do a television show at PBS.

He makes it sound so easy.

God had now planted a Christian in the midst of a very cynical environment, intending Hugh to use the tools controlled by the secular elite to advance the gospel. As before, Hugh had no doubt about his mission or his environment. He wrote his book, *The Embarrassed Believer*, during his tenure at PBS. In it, he describes the mission field where God placed him:

> Intellectual elites have never been so far removed from the normal distribution of religious attachment or practice as they are today. And no segment of the intellectual elite is more estranged from faith, and specifically from Christianity, than the media elite. . . . The prestige media is populated by professionals who by and large share a sense of their own significance and their own wisdom. . . . I work for PBS, which simply cannot be trumped when it comes to its own high opinion of itself. . . . I'm surrounded by people who, upon learning that I am a true believer in Christianity, treat that part of me as either a charming lunacy or an irrelevant eccentricity.[11]

But this "irrelevant eccentricity" quickly gained relevance in terms that the response-driven media elites understood—callers and ratings. While at KFI, Hugh would frequently turn his back on the normal talk-show fare—O. J. Simpson's trial, for example—in favor of a thought provoking religious question. Like the time he asked whether it was right to pray for the dead. "My little question lit up the board," Hugh recalls. "All incoming lines were jammed with callers. I had a 'full board.'"[12]

A few weeks later, Hugh discovered that the writings of C. S. Lewis as memorialized in the book *Mere Christianity* had originally been read as part of a radio show during World War II in Britain. The writings of Lewis had been an enormous influence in Hugh's life. Since he hosted the late night shift on Sunday, he was pretty sure that KFI management was not listening. If it was good enough for Lewis, it's good enough for me, Hugh decided. For six straight weeks he did nothing but read *Mere Christianity* on a secular radio station that dominated the Los Angeles market. The results? *Six* full boards, week after week.

Then it was on to PBS, where success was measured not by full boards but by ratings. The first spike came when Hugh interviewed Robert Funk, the organizer of the Jesus Seminar, a group of self-appointed scholars who sit around and take votes on how much of Scripture they want to believe. Hugh asked the tough questions the liberal media had never asked. Ratings soared. Other religious interviews followed with the same results. Soon, the liberal PBS management asked Hugh to do a special called "Searching for God in America."

"There was only one requirement," says Hugh. "I couldn't have more than fifty percent of the show be evangelical Christians. So we started with Chuck Colson and ended with the Dalai Lama. We covered the gamut." But the gospel message came across clear through the testimonies of Colson, Greg Laurie, and others. The response of the Christian community was overwhelming. They weren't used to seeing their faith treated so fairly by the mainstream media. And others responded favorably as well, thankful that somebody was finally talking about the issues that everybody else ignored.

Today, Hugh teaches law school and hosts his own radio show, addressing current events through talk laced with common-sense wisdom and biblical values. He sees his radio show as a stewardship, and is not afraid to talk about his faith and plug his favorite ministries. Though he's certainly not immune from criticism—"fringe groups assault you whenever you talk about faith"—he's content in the knowledge that God is using him to make a difference in the lives of people he'll never meet.

A news junkie. A Harvard grad. A Reagan staffer. A PBS talent. A talk show host and a law school professor. What does God have in store next?

Hugh Hewitt knows better than to guess at that one. He has learned to expect the unexpected. After all, who would have thought that a lawyer trained by the vaunted D.C. circuit would help lead a search for God in America by PBS? Yet the outcome of Hugh's calling, like the fall of communism, was never really in doubt. Turning the world upside down. Hugh Hewitt understood that concept from day one.

NOTHING IS IMPOSSIBLE WHEN GOD'S IN IT

Governor Sonny Perdue. When you run for governor in a state that hasn't had a governor from your party since Reconstruction, and your incumbent opponent outspends you seven to one, most people don't expect you to win. That was the case in 2002 when Republican Sonny Perdue ran against incumbent Roy Barnes for the governor's mansion in Georgia. Throughout the campaign, most Democrats and even quite a few Republicans were saying that Sonny didn't have a chance. Some were even suggesting that the incumbent governor would win by a landslide.

That was just fine with Sonny. He liked playing the "aw shucks" underdog. Besides, "winning" wasn't the reason Sonny Perdue was running for the governor's office in the first place. For him, it was all about obedience—obedience to a call that he and his wife, Mary, knew God had placed on their hearts months earlier. They realized that even in defeat they would have the opportunity to grow in obedience, humility, grace, and character. Long before they made the decision to run, Sonny had decided that he would honor principles over politics. He made that choice at a crossroads years earlier.

> After four years of serving in the state legislature I was elected majority leader in the state senate and after six years I found myself as president pro tem which is the highest elected office in the body of the state senate. Nobody was more surprised than I.
>
> But when you're president pro tem of the state senate, the typical questions start being asked of you: Are you going to run for Congress? How about the U.S. Senate? Is the lieutenant governor a consideration? And on and on the questions go. As 1998 neared, the Democrats began to focus on the lieutenant governor's seat. As the Democratic leadership met with me, they were checking off all the blocks. They asked if I were pro-choice. When I told them I was pro-life they said, "What do you mean? You're a Democrat." I said, "I guess that means I'm a pro-life Democrat."[13]

Their response was fast and firm. "Sonny, you'll have to change if you ever want to get elected." And so he did. But it wasn't the change they expected.

Sonny changed political parties, effectively eliminating any hopes for statewide office in Georgia.

But then came a story from an unlikely source about *change* that really precipitated my decision to run for governor. I had absolutely no vision of statewide office, and God seemed to have extinguished any desire for such a role. During the summer of 2000, we had a missionary come to our church whom we had supported in Brazil. He was a retired fireman, and he and his wife had settled down in a cul-de-sac outside Louisville, Kentucky. But God came and clearly called him out of retirement and back to Brazil. A year later, in the summer of 2001, he came to our church reporting to all of us another major change, "You know, I just don't understand it, but God has asked us to get out of our comfort zone again and move from our present city in Brazil to Sao Paulo and start another new work. While I don't understand it, I know God blessed our obedience the last time, and I feel He will surely do it this time."

For Sonny Perdue, the missionary's simple story of obedience started a still, small whisper that summoned him out of his comfort zone. Restless and uncertain, Sonny read the Declaration of Independence. Then he read the stories of the men who signed the Declaration and the risks they took with their fortunes, their families and their lives. Many of them paid terrible prices. In addition, he went to one of his standard points of comfort, the hymnbook. When he turned to *Battle Hymn of the Republic*, it was as though the still, small voice turned into a marching cadence.

He has sounded forth the trumpet that shall never sound retreat

Oh be swift, my soul, to answer Him, be jubilant my feet!

I felt this steady drumbeat deep in my heart that said, "Get ready." That's when I went to the church and said, "I don't know what God is doing in my life and Mary's. I think it's something in the field of politics and leadership, but I'm fearful of being seduced for the wrong reasons."

Sonny asked his church to pray for him and Mary. She was headed for a women's retreat, and they didn't have much time to talk about what was happening. But the retreat had been scheduled for just after September 11, 2001, so all the special women's speakers who were traveling long distances cancelled and substitutes were brought in. Mary couldn't believe it when one of the substitutes challenged the women to get out of their comfort zones and go wherever God called them.

That sealed it. In November of 2001, Sonny agreed to run as the Republican candidate for governor.

> I realized that this could be God's way of giving me a huge dose of humility, but this was something we were sure we were absolutely called and compelled to do by the Christ we serve, and the results were totally up to Him.

Before the campaign began in earnest, Sonny went to his church again and asked if they would pray for him and Mary. They felt a divine mandate to run, and they asked the church members to pray for obedience, not necessarily victory. The church gathered around and prayed over him just like they would when they commissioned a missionary. As Sonny described this event to Bob he literally wept, saying he believed that churches should do the same with business people, professionals, and other political leaders.

For Sonny and Mary, the call meant months of travel, endless speeches and fundraisers, tireless campaigning, relentless interviews, and the consumption of more barbecue and chicken than most of us see in a lifetime. Sonny ran a grassroots campaign, both because that's his strength—meeting and relating to people—and because he couldn't afford anything else. The results? A stunned incumbent party. Late on election night it became clear that Sonny Perdue had engineered perhaps the greatest upset in Georgia's political history.

One of the first things the new governor did was pull the capitol staff together and speak to them about principle-centered leadership. Sonny made it clear that one of his goals was to build a culture based on Judeo-Christian values and high ethical standards. He let them know that he would be asking for a revision and tightening of the ethics rules throughout the state and in the government's policies and procedures.

Governor Perdue also brought a passionate heart for prisoners and their families, and found increased ways to minister to them with hope and an opportunity for the future. He also focused on the needs of the illegal immigrants who had flooded the Atlanta area, defying the stereotype of a Republican governor who would turn a deaf ear to such concerns.

In addition, he rallied the faith-based community to get more involved in foster care, a vital ministry that he and Mary had modeled in their own family. For about five years, they were foster parents for newborn, preadoption children whose mothers couldn't keep them for a variety of reasons. "We have seen the joy of the families who eventually take the children and how their faces light up the first time they realize this is now their child. I feel if we take care of the needs of the children of Georgia we will eliminate a lot of the problems that would otherwise occur later on."

When we asked Sonny if he had seen God move around the governor's mansion since he inhabited it, tears again formed in his eyes.

> As God tells us, to whom much is given, much is required. We've been afforded a great opportunity to live in this, the people's house. We have had a tremendous opportunity to talk unashamedly about our faith and the importance of faith in all people's lives regardless of their beliefs. We have also come to understand that ministry still happens one-on-one.

He shared an example of how those one-on-one opportunities work. A staff member working in the governor's detail began asking a lot of questions about the faith he saw and heard in the governor and his family. As the questions mounted for this staff member, an opportunity came for him to personally experience Christ's loving plan for his life right in the midst of his duties for the governor. Today, he is growing as a new Christ-follower. Others are now asking the same questions on their own time and during personal and private conversations.

Sonny and Mary Perdue believe that they have been placed in the gubernatorial role to lead the state, and to represent their Lord. "As the governor and first lady we must respect the office, but at the same time we intend to live a lifestyle that will encourage people to look for what the difference is. And we will be ready to tell them the difference is Christ."

What once seemed impossible, and still seems like a political miracle, also feels like the most natural thing in the world. Fortunately for Sonny, the pundits don't get to call the election. The people still get to vote.

In the unpredictable world of Georgia politics, they voted in a Republican governor who is helping prisoners, immigrants, and foster children. One who relishes the role of ministering to individual members of the governor's staff. And one who sees his calling as a chance to serve, not just a steppingstone to power. It's a political world turned upside down. Just the way Sonny likes it.

IMPACT IS ONLY A PRAYER AWAY

Some say it's the most cutthroat businesses in the world. Others say it's one of the greatest opportunities for success if you're good and the hardest business in the world if you're not.

Real estate. Fast-paced, hard-charging, demanding. And **Jenny Pruitt** has found it to be a great platform for serving Christ.

That's not the way she started, however. When she began as an agent for Northside Realty in Atlanta, Georgia, from 1968 to 1976, she was all business. Each year brought more success, more attention, higher production, and longer working hours. She thrived on it. After all, the more real estate she sold, the more "stuff" she could have. That became her purpose—to enjoy the ride, get the toys, and make a name in a very competitive industry, especially for a woman. "My heart was just not in the right place. I was very materialistic, and my purpose in life was focused solely on a career."

In the midst of the climb, one person continued to be unnerving—her boss. He was one of the most gentle, kind, and godly men she'd ever been around. She'd rubbed elbows with a lot of people from church life, but she'd never seen a man who lived it out and modeled the Christian walk like this man. He took Jenny under his wing and helped her navigate the incredible pressures and pitfalls of the real estate industry. He gave her a proverb, which he said happened to come from the Bible, urging her to constantly keep it in front of her. "As [a man] thinks in his heart, so is he."[14] And that proverb began to haunt Jenny. She realized that her boss had something in life that she was missing. Despite her success, there was still a huge vacuum in her heart, and nothing seemed to be filling it.

With time, patience, consistency, and persistence, the boss's lifestyle and occasional sharing led Jenny to a one-on-one relationship with Jesus Christ. The change was just as dramatic for her as it had been for him. And Jenny began to experience what happens when God decides to bless a business. Six months later she was offered the opportunity to become the first woman manager in real estate—not just in Northside Realty, but in the entire city of Atlanta.

The big promotion did have a few pitfalls. "When I went to the new office, it was not in a great location, I found out I didn't have any staff, and I didn't have any agents. Other than that it was fine!"

It was a depressing first few days until her mentor dropped by. He gave her the simple and straightforward advice she had learned to appreciate so much: "Jenny, you know that unless the Lord builds a house, it's built in vain. I think we just need to pray together that God will open the windows of heaven and bless you in this new work." To Jenny's amazement, her mentor invited her to kneel down on the floor of the empty office and pray a prayer of dedication—not just that God would bless the business, but that He might be honored in everything that happened there.

> It was like my whole purpose changed, and I began to think of my business as a ministry. I began to reach out to those around me and focus on growing people and trusting God to grow the business. I was committed to working according to His plan and doing whatever He wanted me to do.[15]

That was in 1976. Today Jenny owns her own real estate company, one of the largest in metro Atlanta. In 2002, the residential sales volume for Jenny Pruitt and Associates reached $1.07 billion.

But that's just the business side of things. Remember how Jenny prayed that God might be honored in everything that happened? Well, He answered that prayer in an amazing way, showing Jenny that God's most powerful work can sometimes come in our most desperate moments.

Jenny recalls how in April of 1996, a strong impression came to her while she was driving to one of her offices. God was getting ready to do something in her life. Quietly in her heart, she sensed God saying, "Jenny, my child, I'm going to take you through a valley, and it's going to be very dark and deeper than it's ever been before, but I'll be with you. Never fear and I'll hold you close to my bosom and in the palm of my hand."

> It was a very fearful thought because I knew something was coming down the pike and I wasn't sure what it was. I just took a deep breath. I remembered that God had said "never fear" so that was a warning that God used to prepare my life. Three months later, after being checked by two doctors and nothing showing up, I sought a third opinion at which time the doctor did a biopsy and gave me the report that everybody's scared to death to hear: "You have cancer."

The options that Jenny faced were surgery that would lead to a colostomy or radical chemo and radiation. She chose the latter. After thirty-seven treatments of radiation and two rounds of chemo, the doctors reported to her that the aggressive treatment had accomplished its goal. And while the chemo treatment was doing a job on her disease, she also allowed it to do an amazing thing in her business.

Jenny decided to be transparent and vulnerable with her three hundred agents and sixty-five employees while walking through cancer.

> I told them that I was totally at peace and that God was in control and that He had the power and strength to heal me, without question. But even if He didn't, the ultimate healing would be that I knew where I was going if life on this earth ended, and I would be immediately in the presence of Jesus who had become my Savior. If He left me here, He wasn't finished with me and had more work for me to do.

Jenny watched as God used her new weakness for His power. She describes three things that happened because of her transparency and vulnerability:
- I bonded with a lot of people because they were allowed to share my trial and weakness, and that vulnerability opened their hearts to mine.

- Through that vulnerability and heart connection, I was able to introduce a number of people to a personal relationship with Jesus Christ.
- My transparency led several people to check on some medical issues they had been putting off, and at least fifteen people were found to have precancerous conditions that were treated and resolved, that otherwise might have been missed.

Jenny has seen how the Lord can soften hearts in one of the toughest industries around. And having experienced God's grace in a powerful new way through her cancer experience, Jenny is more determined than ever to see her business as an opportunity to be *on mission* to meet the spiritual needs of others. Here are some of the practical ways she implements that philosophy:

1. The success of Jenny's company is based on serving others. "My business has become my ministry. One of my slogans in business is that if you care about people first, the bottom line will come! After all, people don't want to be led, they want to be served."

2. Because of the success that Jenny has experienced, she's often asked to give business talks. But she will accept the invitation only if they allow her to share with sensitivity the importance of faith in her life. "If they say no, then I tell them to find another speaker. That's the only way I'll do a talk, and so far I've never had anybody turn me down. It all goes back to a covenant I made with God when He gave me this company. I promised Him, 'Lord, I'll go anywhere You send me to talk about Your love for me from this day forward.'"

3. With each new opening of a real estate office, Jenny invites a local Christian leader to come and participate in the dedication. She knows firsthand how powerful a prayer of dedication can be.

4. Every year in December, Jenny hosts an Inspirational Prayer Breakfast. "We focus both inside our company and to the outside business community. For twenty-two years now we've had over 400 people attend the breakfast each year. It's amazing how God has used this event to touch the lives of so many. Many have entered into a personal relationship with Christ!"

5. But perhaps the most powerful practice that Jenny employs may also be the simplest. She is mindful of the need to share her faith with sensitivity in the workplace, and she doesn't want to come across as offensive or overly aggressive to those around her. She has learned to use a few simple questions, in a multitude of circumstances, to open doors in a nonthreatening manner: "What can I

pray about for you? I really believe in the power of prayer, so is there anything in your life that you would like for me to lift up to God for an answer?"

Those simple questions have a way of surfacing deep spiritual needs. Few people will refuse the blessing of having somebody else pray for them. Jenny knows. And she'll never forget the power of that simple prayer of dedication that her mentor spoke into her life when he prayed that God would be honored in everything that happened and everything she did.

GOD'S AMBASSADOR TO A LONELY WORLD

Graham Lacey is an international businessman and entrepreneur, a friend to England's royal family, and to politicians and religious leaders throughout the world. But if you look at his background, you'll see that he didn't follow the path that would normally open those doors. Instead, God in His sovereignty led Graham down an entirely different path, placing in his heart a desire to impact not just the rich and famous but the down and out as well.

> I grew up in a very strict Christian church. We had no television in our house; we never went to a theater. I attended church four times every Sunday and twice during the week. I thank God today for that Christian heritage that grounded me in the Word. However, I felt at a very young age that we were great at being Christians in a very introverted way in our church, but we made no impact on the outside world. And I had a hunger for all those people out there.

One Sunday night at age fourteen, Graham brought a tramp to church so he could hear the gospel. It was a night that changed his mission forever.

> When I got home, my mother told me never to do what I'd done that night, that I'd somehow brought disgrace on the family. I'd taken this man out of his natural environment and made him uncomfortable by bringing him into the church. I knew with every fiber of my being that she was wrong. That day I made a secret commitment that no matter what my mother thought, I would find a way to leave home and make a difference for lonely and beaten down people.

Made to Count!

When Graham was fifteen, he was severely beaten by a group of neighborhood bullies and spent three months in the hospital. As a result, he missed a critical exam at school, which ended any plans for college.

> Within a year, I went into business on my own, and since then I've never worked for anyone but myself. It has enabled me to do what I'd always wanted to do, share the gospel with people I never saw in church. That is a hunger that has stayed with me my entire life.

Graham was a gifted entrepreneur. At sixteen, he built the first out-of-town shopping mall in the United Kingdom, then he went on to significant success in real estate. But before he reached age twenty-five, Graham experienced his share of trauma. His father died, his older brother died, and Graham was put on the Irish Republican Army's assassination list. Yet God pulled him through every challenge in ways that Graham still finds remarkable. And it has only deepened his resolve to trust Christ with every aspect of his life.

> I've been involved in hostage negotiations in some of the most unfriendly parts of the world. I've known all manner of positive and negative experiences, but nothing has taken away the burden I have to make a difference for Christ by thinking outside of the box, of being different, by daring to think big. I think we've got a God who can outthink all of us and outperform all of us if we'll just trust Him.

Graham demonstrated this in a tangible way when he befriended an ambassador to the United Nations from a Muslim country. This country had come under great criticism and pressure due to their actions on the international scene, bringing tension between the United States and this nation. At the time, Graham was involved in a Bible study group in New York City. Most of the group had recently come to faith in Christ. They met each week and shared a common desire to impact New York. "We felt that if we made a difference in New York, one of the most cosmopolitan cities in the world, it could in turn touch the world."

The group planned to have a Thanksgiving lunch, and Graham suggested that they invite the loneliest couple in New York. When asked who that might be, he quickly named the ambassador and his wife. The prayer group suggested that Graham write the invitation to the ambassador. Weeks went by with no response, but the group continued to pray.

The day for the luncheon arrived and just as the group sat down to eat, the intercom in the apartment sounded. It was the ambassador and his wife, their security detachment, the Secret Service, and the FBI. Two additional places were quickly added to the table as Graham introduced the couple to the Bible study group.

> We sat around the table, and I asked a group member to pray. During the prayer, the ambassador started to cry uncontrollably. At the end of the prayer I asked the ambassador if anything had been said that offended him. He said, "No, but as I listened to your friend praying, I was so moved that you would invite us into your home. If the people in New York knew who we were, they'd spit in our faces, yet you invited us to share your Thanksgiving meal. You showed us friendship."

That Thanksgiving luncheon led to an extraordinary relationship between Graham and the ambassador.

> I got to know him and his wife as well as his family. I took him to a Baptist church to hear the gospel. I met with him one on one and talked to him about Christ. I prayed with him on numerous occasions in his office.

As a result of a mutual trust and respect, Graham was invited to go to the ambassador's homeland. While there he met with the Islamic leadership and, at their request, shared his faith in Christ. He spent an hour and twenty minutes with the country's leader and his translator.

> I started by giving him an Arabic copy of the New Testament and Psalms and then shared my faith and talked to him about Christ. It was a very energetic conversation. At the end of our time, I asked him if I might pray with him. There was some discussion in Arabic and

then he invited me to pray with him. I got down on one knee and prayed for him, his wife, and his family. I prayed that the Holy Spirit would break out in revival power in his country. When I finished praying, the leader embraced me, kissed me three times, and then once again spoke in Arabic to his colleague. The translator said that the distinguished leader would like me to pray again. When I asked why, he told me that no one had ever prayed for him before, and this leader wanted their television cameras to film me praying for him.

While the cameras rolled, Graham prayed again for revival to fall on the nation.

From that time up until the present day, this country's government-sponsored television station opens and closes with excerpts from that prayer for revival. I believe that God is limited in what He can do by the limitations we place on Him through our lack of faith in His promises. If we'll just dare to believe Him and challenge Him, God will open the windows of heaven and pour out blessings so great that our storehouses won't be able to contain them. We just have to dare to believe and find that the God of Abraham is the same yesterday, today, and forever.

Where Is Your Corner of the World?

Hugh Hewitt, Graham Lacey, Sonny Perdue, Jenny Pruitt. A Harvard grad. A high school education. A political survivor. A cancer survivor. Four people without much in common except an uncommon faith and a desire to turn their corner of the world upside down.

Maybe God has placed you in a challenging secular environment. Or maybe He hasn't yet, but will soon. Could it be any more hostile than PBS? More cutthroat than real estate? More cynical than politics? Yet in every one of these areas, and dozens of others profiled in this book, God has called men and women against the tide, asking them to demonstrate the heart of Christ while they change their corner of the world.

Where is your corner of the world? How has it changed since you've been there? What mind-numbing thing do you think God wants to do *through you* to turn that corner upside down? Now, multiply it by a thousand and think bigger, more radically, more creatively. Remember, His thoughts are not our thoughts. His ways are not our ways. Pray for His thoughts. Pray for His ways.

Is your corner right side up from the world's perspective? Is it a place where things make perfect sense, with everybody running hard after the world's definition of success? If so, it's time to shake things up. It's time to rattle a few cages with uncommon authenticity, integrity, love, and obedience to Christ. It's time for a few folks to be standing around the water cooler, shaking their heads and saying: "Those who have turned the world upside down have come here too."

18

The List

This book is the story of God calling men and women of faith. "Now faith is being sure of what we hope for and certain of what we do not see."[1]

In the eleventh chapter of the book of Hebrews, the Bible contains what many refer to as the "faith hall of fame." Noah is there, commended for building the ark, when warned about the rains he had "not yet seen."[2] Abraham is lauded for following God's call to a far-off land, "even though he did not know where he was going."[3] Moses made the list because he threw his lot in with the Israelites, the people of God, rather than claiming the privileges he had as the son of Pharaoh's daughter.[4] And many of the others mentioned in the pages of this book are there as well, including David, Gideon, and a reference to our friends from the book of Daniel who "shut the mouths of lions" (Daniel) and "quenched the fury of the flames" (Shadrach, Meshach, and Abednego).[5]

As we mentioned previously, the list is remarkable for those who made it and those who didn't. There are no priests and there is just one prophet on the list. It is largely a list of laymen and laywomen, ordinary folks, called by an extraordinary God to turn their world upside down. They are distinguished not by their abilities, but by their faith. As our friend Henry Blackaby once said to Bob, "In Scripture, God didn't call the qualified; He qualified the called!" These men and women are there to inspire us and cheer us on, says the writer of Hebrews. "Therefore, since we are surrounded by such a great cloud of witnesses, let us throw off everything that hinders and the sin that so easily entangles, and let us run with perseverance the race marked out for us."[6]

In many respects, this book is the continuation of that list. We have told the story of modern-day men and women of faith, those who are running the race with perseverance and passion. They are a list of Christ-followers called to make a difference in areas long viewed as secular by coming alongside those called into vocational leadership roles in the church. We have profiled them not to lower the high call of those responding to full-time ministry, but to raise the view of the call of every Christ-follower, allowing the church to penetrate every aspect of our culture with the gospel.

Peggy Wehmeyer and Phillip Johnson are on the list, having discovered that God designed them for a destiny. For Wehmeyer, it was the irresistible call to make a difference in media, despite those who warned her against it. For Johnson, it was the never-ending battle against the intellectual elites as he exposed the fatal flaw of Darwinism. For both, it was the life-changing realization that God had prepared a unique plan and calling for them before they were born.

The list is the story of dramatic changes when God calls people to a life-changing relationship with Christ. Consider Marvin Olasky's journey from a cynical communist to a compassionate Christ-follower. Or Jay Sekulow's saga—a Jewish kid from Brooklyn defending the rights of Christ-followers to carry out the Great Commission. These are not motivational self-help stories, with Olasky and Sekulow boot-strapping their way to high achievement. These are lives totally transformed by Christ, and then being used in a life-changing mission far bigger than either of them.

These modern-day followers of Christ started their mission right where they were, wasting no time in responding to God's call. They lived *on mission* at home like the Frost family and their forty-eight foster children, or Jeanine Allen, teaching her girls how to follow Christ while battling cancer, or J. C. Watts, leaving the power of our nation's capital for the prospect of being a better dad. They were *on call* at work, winning admirers with their commitment to excellence, and their creative willingness to meet needs and share Christ. And they did their work as though Christ Himself were their boss, resulting in some of the best organized client lists and cleanest port-a-johns you've ever seen!

The list is the story of a God who guides His followers and reveals His mission through His Word, His Spirit, wise counsel, and His work in circumstances. Who could forget the story of Ruth Okediji, rising so early each morning, desperately seeking God's direction for her life? "He speaks! He speaks!" she exclaimed to her roommate on that morning when God broke through with His Holy Spirit. Or the way God guided Jenny Pruitt, less dramatic but no less impactful, through the quiet and consistent witness of a mentor in the workplace.

This list of modern-day Christ-followers is replete with those who chose God at the crossroads. Karen Covell had to choose her own private lions' den, following God's call to be a loving witness to Hugh Hefner. And Graham Lacey decided to befriend the loneliest couple in the United States, rather than stay in his comfort zone with friends and family on Thanksgiving. The result? An opportunity to touch an entire Muslim nation with Christ's love.

It's faith that allowed these Christ-followers to carry out their mission one step at a time, seldom seeing beyond the next bend in the road. Janet Parshall did not set out to be a national voice for Christ-followers but simply took a step of obedience to defend her family's values at school. She continued following each step of the way, ultimately ending up ministering to her own "lost tribe," the politicians and power brokers of Washington, D.C. And how could anyone argue that Mark Earley was not guided step by step, first to the mission field, then to politics, and finally to head the Prison Fellowship ministry that will draw on a combination of all his experiences and passions? Perhaps the same could be said about his resume, or the resume of Janet Parshall, as was said of coauthor Bob's: Either these are some of the dumbest career moves ever seen, or God has been preparing them for their present role at every step of the journey.

And ultimately, the list is the story of a world turned upside down by those who answer God's call. By a nineteen-year-old kid who runs for mayor. By a Midwestern homemaker who goes into talk radio. By a father who chooses to bless his son's dreams. By a governor who takes his own private time to witness to a staff member in the governor's mansion. And by the world's best cleaner of port-a-johns.

Made to Count!

It's not a list about those who took the easy path at the crossroads. You'll read nothing about the college students who didn't run for mayor, or the law school professor who kept writing law review articles instead of taking on the scientific establishment. The port-a-john cleaners who just spray a little Lysol around are a dime a dozen. This is a book and a list about people of faith—not in their own abilities but in the abilities of a loving and trustworthy God. It's a book about faith in God's creative power, and the belief that He created us to count.

Unlike earlier chapters, this chapter contains no new stories of those who have made a difference. This chapter is not about them but about you. Like the heroes in Hebrews 11, the people we have profiled in this book are not here to be dissected, studied, and put on a shelf. They are here to inspire. They are here to personify how a great God uses ordinary people, not just in biblical times but today.

So this chapter is your story. Add your name to the list. What unique mission has God placed on your heart? Go back to page 198 where you wrote the mission that God emblazoned on your life. Take a moment to review it now. It's a mission that's bigger than you are but not too big for God. It's a mission that God uniquely created you to fulfill, molding you with both the strengths, *and the weaknesses,* that will allow God to work through you in bringing it to pass.

With that in mind, take one more look at Hebrews 11. Those men and women believed that God would fulfill their mission even when it looked impossible. They could have downsized their mission or balked at the step of faith God required, but instead they chose obedience. Noah built the ark before it rained. Abraham's wife, Sarah, bore a child when she was half a decade past the age for bearing children, "because she judged Him faithful who had promised."[7] Moses chose the Israelites before God sent the plagues. And the walls of Jericho fell down because Joshua and his army *first* circled the city seven times and shouted, just like God told them to do.

Now it's your turn. Are you willing to step out with the type of insane obedience we mentioned earlier, even before you know how God might pull this one off? Are you willing to pay the price of the rough and narrow path at the crossroads, knowing that it's the only path that leads to greater responsibility?

God wants your name on the list of faith. He loves you and calls you by name. He has constructed an unbelievable plan for your life and given you a mission that will turn your world upside down. He has created you with every tool you need to fulfill His purpose! He is right now whispering over your shoulder, guiding your very next step and painting a beautiful story on the canvas of your life. It's a story that will rival any of those contained in the pages of this book. It's a story of a life lived large—the story of a life that counts!

If you believe this, then we urge you to adopt the simple but powerful prayer of David Livingstone, a medical missionary who opened the continent of Africa to the gospel. It's a prayer that God will honor with a life of impact *wherever* He calls you. As a teenager, this prayer changed David Livingstone's life. If you're willing to apply the biblical principles in this book and make this the prayer of your heart, it will change yours as well.

> Lord, lead me anywhere, just go with me;
> Lay any burden on me, only sustain me;
> Sever any tie in my heart except the tie that binds me to you.

Appendix A
Auxiliary Insights for Online
Temperament Analysis Profiles

As you have by now gone to the Uniquely You website and had the enjoyment of completing your personality temperament profile, the key will be what you do with the information. One of the maxims of life is . . .

Information without application leads to stagnation.

So, let's take a look at some of the application opportunities for what you've learned about yourself. Following you will find some very helpful charts concerning your personality temperament profile. You've already found some on the Uniquely You website, and those on the following pages are auxiliary tools.

To use them well, find where you fall on the following charts and then observe the information that helps you determine things like...

- How those with differing temperaments can see you, when you don't even realize that you may be coming across in certain ways.
- How your temperament best mixes with other temperaments.
- Things that people with your temperament need to work on in order to be effective in people skills and team orientation.
- How to better understand where people are coming from when they address an issue from a different temperament than yours.

Appendix A

We hope these additional analysis charts will prove to be helpful in the interpretation of the information you received on your personality temperament. Now the ball is in your court as you have the opportunity to apply what you've learned in your relationships with those with whom you live and work.

Appendix A

A1. Improving Your Versatility

Versatility is the ability to adjust your behavior in order to reduce tension and meet the needs of your family or team members. Here are some actions/steps you can take to improve your versatility.

If you are a High "D"
- Learn to listen; be patient.
- Develop greater concern for people.
- Focus more on personal relationships.
- Be more flexible with people.
- Be more supportive.
- Explain "why."
- Be warmer . . . more open.

If you are a High "I"
- Be less impulsive.
- Be more results oriented.
- Control actions/emotions.
- Focus attention on details/facts.
- Slow down pace.
- Listen, don't talke as much.

If you are a High "S"
- Be less sensitive to what people think.
- Be more direct.
- Be more concerned with the task.
- Face confrontation.
- Be more decisive.
- Increase pace.
- Initiate
- Learn to say "No."

If you are a High "C"
- Develop focus on right things, not just doing things right.
- Try to respond more quickly.
- Trust your intuition.
- Be less fact oriented.
- Look ahead.
- Develop relationships.
- Be more open/flexible.

Used by permission of Leadership Dynamics

Appendix A

A2. HOW YOUR BEHAVIOR CAN CAUSE TENSION IN OTHERS

If you are a:	And your family/team member is a:	Your behavior which may cause tension for them is as follows:
D	D	Your tendency to over-control a situation, which may reduce their freedom and ability to control.
	I	Your concern for results, accompanied by an apparent lack of concern for a motivational environment.
	S	Your tendency not to take enough time to listen. Your priority of time over relationships.
	C	Your being so quick, but perhaps not thorough enough.
I	D	Your apparent lack of results orientation/too emotional.
	I	Your desire for visibility – especially if it reduces their visibility.
	S	The lack of depth in some of your relationships/your quickness.
	C	Your lack of attention to detail/your impulsive tendencies.
S	D	Your time engaged in too much small talk.
	I	Your apparent lack of quickness.
	S	Your lack of initiative, especially if it means they have to initiate.
	C	Your people/small talk orientation – not task orientation.
C	D	Your slower and more methodical pace.
	I	Your attention to detail.
	S	Your lack of letting them know how you "feel."
	C	Your desire to be more right/correct than they are.

Used by permission of Leadership Dynamics

Appendix A

A3. LEARNING TO WORK TOGETHER

DOMINANT		INFLUENCE	
Harsh Pushy Dominating Severe Tough	Decisive Independent Efficient Practical Determined	Excitable Egotistical Reacting Manipulative Talkative	Stimulating Enthusiastic Dramatic Outgoing Personal
⬆	⬆	⬆	⬆
Others May See	Those with Similar Pattern	Others May See	Those with Similar Pattern
STEADINESS		**COMPLIANCE**	
Conforming Awkward Dependent Slow Retiring	Supportive Willing Dependable Reliable Agreeable	Critical Stuffy Indecisive Moralistic Picky	Thorough Persistent Orderly Serious Industrious
⬆	⬆	⬆	⬆
Others May See	Those with Similar Pattern	Others May See	Those with Similar Pattern

Used by permission of Leadership Dynamics

Appendix A

A4. Blending Strengths Summary

	D	I	S	C
Value to the Team	Takes initiative	Contacts people.	Performs specialized follow-throughs	Concentrates on details.
Major Strength	Strength of purpose, goal oriented, gets things done.	Enthusiasm, gets people motivated, involved.	Good people skills, good team player or leader.	Thoroughness, accuracy in analyzing all the data.
Major Weakness	Can be insensitive to feelings of others, impatient.	Impulsiveness, may not focus attention on detail/facts.	May sacrifice results for harmony, reluctant to initiate.	Overly cautious, can be too thorough and lose sight of time.
Motivated By	**Results** challenge, action.	**Recognition** approval, visibility.	**Relationships** appreciation.	**Being Right** quality.
Time Management	Focus: **Now** Efficient use of time…likes to get to the point.	Focus: **Future** Tends to rush to the next exciting thing.	Focus: **Present** Spends time in personal interaction sometimes to the detriment of the task	Focus: **Past** Works more slowly to ensure accuracy.
Communication	One-way…not as good a listener, better at initiating communication.	Enthusiastic, stimulating, often one-way, can inspire others.	Two-way flow, a good listener.	Good listener, especially in relation to tasks.
Decision Making	**Impulsive** Always makes decisions with goal in mind.	**Intuitive** quick. Lots of wins and losses.	**Relational** Makes decisions more slowly, due to input from others.	**Reluctant** thorough. Needs lots of evidence.
Behavior under Tension	**Autocratic**	**Attacks**	**Acquiesces**	**Avoids**
Would Improve Effectiveness By	Listening	Pausing	Initiating	Declaring

Used by permission of Leadership Dynamics

Appendix B
Suggested Reading

We offer these recommendations for additional reading to help you find your calling and to build bridges to others who may not have a relationship with Jesus Christ.

Experiencing God, Henry Blackaby and Claude V. King (Nashville: Broadman and Holman Publishers, 1998). Helps us understand that we can join God in what He is doing rather than coming up with our own plan and asking Him to bless it.

Ordering Your Private World, Gordon MacDonald (Nashville: Thomas Nelson, Rev. Ed. 2003). A book that helps us set margins for our lives along with biblical priorities when we become quiet enough to hear the still small voice of God.

Called and Accountable, Henry Blackaby and Kerry Skinner (Birmingham: New Hope Publishers, 2002). A six-weeks Bible study dealing with a biblical basis of calling for every Christian.

The Call, Os Guinness (Nashville: W Publishing, 1998). A book focused on helping us understand our unique life purpose by benefiting from both Scripture and history in discovering that purpose.

Appendix B

The Power of the Call, Henry Blackaby and Henry Brandt (Nashville: Broadman and Holman, 1997). This book is specifically geared toward those sensing God's call to vocational missions or ministry and how best to become a strategic equipper of God's people for their work in being *on mission*.

The Purpose Driven Life, Rick Warren (Grand Rapids: Zondervan, 2002). A 40-day spiritual journey that allows the reader to grapple with the question, "What on earth am I here for?" Unlike self-help books that start wi th you, this book rightly starts with God.

Life Keys: Discovering Who You Are, Why You're Here, What You Do Best, Jane Kise, David Stark and Sandra Krebs Hirsh (Minneapolis: Bethany House, 1996). An excellent tool to guide you in discovering just how unique you are as a masterpiece (Ephesians 2:10) created by the Master Creator. It will help you fulfill what you were designed to do.

Loving God, Charles Colson (Grand Rapids: Zondervan, 1996). An insightful view of what it really means to love God and live accordingly. One of the greatest strategic thinkers of our day blends stories from history with the truths of God's Word in showing how a loving God can transform your life.

How Now Shall We Live? Charles Colson and Nancy Pearcey (Wheaton: Tyndale, 1999). This thought-provoking book will inspire you to put into practice your *on mission* lifestyle by penetrating your culture with the gospel.

*The Search for Significance,*Robert McGee (Houston: Rapha Publishing, 1998). A great manual to help you handle step by step those tripping points in your life over which you may be stumbling - past hurts, emotional and spiritual wounds, lack of forgiveness and many more.

Roaring Lambs, Bob Briner (Grand Rapids: Zondervan, 2000) and *Final Roar*, Bob Briner (Nashville: Broadman & Holman, 2000). Both books call believers to step out of their comfort zones and into the secular world to be heard. They are one Christian's challenge to impact the culture, specifically the media, art and entertainment worlds, in a practical way on a daily basis. The late Bob Briner was an Emmy-award-winning television producer and long-time president of Pro-Serve Television.

Great Commission Companies: The Emerging Role of Business in Missions, Steve Rundle and Tom Steffen (Downers Grove, Illinois: Intervarsity Press: 2003). This resource explores the growing importance of business leadership in taking the gospel global.

You Are Talented! Patrick Kavanaugh (Grand Rapids: Chosen Books Publishing Company, 2002). Kavanaugh helps readers find their talents and teaches them how to use their abilities at home, in the local church, and in the world.

The Day I Met God, Jim and Karen Covell and Victorya Michaels Rogers (Sisters, Oregon: Multnomah Publishers, Inc., 2001). A compilation of stories about Hollywood stars, musical artists, and athletes and how they found God at the pinnacle of their careers or in the valleys of defeat.

The Embarrassed Believer, Hugh Hewitt (Nashville: Word Publishing, 1998). This contemporary classic is an inspiring and challenging call to all believers to be serious about their faith, to know why they believe it and to learn how to be bold with the gospel in their communities and in the workplace.

The Passion Promise, John Avant (Sisters, Oregon: Multnomah Publishers Inc., 2004). John Avant challenges readers to put an end to a boring life of low-risk living. He brings to life God's promise that God will do "immeasurably more than all we ask or imagine" if we commit our lives to Him.

Life According to Jesus, Jack Graham (Wheaton: Tyndale House Publishers, 2004). A collection of eighty devotional lessons divided into five sections, this compendium of wisdom provides present-day saints with insight for living every day to the fullest in our homes, churches, and workplaces.

On Mission magazine. This quarterly helps you reach your potential as an on mission Christian by introducing you to laypeople who daily live their faith out loud, sometimes successfully, sometimes not. They're *real* people sharing Christ in the real world. Like you, they want their lives to count for Christ in the career arena as well as their time away from work. To subscribe, call 888-239-3990 or visit www.onmission.com.

Also, we recommend you read about the leadership philosophy of people like Max Dupree, who was CEO of Herman Miller Furniture, in *Leadership is an Art,* Max DuPree (New York: Doubleday, 1989). Bob Buford, president of a successful cable television company and founder of Leadership Network, has two outstanding books about determining the course of life entitled *Half Time* (Grand Rapids: Zondervan, 1997) and *Game Plan* (Grand Rapids: Zondervan, 1999). Bill Pollard's principle-based leadership of Service Master is powerfully told in *Soul of the Firm,* Bill Pollard and Carlos Cantu, (Grand Rapids: Zondervan, 2000), where he describes how his Bible-centered beliefs and faith in Christ entered into everything from developing corporate values to establishing a high work-ethic environment and culture.

Also read stories of historical leaders who have stood strong through the ages. Examples are John R. Mott, Adoniram Judson, Helen Keller, John and Charles Wesley, John Bunyan and David Livingstone, to name a few.

And read books about men and women whom God has powerfully used in recent days. You can glean great counsel from books on the lives of Joni Eareckson Tada, Chuck Colson, Bill Bright, Dawson Trotman and Billy Graham.

Notes

Introduction
1. Jeremiah 29:11.

Chapter 1: Made to Count!
1. Galatians 2:20.
2. Jeremiah 29:11–13.
3. Jeremiah 29:13 (NKJV).
4. Ecclesiastes 11:1.
5. Isaiah 30:21.

Chapter 2: Designed for a Destiny
1. Unless otherwise noted in this section, quotes from Mr. Sekulow are based on his testimony contained on the Jews for Jesus website at www.jewsforjesus.org/stories/sekulow.html. Information regarding cases he is presently handling and the results of prior Supreme Court cases is found at the website for the American Center for Law and Justice—www.aclj.org/about/aboutj.asp.
2. Jeremiah 1:5.
3. Isaiah 45:9–12 (NLT).
4. Galatians 1:15.
5. Ephesians 2:10 (NKJV).
6. Interview with Baptist Press, February 11, 2003.
7. Hebrews 12:1.

Notes

Chapter 3: God's Calling Is for Everyone, Not Just Ministry Professionals
1. Matthew 10:1–4; Luke 6:12–16; John 1:33–51.
2. Mark 10:46–52.
3. Acts 9:15–16.
4. Mark 10:21 (NKJV).
5. Matthew 8:8 (NKJV).
6. Matthew 8:10 (NKJV).
7. Matthew 8:13 (NKJV).
8. Luke 19:2–10.
9. Mark 15:42–43 (NKJV).
10. Mark 5:19 (NKJV).
11. Galatians 3:28.
12. Acts 1:8 (NKJV).
13. Acts 6:2 (NKJV).
14. Acts 6:3 (NKJV).
15. Acts 8:8 (NKJV).
16. "Catch the Vision," Mission Frontiers, November/December 1996, http://www.missionfrontiers.org.
17. Acts 8:1 (NKJV).
18. Acts 1:8 (NKJV).
19. V. Raymond Edman, *Finney on Revival* (Bethany House Publishers 2000). Facts on the life of Finney are taken from Edman's book. Quotes attributed to Finney also are drawn from Edman's work, which in turn relied on Finney's own autobiography— Charles G. Finney, *The Autobiography of Charles G. Finney* (New York: Revell, 1876).
20. Quotes from Mark Earley are from the author's interview on July 1, 2003.
21. 1 Corinthians 1:9.
22. Joe Musser, *The Infidel* (Nashville: Broadman and Holman, 2002). This account of the meeting between Newton and Wilberforce is taken from Musser's excellent book, pages 349–350. A meeting between Newton and Wilberforce is well-documented, as is Newton's influence on a young Wilberforce and the friendship of the men as they battled slavery together. Precisely what was said in this first meeting is a product of Mr. Musser's informed imagination based on known historical facts.

Chapter 4: Finding God's Unique Plan Outside the Box
1. From *A Quest for Godliness* by J. I. Packer, © 1994, pages 23–24. Used by permission of Crossway Books, a division of Good News Publishers, Wheaton, Illinois 60187.
2. Quotes from Peggy Wehmeyer are from the author's interview on March 17, 2003.
3. Romans 1:6–7.
4. Reprinted by permission. *The Call*, Os Guiness. (Nashville: W Publishing, 1998), 10. All rights reserved.
5. Ibid., 4.
6. Ibid., 118.

7. John 3:16.

8. Romans 5:8.

9. 2 Corinthians 5:21.

10. Acts 4:12.

11. Acts 16:31.

12. Findley Edge, *The Doctrine of the Laity* (Nashville: Convention Press, 1985), 44.

13. Ibid., 37.

14. Psalm 32:8 (NLT).

15. Isaiah 30:21.

16. Proverbs 3:5–6.

17. Galatians 1:15.

Chapter 5: "The Power Lies Within You" and Other Self-Help Lies

1. Ephesians 1:1.

2. 1 Corinthians 2:1–3.

3. Acts 20:9.

4. Acts 20:12.

5. 1 Corinthians 2:4–5.

6. 2 Corinthians 5:17.

7. John 10:10 (Amp.).

8. Acts 4:12 (Amp., italics ours).

9. Matthew 7:13–14 (Amp., italics ours).

10. Matthew 7:13–14 (MSG).

11. Quotes from a speech given by Dr. Olasky to the Council for National Policy on April 25, 2003, on the Web site www.Olasky.com. Dr. Olasky is editor-in-chief of *World* and its daily editor, www.worldmagblog.com.

Chapter 6: "It's All About My Strengths," Another Self-Help Lie

1. John 15:4–5 (NKJV).

2. 2 Corinthians 12:10 (NKJV).

3. 2 Corinthians 12:9.

4. 1 Corinthians 1:31 (NKJV).

5. Psalm 139:13–16 (MSG).

6. Donald Clifton and Paula Nelson, *Soar with Your Strengths* (New York: Doubleday Dell Publishing Group, 1992), 43–56.

7. James 1:17 (NKJV).

8. Clifton and Nelson, *Soar with Your Strengths*, 11 (parenthetical ours).

9. 2 Corinthians 12:7–10 (MSG).

10. For a more thorough discussion, see Bob Reccord, *Forged by Fire* (Nashville: Broadman & Holman, 2000).

11. Psalm 119:71 (italics ours).

12. James 4:7–8.

Notes

Chapter 7: A Life-Changing Mission Bigger Than You

1. Reprinted with permission. *Wild at Heart,* John Eldredge. (Nashville: Thomas Nelson Publishers, 2001), 141–42. All rights reserved.
2. Ibid., 174.
3. Ibid., 175.
4. Matthew 16:18.
5. Mark 16:15.
6. Matthew 16:18 (NLT).
7. Ephesians 5:15–16 (NKJV).
8. Colossians 3:23.
9. Ephesians 4:11–12 (NKJV).
10. Ephesians 5:25–27 (NKJV).
11. Romans 7:19.
12. Hebrews 10:24–25.
13. Matthew 28:19–20 (NKJV).
14. Myron Augsburger, *Invitation to Discipleship* (Scottdale, Penn.: Harold Press, 1964), 16.
15. Genesis 17:1–4.
16. Exodus 4:10–12.
17. Judges 6:15–16.
18. Esther 4:11–17.
19. 1 Corinthians 2:1; Acts 9:15.
20. Luke 1:26–35.

Chapter 8: On Mission at Home

1. Quotes from J. C. Watts are from the authors' interview on June 13, 2003.
2. 1 Timothy 5:8 (KJV).
3. Mark 5:5.
4. Mark 5:3 (NKJV).
5. Mark 5:15 (NKJV).
6. Mark 5:18–19.
7. Quotes from LaRue Coleman are from the authors' interview on April 13, 2003.

Chapter 9: Your Home As a Nerve Center for Ministry

1. Luke 12:48.

Chapter 10: On Mission at Work

1. Kenneth A. Tucker, "A Passion for Work" *Gallup Management Journal* (February 18, 2002).
2. Colossians 3:23.
3. Quotes from Victorya Rogers are from the authors' interview on May 12, 2003.
4. Reprinted by permission of Thomas Nelson, Inc., *It's Easier to Succeed Than to Fail,* Truett Cathy. (Nashville: Oliver Nelson, 1989), 19. All rights reserved.

5. Ibid., 47.

6. Quotes from Jim and Karen Covell are from the authors' interview on May 20, 2003.

7. 1 Peter 3:15.

8. Ibid.

9. Isaiah 55:8–9 (Amp.).

10. Deuteronomy 7:17–19, 22 (italics ours).

11. Information on Steve Puckett is from the authors' interview on April 9, 2003.

12. Quote from Governor Sonny Perdue is from the authors' interview on June 1, 2003.

Chapter 11: Understanding How God Wired You

1. Philippians 2:13.

Chapter 12: How God Reveals Your Mission

1. 2 Timothy 3:16–17 (NLT).

2. 2 Timothy 3:16–17 (Amp.).

3. Deuteronomy 32:46–47 (italics ours).

4. John 6:63 (italics ours).

5. Matthew 7:7–8.

6. Jeremiah 33:3.

7. I Kings 19:9–13.

8. Psalm 46:10 (NKJV).

9. John 10:3–5.

10. Acts 21:13.

11. Acts 21:14.

12. Acts 9:15 (NKJV).

13. Henry Blackaby and Claude King, *Experiencing God* (Nashville: Lifeway Press, 1990), 14.

Chapter 13: A Fleece, a Closed Door, a Sense of Peace—Does God Guide Like That?

1. Judges 6:14–16.

2. 1 Corinthians 16:9 (italics ours).

3. Colossians 4:3.

Chapter 14: God at the Crossroads

1. Matthew 25:21.

2. 1 Samuel 17:35 (NLT).

3. Daniel 1:5.

4. Daniel 1:8 (NKJV).

5. Matthew 7:13–14.

6. Daniel 1:8 (NKJV).

7. Psalm 119:11.

Notes

8. Isaiah 30:21 (Amp.).

9. Psalm 37:23–24 (Amp).

10. William Shakespeare, *Julius Caesar*, Act IV Scene 3 lines 218–23.

11. 1 Samuel 15:22–23.

12. Quotes from Phillip Johnson are from the authors' interview on June 27, 2003.

13. Stephen Gould, "Impeaching a Self-Appointed Judge," *Scientific American*, July 1992, 119.

14. Tim Stafford, "The Making of a Revolution," *Christianity Today* 41, no. 14, (December 8, 1997).

15. Ibid.

Chapter 15: In Step with God

1. Harry Reasoner, when he was an ABC News commentator, reported this on ABC *Nightly News* on February 16, 1971 (during the Vietnam War).

2. Job 38:2–21.

3. Isaiah 30:21 (Amp.).

4. Psalm 37:23–24 (Amp.).

5. Psalm 32:8.

6. Isaiah 55:9.

7. Proverbs 16:9.

8. Quotes from Janet Parshall are from the authors' interview on July 10, 2003.

Chapter 16: Follow God's Plan and Experience His Pleasure

1. 2 Corinthians 5:9.

2. 1 Thessalonians 2:4.

3. 1 Corinthians 1:1 (NKJV).

4. 2 Corinthians 11:25–28.

5. Acts 9:15–16 (NKJV).

6. James 1:2.

Chapter 17: Follow God's Plan and Change Your World

1. John 14:30.

2. John 16:11.

3. 2 Corinthians 5:17; John 16:11.

4. Acts 17:4.

5. Acts 17:5.

6. Acts 17:6–7 (NKJV).

7. Isaiah 55:8.

8. Acts 17:32–34 (NKJV).

9. Proverbs 16:9.

10. Unless otherwise noted, quotes from Hugh Hewitt are from the authors' interview on July 3, 2003.

11. Reprinted by permission. *The Embarrassed Believer*, Hugh Hewitt. (Nashville: Word Publishing, 1998), 1–2. All rights reserved.

12. Reprinted by permission. *Searching for God in America*, Hugh Hewitt. (Nashville: Word Publishing, 1996), xiv. All rights reserved.

13. Quotes from Governor Sonny Perdue are from the authors' interview on August 6, 2003.

14. Proverbs 23:7 (NKJV).

15. Quotes from Jenny Pruitt are from the authors' interview on August 6, 2003.

Chapter 18: The List

1. Hebrews 11:1.

2. Hebrews 11:7.

3. Hebrews 11:8.

4. Hebrews 11:24–25.

5. Though not mentioned by name, this reference from Hebrews 11:33–34, is referring to the feats of the Old Testament prophets and is clearly an allusion to Daniel, Shadrach, Meshach, and Abednego.

6. Hebrews 12:1.

7. Hebrews 11:11 (NKJV).

MADE TO COUNT
Study Questions

CHAPTER 1: MADE TO COUNT!

1. "To make life count, we must first die to ourselves and be willing to do whatever God asks us to do." (pg 3) . . . What would 'dying to yourself' look like in your life?

2. What areas of your life pull you away from following the hunger God placed in your life to make it count?

3. In Jeremiah 29:11, God says, "For I know the plans I have for you . . . .plans to prosper you and not to harm you, plans to give you hope and a future." When you look at your personal business plan or yearly goals, how many of them reflect God's plans? Do they express your belief that you were made to count for God?

4. Is it easy to trust God with your life in matters related to home and work? Why or why not?

Principle 1: God prepared a unique plan and calling for your life even before you were born.

Key scriptures:

- "Before I formed you in the womb I knew you; before you were born I set you apart; I appointed you as a prophet to the nations" (Jeremiah 1:5).

- "God, who had set me apart before I was born and called me through his grace . . . " (Galatians 1:15 NRSV).

- "For we are His workmanship, created in Christ Jesus for good works, which God prepared beforehand that we should walk in them" (Ephesians 2:10 NKJV).

Key points:

- God designed you with your destiny in mind, creating you with every gift and resource necessary to perfectly accomplish His will.

- Everyone is designed with a unique plan and calling in mind, not just those in full-time ministry.

- It's time to let God "out of the box" as you search for His unique plan and calling for your life.

CHAPTER 2: DESIGNED FOR A DESTINY

1. Read Isaiah 45:9-12. Based on this section of God's Word, who is the "shaper" of the pot? Who does the pot represent? How have you responded to the Potter's shaping of your life in the last 6 months?

2. Have there been times in your life when you questioned God's plan for you—or if there even *was* a plan? Explain.

3. God's calling is primarily to *Someone (Jesus Christ)* and only then to do *something* that will take place *somewhere*. Describe a time when the "something or somewhere" came before the Someone. What was the result?

4. In Isaiah 43:1, God says, "Fear not, for I have redeemed you; I have summoned you by name; you are mine." In a social setting, would you prefer to be greeted by name or with only a general greeting? When someone calls you by name, what does that imply about his or her perspective on the relationship?

5. A designer takes into account the individual(s) involved at the same time he plans for the overall purpose of the design. As you view the design of your life, what defines success for you? Has that definition changed in the last five years? If so, in what way?

6. Read Ephesians 2:10 and Hebrews 12:1-4. How does the race compare to our individual and collective destinies?

CHAPTER 3: GOD'S CALLING IS FOR EVERYONE, NOT JUST FOR MINISTRY PROFESSIONALS

1. Make a list of 10 people you know that probably do not have a personal relationship with God. Next, put a check mark by the ones who do NOT regularly attend church. If you cannot list 10 people you personally know who need Christ, what does that say about your relationships?

2. Jesus did not encourage everyone to physically follow him but encouraged some to stay where they were. Who did these biblical examples impact by staying in their area of giftedness and calling? Roman Centurion (Matthew 8:8-10), a man called "Legion" (Mark 5:19), Ethiopian (Acts 8:26-39), Joseph of Arimethea (Mark 15:42-43).

3. Describe people you know who might be "lights" for God in their workplace, community, government, or home.

4. Read Acts 1:8. The power is universally available, and the call is universally applicable. Is "no" an option for Christians? Why?

5. Mark Earley states, "I discovered that God's calling is really to Himself . . . In that context, God will place me wherever He wants me to be, and that pursuit will become holy." How is Earley's view of a calling similar or different than yours?

6. Finney, Newton, Wilberforce, and Earley all finally obeyed God. Is there anything in your life that, like Wilberforce early on, keeps you from obeying God's call?

Chapter 4: Finding God's Unique Plan Outside the Box

1. Do you find yourself in a secure, but boring box? Explain. If so, what steps are you willing to take to get outside the box?

2. As many journey into adulthood, the sense of adventure wanes and routine seeps into our lives. Write down some outcomes of allowing our "Christianity" to become a matter of convenience rather than conviction.

3. Are there well-meaning individuals who might be causing you to second-guess God's direction in your life?

4. Read Hebrews 11. How many priests and prophets are listed by name in the *Hall of Faith*? What were some of the occupations of people honored in this chapter?

5. Up until the 18th century, *calling* served as the basis for the word *vocation*. Even today, *Webster's Dictionary* still carries that emphasis of calling as . . .

> A strong inner impulse toward a peculiar course of action, esp. when accompanied by conviction of divine influence.

> The vocation or profession in which one customarily engages.

How would you define "calling?"

6. God's calling is two-fold: first to a life-changing relationship with Him and then to a life-fulfilling mission alongside Him. Review pages 48-49. Are you sure you are in a personal, intimate relationship with the Creator of all life?

7. Why is it sometimes difficult to give up control of the planning, guiding and directing of activities?

8. Discuss a time when you missed God's best because you wouldn't give up the planning, guiding and directing of your life.

Principle 2: God calls you to a life-changing relationship with Him through Jesus Christ.

Key scripture:

- "Therefore, if anyone is in Christ, he is a new creation the old has gone, the new has come!" (2 Corinthians 5:17)

Key points:

- Surrender to Christ radically changes our mission in life.
- The power to complete our mission comes not from ourselves, but from Christ at work in us.
- When we abide in Christ, even our weaknesses can be used for His glory.

CHAPTER 5: "THE POWER LIES WITHIN YOU" AND OTHER SELF-HELP LIES

1. Compare some of the differences between the self-help (*me* focused) philosophies and the biblical view of "calling."

2. In the last year, what have you experienced that could *only* be attributed to God?

3. List some of the differences between religion and relationship.

4. Matthew 7:14 says, "The way to life—to God!—is vigorous and requires total attention." (MSG) How is this verse different from the world's perspective? How is it different than the perspective of some inside the church?

5. Are you willing to go anywhere God calls you and to do anything He asks you to do? If the answer is "no" or "not yet," what is holding back your affection for Christ?

CHAPTER 6: "IT'S ALL ABOUT MY STRENGTHS," ANOTHER SELF-HELP LIE

1. The self-help philosophy tells you to focus almost exclusively on your strengths—unlock their full potential and you will change your world. The Bible tells us to focus on two areas for a balanced, powerful life. What are those two areas?

2. In order to maximize our strengths, consider the following: listen for yearnings, watch for satisfactions, watch for rapid learning, catch glimpses of excellence, and note patterns of excellence in performance. Do any areas of strength in your life stand out to you?

3. Make three columns. List some of the weaknesses you will trust God to use for his glory: weaknesses from unrestrained strengths, personal weaknesses to manage, or circumstantial weaknesses.

4. Strengths left unchecked can become weaknesses. Are there any areas to be aware of in your life?

5. Stan Thomas once said, "Strengths make you a better leader and weaknesses make you a better follower and servant. Both are critical in the eyes of Christ."

   Describe a supervisor, team mate, or friend in your life who was challenged in this area. Describe a supervisor who was a strong leader and servant. What was the response of the employees to the two supervisors?

Principle 3: God calls you to partner with Him in a mission that is bigger than you are.

Key scriptures:

- "So do not be ashamed to testify about our Lord, or ashamed of me his prisoner. But join with me in suffering for the gospel, by the power of God, who has saved us and called us to a holy life—not because of anything we have done but because of his own purpose and grace . . . And of this gospel I was appointed a herald and an apostle and a teacher" (2 Timothy 1:8-9,11).

- "On this rock I will build My church, and the gates of Hades shall not prevail against it" (Matthew 16:18 NKJV).

Key points:

- God's mission for our life is bigger than anything we could do on our own.

- God calls each of us to be part of an institution that will outlast us—the local church.

- God calls each of us to be part of a cause far greater than us—the Great Commission.

Chapter 7: A Life-Changing Mission Bigger Than You

1. God does not ask us to work independently of His church and His Great Commission, nor does He tolerate those who work against them. If you are not involved in a local church or in sharing Christ, what steps can you take to change your course? This chapter lists several "excuses" that we use for not attending church. Have you ever used them or are you using them now? If so, which ones?

2. If you are involved in the local church, what two areas of service fit your passions and abilities? (We will discuss this more in chapter 11).

3. Read Hebrews 10:24-25. What command does God give us? What are the benefits of following this command?

4. One thing we can do now that we won't be able to do in heaven is to lead others to a personal relationship with Christ. When was the last time you shared Christ?

5. What are you part of that is bigger than yourself? Are you part of a cause worth dying for?

Principle 4: God calls you to be on mission with Him right where you are—starting now.

Key scriptures:

- "As Jesus was getting into the boat, the man who had been demon-possessed begged to go with him. Jesus did not let him, but said, 'Go home to your family and tell them how much the Lord has done for you, and how he has had mercy on you.' So the man went away and began to tell in the Decapolis how much Jesus had done for him. And all the people were amazed" (Mark 5:18-20).

- "Whatever you do, work at it with all your heart, as working for the Lord, not for men" (Colossians 3:23).

Key points:

- You are called to make your family a top priority. Family responsibilities cannot be delegated to others or relegated to less than first place.

- Your home should be a nerve center for ministry as you reach out to your friends and neighbors.

- You should be "on call" at work, looking for creative opportunities to share the gospel with those around you.

- Your gospel witness at work will only be as credible as the quality of your work.

CHAPTER 8: ON MISSION AT HOME

1. In your own words, what does "Jesus is head of this home" mean?

2. List the names of your spouse and children. As you list their names, can you recall the last time you prayed for them? With them?

3. Take time to write out a blessing for each child. Ask God to give you special time to share it with them.

4. What specific ways can you encourage your child or spouse to follow God's calling on his or her life?

CHAPTER 9: YOUR HOME AS A NERVE CENTER FOR MINISTRY

1. When you read the stories about the Hammonds, the Frosts, Cheryl and Jeanine, what was your first thought? Did you have a sense of excitement or frustration? Explain.

2. Where you live is very important to God. He placed you and your family in your home for a specific purpose. Describe a time when you knew for certain you were right where God wanted you.

3. You might want to make a list of the neighbors on your street. Begin to ask God to give you opportunities to care for them and talk to them about Christ.

4. List specific abilities or life situations God might use in your ministry at home and from the base of your home. Don't forget the children! Sometimes they're the best outreach of all.

Chapter 10: On Mission at Work

1. In what ways do you find significant productivity, fulfillment and influence at work?

2. Keeping a balance between productivity and influencing work for Christ is challenging. Share some creatively intentional ways you reached out to co-workers or customers.

3. Read 1 Peter 3:15. Why are gentleness and respect necessary when you're on a mission at work—or anywhere?

4. What creative ways have you discovered to be "salt and light" for Christ at work with grace and good taste?

5. Is there a person at your workplace who is a strong witness for Christ? If so, what does he or she do that makes this person a bold and effective witness? What can you learn from him or her?

6. How does the quality of your work and the effort you put forth compare to your co-workers? What does this say to others about Who your ultimate boss is?

Principle 5: God reveals His mission through His Word, His Spirit, wise counsel, and His work in circumstances around you.

Key scriptures:

- His Word – "All Scripture is God-breathed and is useful for teaching, rebuking, correcting and training in righteousness so that the man of God may be thoroughly equipped for every good work" (2 Timothy 3:16-17).

- His Spirit – "But when he, the Spirit of truth, comes, he will guide you into all truth. He will not speak on his own; he will speak only what he hears, and he will tell you what is yet to come" (John 16:13).

- Wise counsel – "Plans fail for lack of counsel, but with many advisers they succeed" (Proverbs 15:22).

- His work – "And we know that in all things God works for the good of those who love him, who have been called according to his purpose. For those God foreknew he also predestined to be conformed to the likeness of his Son, that he might be the first-born among many brothers" (Romans 8:28-29).

Key points:

- When God formed you, He hard-wired you for success in your mission. He will not work at cross–purposes with His own creative work.

- The Bible is the owner's manual for our life. God will never call us to do anything inconsistent with His will as revealed in Scripture.

- God does not play guessing games with our lives. If we earnestly seek Him, He will guide us through His Spirit and His work in circumstances around us.

- We should seek the counsel of mature Christians who can help us discover God's will for our lives. But we should remember that God will ultimately reveal His plan for our life to us, not them.

- There are no shortcuts or gimmicks that reveal God's will. Fleeces, our feelings, and "open doors" can sometimes steer us wrong.

CHAPTER 11: UNDERSTANDING HOW GOD WIRED YOU

1. Read Philippians 2:13. What two areas does Paul reference as being part of our fulfilling God's good purposes?

2. Questions are a great way of sifting through the "fluff" of our existence. Review pages 143–44 and write down your responses to the questions. Ask God to use these to provide insight into your passions.

3. You may also wish to go online to www.uniquelyyou.com to determine your personality type and how this impacts your perceptions and expectations, and your work with others.

4. How might understanding your passions and personality aid you in your pursuit to impact others for Christ?

CHAPTER 12: HOW GOD REVEALS YOUR MISSION

1. Define why the Bible is sometimes called the "Owner's Manual."

2. Read Deuteronomy 32:46-47. The passage states, "they [God's scriptures] are your life." What does that mean?

3. God desires for us to come to Him in persistent asking, continuous seeking, and relentless knocking. How often can your prayers be characterized by those traits? What might be keeping you from persistent, continuous and relentless praying?

4. Psalms 46:10 (NKJV) says, "Be still, and know that I am God." What steps would you need to take in your busy world to be still before God? List the benefits of doing so.

5. Wise counsel can confirm God's mission. What qualities would you look for in someone who might provide wise counsel?

6. God may be calling you to participate in the sowing stages where the results are not evident at the moment. Henry Blackaby states, "The focus needs to be on God, *not my life*." Why is that a challenging way to live?

CHAPTER 13: A FLEECE, A CLOSED DOOR, A SENSE OF PEACE— DOES GOD GUIDE LIKE THAT?

1. Read 1 Corinthians 16:9. Paul saw an open door although there was much opposition awaiting him if he went through it. Did Paul solely use the open door as his determination of the right course?

2. What steps will help you determine if an open door is the correct door?

3. Describe a time when your feelings determined your steps. Did that course take you where God wanted you?

4. Have you ever experienced "peace" while you were moving in the opposite direction of God's will? Why? How long did the "peace" last until God got your attention?

Principle 6: God will repeatedly bring you to cross-roads of choice as He forges you for His mission.

Key scripture:

- "But Daniel resolved not to defile himself with the royal food and wine, and he asked the chief official for permission not to defile himself this way" (Daniel 1:8).

Key points:

- God will bring us to critical junctures in our life and give us the choice of whether to follow Him.
- When we choose God at the crossroads for seemingly minor things, He will send us down a path toward greater responsibility and impact.

CHAPTER 14: GOD AT THE CROSSROADS

1. Describe a crossroads of choice in your life. Which path did you choose? How has that choice affected your life and those around you?
2. The crossroads choice is a tough choice, a crisis choice, and usually a low-profile choice. Read Psalm 32:8 and Proverbs 16:9. How might the practices in these verses ease your decision?
3. Share a time when God's Word not only confirmed the turn to take, but also gave you the strength to follow the God-pleasing path.
4. *God wants complete obedience, even in the little things, even when nobody else is watching.* Why is this principle foundational to making the right choices in the crossroads?
5. Philip Johnson states, "I'm like a kid in a candy store. I can't think of anything I would rather be doing." Have you found your candy store? Share where God has made you count.

Principle 7: God guides you and provides for your mission one step at a time.

Key scriptures:

- "I will instruct you and teach you in the way you should go; I will counsel you and watch over you" (Psalm 32:8).
- "The steps of a [good] man are directed and established by the Lord when He delights in his way [and He busies Himself with his every step]" (Psalm 37:23-24, Amp.).

Key points:

- Though God reveals His mission for us in advance, He reveals His plan only one step at a time.
- Sometimes God is calling us to take a step that just doesn't make sense. Take it anyway.
- God is not just guiding the steps of your vocational mission, He is also guiding your steps as you seek to bring others into a personal relationship with Christ.

CHAPTER 15: IN STEP WITH GOD

1. Read Isaiah 30:21. What does God say He will show you?
2. God's mission is redemption. If you are on mission with God, should you expect God to call you only to the "fun" people and situations? Why or why not?
3. God guides you and provides for you to carry out your mission one step at a time. Share some of the steps God lead you through.
4. Janet Parshall didn't jump right into her role as a radio show host. What did God teach her in the years before? What did He use to teach her those things?
5. On page 198, take a few moments to write out your mission, crossroad decisions, and some specific steps toward your mission where God has provided and guided.

6. Spend time in prayer thanking God for His involvement in your life and ask Him to give you a willing heart to continue following His steps for your life.

Principle 8: When you answer God's call, you will experience His pleasure and change your world.

Key scriptures:

- "So we make it our goal to please him, whether we are at home in the body or away from it" (2 Corinthians 5:9).

- "On the contrary, we speak as men approved by God to be entrusted with the gospel. We are not trying to please men but God, who tests our hearts" (1 Thessalonians 2:4).

- "But when they did not find them, they dragged Jason and some brethren to the rulers of the city, crying out, 'These who have turned the world upside down have come here too'" (Acts 17:6 NKJV).

Key points:

- When we find ourselves doing what God created us to do, we will experience His pleasure.

- God calls us to turn the world "upside down," radically changing those we come in contact with and the professions we pursue.

CHAPTER 16: FOLLOW GOD'S PLAN AND EXPERIENCE HIS PLEASURE

1. What will a person gain if he or she follows God's steps for their lives?

2. Read 2 Corinthians 11:25-28 and Acts 9:15-16. What situations did Paul experience? Were they part of God's plan for Paul?

3. Today, we often focus on the things we must *succeed in* to make a difference, rather than the things we must *suffer through*. How might God use personal suffering in our lives to bring about His plan and purposes?

4. How would you define the difference between *passion* and *emotion*?

5. Share a time when you experienced God's pleasure in the midst of a terrible time.

CHAPTER 17: FOLLOW GOD'S PLAN AND CHANGE YOUR WORLD

1. Share a time God worked in an unexpected way or place.

2. Think back over the last few years. Have any of the people around you changed for the better because of the influence you have had?

3. How might an individual outside of a church's staff be even more effective in reaching the culture?

4. Are you prepared to see God do something radical through you? Why or why not?

CHAPTER 18: THE LIST

1. What unique mission has God placed on your heart?

2. Are you willing to step out with the type of insane obedience we mentioned earlier, even before you know how God might pull this one off?

3. Are you willing to pay the price of the rough and narrow path at the crossroads, knowing that it's the only path that leads to greater responsibility?

A Free Offer from

Uniquely You

DISCOVER YOUR OWN UNIQUE PERSONALITY and your own unique giftedness! Dr. Mels Carbonell of Uniquely You Leadership Center has helped the authors provide an online diagnostic tool to help you explore these areas of your life.

To access these excellent online instruments, you must have a personal access code. This individually numbered eight-digit code is located under the front flap of the dust jacket of this book.

When you find your personalized code, use it to enter the Uniquely You website: www.uniquelyyou.com. You will then be allowed to complete one personality temperament profile, as well as one evaluation of the spiritual gifts profile.

After you complete your own profile, if you would like to have your spouse, family, leadership team, or others use the profiles, you will be able to do so for a very reasonable fee.

When you have completed the online profile assessment, please turn to Appendix A in the back of this book for some interpretative information provided by Dr. Carbonell and the authors to help you understand how to best relate to others based on these personality assessments.

Why not take advantage of this free offer right now?

www.uniquelyyou.com